BEGGARS WAY

Readers of the Martin Cole series of novels will be familiar with the cosy side of the fictional Devon town of Roselake. In his new novel Alan Tootill pulls the curtain aside to reveal some of what goes on behind Roselake's normally tranquil façade.

Alan recently moved back to the Fylde, where he grew up, but still retains his affection for Devon. Much of the time he is to be found in Puglia, southern Italy, or travelling in India.

The Roselake Novels

Beggars Way

BEGGARS WAY

ALAN TOOTILL

PROLOGUE

It is not often that the Midweek Gazette contributes to the making of news, rather than reporting it. Such a vital organ of the free press indeed rarely reports to its Roselake readership any news of significance.

You will appreciate that we use the word "free" to indicate that nobody pays for the paper except for its advertisers, as opposed to suggesting that the paper has an editorial viewpoint independent of its owners, who have spent many years and many pounds supporting the local Conservative party and keeping the Roselake map blue, as they believe nature intended. Not that Roselake is a town fomenting with political discord. Incomers to the town - and an incomer is usually defined as anyone not born here and not having a minimum twenty-year residence - don't dare make waves, and the old Roselakeians are set in their ways. They tolerate a couple of members on the Town Council who declare themselves as Liberal Democrats, largely on the grounds that the pair are demonstrably ineffective, and they even smile on a single Labour member, on the grounds that his farcical frustrated Bolshevistic outbursts make every other councillor look well-balanced and right-minded. True, lately, an active Green Party member started making a reputation for herself doing many busy and praiseworthy deeds in the town, but then the people of Roselake, like a majority in the area, or even in the country, were under the false impression that Greens were only Tories with a passion, and an ability, for growing organic vegetables. So our Green stalwart was left to her good works unmolested, sowing the seeds of a greener future and a greener Roselake.

However, if social and political news is in the main absent from the Gazette's pages, the paper does have some justification in its claim that it serves the community in a praiseworthy fashion. To quote just a few examples, the Gazette gives many page inches to the meetings of the local WI, to exhibitions of the local Watercolour

Society, to the Roselake Ferret Appreciation Society and to the selection of the Carnival Queen and Princess (supposedly annual but occasionally needing by-elections during the year due to unexpected pregnancies). The paper prints press releases from the Roselake Ramblers announcing their next hike, and regretting that their last meeting was called off due to inclement weather. It reserves column space for local Church news - seldom called upon except to report eminent members of the congregation being called to a higher place - and generally performs such and similar duties to local approval. It illustrates its reports of these various events with sufficient photographs to make its readership happy, across the range of thrusting local politicos, cake decorators, prize vegetable growers and proud mums. Once in a blue moon an item of interest crops up on the local council, but coverage of the town's elected members usually consists of the annual photo-opportunity for the newly-elected mayor in his – or her - regalia of office, the tricorn hat, the gold chain with the enamel medallion and the ermine-trimmed cloak.

This is not to say there is never any serious news printed, but the dissemination of news is not the main reason for the paper's existence. It promotes local feel-good factor. More significantly, it keeps its advertisers happy and lines the pockets of its owner. Over half of each week's edition is, of course, dominated by estate agents' adverts, car showroom offers, and other regular advertising. The dating and introduction section has been growing recently, but whether this represents - especially the "no strings attached" section – a new lax morality amongst the population of Roselake is not for us to judge.

The Midweek Gazette is not Roselake's sole free newspaper. It is one of the two weekly tabloids which circulate around the town. The Gazette and Echo have long been rivals, but the Gazette has always maintained pole position in the race for readership and hence advertising income. The Midweek Echo attempted to steal a march on the Gazette by changing its day of appearance to Tuesday, rather than the Wednesday its title might imply. The Gazette switched to Monday, to scoop its rival. The Echo folded, the Gazette reverted to Wednesday. The Echo was resurrected and stuck to appearing on Tuesday. However the Gazette always had one big advantage. As the longer established of the two, it had maintained a far broader advertising base, which enabled it to fund a home delivery throughout the town. Whether this was a good thing is debatable. After all, some might say the town's youngsters should be doing their homework on a Wednesday evening rather than lugging newspapers around the streets for a pittance. But the delivery was much appreciated by the Roselake public, most of whom were of an age where the sound of a newspaper landing on the doormat caused a warm bout of nostalgia for days gone by, when milk and newspapers appeared at everybody's door, brightening up the day's start at breakfast time, and when post was looked forward to, dropping in twice a day. Not only were memories of the past rekindled for the older section of the population, but the Gazette's delivery saved ageing legs. Readers of the Echo had to make the effort to walk into Roselake on a Tuesday to find a copy in one of the retail outlets in the town. And Mondays were of course the traditional days for stocking up after a weekend's larder-emptying, so a Tuesday shopping trip was an unwelcome burden for those of advanced years and declining numbers, except for those who lived in town and still preferred to shop for fresh meat or vegetables daily.

In consequence, largely because of its guaranteed circulation, the Gazette continued to thrive and the Echo trailed as an also-ran.

The Echo will not thank me for saying so, but the Gazette also benefited from the quality of the staff its superior budget allowed. While the Echo remained semi-professional and often relied on amateurs to fill staff deficiencies, with a resulting mediocre quality of journalism, the Gazette presented good opportunities for budding newshounds. In recent years junior reporters at the Gazette had moved on to career-advancing situations in prestigious locations such as Reading, Basingstoke and Kings Lynn.

However, the Gazette was currently without a permanent editor. The long-standing editor Gervaise Croudace, despite being appointed on nepotistic grounds, was very capable and well-respected. Sadly for the paper he moved on to better things when he divorced his counties wife, married into even posher society and moved to London. The Gazette's owner made a poor choice of replacement. Although able, the new editor was found lacking in upstandingness when his involvement in certain illegal cross-channel activities came to light. He was obliged to resign.

The good news for the paper was that ready to step into the breach was Tanya Blackman. She had joined the Gazette only comparatively recently under Croudace's patronage, but she soon showed that her abilities were head and shoulders above those of her peers and indeed elders. To keep her on the staff, the owner offered her the post of deputy editor and temporary acting editor. Tanya seized the opportunity. But Tanya was an independent-minded woman, and it rapidly became clear that her ideas of what made stories newsworthy were not shared by the owners. She was given a sizeable financial inducement, and a glowing testimonial, to help her up the career ladder elsewhere. A new temporary editor, Carla Davis, was appointed on a one-year contract. She came from a family who ran a large stables complex on the outskirts of Roselake, and was said to spend more time on a horse than off, so her political judgement could be relied on to follow unquestioningly the owner's direction. The best anyone else can reasonably say about her without contradiction is that she can be trusted to stay relatively sober in work hours, definitely drug-free, and to avoid making her own news through illegal activities.

Whilst staff came and went at the Gazette, the Echo, meanwhile, being maintained on a shoestring, had only one permanent member of editorial staff, combining the jobs of editor, journalist and snapper. For this reason Tom Woodacre relied far more on the incoming supply of written news and publicity material from local organisations, padded out by contributions to the paper's letters page. If the Gazette flagged up an issue of potential serious local interest Tom just might think of getting his backside out of the office in the hope of next week's issue of the Echo scooping the Gazette.

Neither paper was in the habit of having a staff member attend Roselake Town Council meetings, unless there was an exceptional reason, for example the need for an illustrated article reporting the appointment of a new town crier, or, more frequently, as we have mentioned, the crowning of the new town Carnival Queen and Princess. Neither paper considered the Town Council's regular meetings of sufficient interest to their readers to make any emerging news urgent or even worthy of casual reading. The Town Council itself had responded to this lack of enthusiasm, and in the interests of democracy, as they would have it, or self-publicity as the Council's detractors would put it, they supplied not only council minutes to the papers but press releases to highlight any matters that were in the Council's opinion too important to be consigned immediately to the editors' waste bins.

On this occasion, the article which sparked off something of an uproar in the town failed to make the Town Clerk's fortnightly press release. Tom Woodacre binned the council minutes without a glance. It was only because the Gazette had a new junior reporter, Anna Shales, whose skills included the ability to distinguish what was never going to be other than inconsequential from what could be turned into an interesting story, that the article made the pages of her paper. Anna had been given the task of perusing the Town Council minutes and agendas on the off-chance that they might contain a human interest story which the Town Council themselves had overlooked.

Anna had been asked to suggest an item or two to fill a few column inches to pad out this week's paper. She had done just that. Carla had rubber-stamped the article without checking against the Council minutes, so whether we saddle Carla, Anna or both with blame for the Gazette being the catalyst for a town scandal is debatable. But who would have thought such an innocent-seeming account would send enormous ripples through the town? I could exaggerate and say the issue set father against son, husband against wife, brother against sister, friend against friend. Maybe that isn't quite the truth, but it gets pretty close by Roselake standards.

Alan Tootill

CHAPTER 1

Laura Ferguson stirred a spoonful of sugar into her husband's coffee, a blank expression on her face. It would have been impossible to guess what she was thinking. It would have been hard to discern even whether she was thinking at all. She herself, if you had asked her the question, would have maybe replied she didn't know. Or maybe she would have said she was wondering whether to put the dishwasher on, or whether to leave it until tomorrow when it was fuller.

It would be a mistake to judge from this that Laura had an empty life, or was dissatisfied with it in any way. She might have wished for more in the past, particularly for a family, but that didn't happen and she had settled contentedly into middle age and beyond, with a husband who was dull but loyal and undemanding, and whose career in company accountancy had provided a comfortable enough lifestyle. His pension continued to do that following his retirement.

Her life centred on Graham, true enough, as far as the practical side of marriage was concerned, the business of who cooks, washes, looks after the bills and more on her husband's behalf, but Laura herself did not see this as demeaning or confining. She had her friends and her regular activities. Graham never had been a joiner, and Laura had given up hope long ago of enticing him to share her interests in fitness training, yoga, watercolour painting, or any other of the activities they could have done together. That was his choice. He went out for an occasional drink and chat with a friend or two, but the Fergusons had no common circle of acquaintances, and many a night Graham would be left at home alone.

Today Laura had no classes, since the Wednesday night well-being and fitness teacher had met with an unfortunate work-related accident and was laid up in Clover Ward until further notice.

This evening would therefore follow a well-rehearsed pattern. Laura would clear the dining table and kitchen while Graham sat in the lounge and took a snooze. Laura would take him a cup of coffee. She would put the coffee on the side table beside his armchair, only knowing for sure whether he was already asleep or not by whether he was snoring. She would retire to the kitchen to finish clearing up. She would then return to the lounge after a short period, and if the coffee had not been drunk would either inform Graham loudly that his coffee was growing cold or give him a gentle tap on his knee if he was snoring. If she was not in a good mood the tap would not be so gentle and the reminder fortissimo. Laura would settle down on the sofa with a book and read. When Graham woke he would turn the television on, skim through the channels for five minutes before either complaining there never was anything worth watching these days or settling on a decades-old drama series repeat. Laura would continue her reading in the kitchen or return to join Graham in the lounge depending on her own personal television choice. At ten Graham would get up and ask Laura if she was ready for bed. Laura's answer would depend on how much she was enjoying her book and where she had reached in the current chapter. Graham's response in either case would be to go to the bedroom with 'See you soon'.

This Wednesday evening started according to pattern. Coffee was served. Five minutes later Laura revisited the lounge. Graham was resting with his head perched sideways against the armchair headrest, his mouth slightly open, usually a sign he was asleep. But it was never easy to tell from visual signs alone.

Graham had a pleasant round face creased with what can euphemistically be described as smile lines, a balding dome above a forehead creased with what we would be obliged uncharitably to call frown lines, and a moustache which led some of his friends to call him "the captain" after one had remarked on the resemblance to Arthur Lowe's character in Dad's Army. Whilst he was not given to frequent pomposity, when Graham did mount his high horse his friends looked at each other knowingly and smiled. Laura knew about Graham's nickname, because his friend Lawrence at number four had told his wife Pat who told Laura, but Laura never mentioned it and let Graham go unaware of his friends' harmless humour.

Laura said 'Tea's going cold, Graham.'

Calling the coffee "tea" was one of Laura's little private and rather humourless jokes, knowing whatever she said would probably fall on deaf ears. Graham did not stir.

'Graham, drink your coffee, now!' was delivered at a decibel level just below what might be described by a reasonable person as shouting.

Graham stirred, snorted once and opened his eyes.

'Yes, dear,' he murmured.

Laura returned to her book. She was interrupted by the sound of a thud on the front doormat. She went to investigate.

It was the Midweek Gazette. Laura picked up the paper and glanced at the front page. The main headline read "Police Hunt Car Vandal" but the front page picture was of a missing kitten and its owner, presumably now distraught, but pictured smiling. Laura took the paper into the lounge, and with 'Gazette's here' placed it on the coffee table. Graham grunted and Laura returned to the kitchen. She had a yen for a Garibaldi.

Graham roused himself and drank his coffee. He fumbled for the paper and his reading glasses. The front page headline hyped the fact that a visitor to the town, a Mr Reynolds, had left his expensive car in Roselake's main car park and found it scratched when he returned to it. This was now the subject of a high priority police investigation. In truth Jamie Reynolds had had a collision with his son's bicycle when he left his Dorchester home that morning. The bike fared better than the Porsche, which is not the most economical car when it comes to bodywork repairs. Jamie cursed his son's carelessness and continued his journey. He'd stopped in Roselake for a coffee. Unusually, a community support officer happened to be nearby when Jamie was exiting the Roselake car park after his latte. Reynolds was half an hour ahead of his schedule, and with insurance companies being far more willing to pay out if a police report endorses a claim, and since his policy contained a clause excluding criminal damage from an excess cost, Jamie was more than happy when he hit on the idea of placing his opportunistic account of the incident in the hands of the officer.

According to the Gazette report, the police claimed there had been a rash of car vandalism in the town recently. This latest event, the scraping of a Porsche, was part of a sinister unwelcome pattern. The police would take all possible steps to stamp out this latest crime wave.

It was true there had been an incident of car vandalism recently in the town. A single incident. The police would not lie, of course. Exaggerate a little maybe, since the community support officer had to show that some liaising was happening, show that the support officers were supporting, and demonstrate to the public that the police were on top of any sign of Roselake lawlessness. The truth was no less dramatic than the crime wave scare story. Darren Hastings of the Beaver Estate had been upset when he discovered that his so-called mate Colin Waring had been humping his girlfriend. He keyed Colin's Volvo.

Darren had as much interest in bending an out-of-towner's bodywork as admitting he was the father of Chrissie's baby, and was definitely out of the frame for the latest outrage. Particularly as Colin had, on finding his car keyed, acted as investigator, judge and jury and put Darren in hospital, which was the only reason the police found out about the business with the car. The reader of the Gazette was not, of course, privy to this information, nor, to be fair, was the paper's editorial staff, who would probably have made a more engrossing story out of the truth than propagating the fiction

Graham humphed and tutted, and turned the page.

Laura's taste in reading was varied. She would read any novel as long as the writer was female. Or, exceptionally, she would be tempted, if her reading circle recommended a particular book, to venture into male territory. Her love affairs with male authors tended to be brief encounters.

Laura liked to have two books on the go, one for kitchen or lounge reading and one for bedroom reading. There was no subject matter choice, the next book was read wherever the first vacancy occurred. Currently her kitchen reading was a Margaret Atwood novel which Laura wasn't, if she were honest to herself, getting on very well with. Tonight her reluctant reading of page seventy-eight was rudely interrupted. Graham pushed open the kitchen door stabbing the fingers of his right hand into a page of the Gazette and muttering.

Laura was a little concerned. Graham's face was flushed and she hadn't seen agitation like this since she accidentally broke the most treasured of his coronation mug collection.

'Do calm down, dear, you know one more run of peaking systolic pressure and the doctor will move you on to the next level of blood pressure pills.' She knew Graham's fear of moving on to the next medication level, it smacked of the next nail in his coffin.

'Have you seen this?' Graham repeated, stabbing the paper again. The page he was attacking had not had time to recover from his last assault and rent.

'You know quite well I haven't seen it, whatever it is. I put it on your table for you to read.'

'Well read this!' Graham pushed the paper into Laura's hands, his speech volume definitely reaching shout level.

Laura looked at page five. The offending article had been mutilated. A V-shaped tear had worked its way down to put the column beyond view.

'Do calm down. If you want me to read it then please do a repair. You know where the Sellotape is.'

This was a wrong move. Laura had underestimated Graham's mood. He told her to just read the thing. He inserted a word he didn't use often before the word "thing". Laura didn't use this word at all, although she found it tended to crop up more and more in the modern books she read. She had no real opinion on that in general terms, she was too much of a realist to want to turn the vocabulary decency clock back, but she was a little perturbed to find Graham swearing at her. These days your ears had to get used to hearing the f word quite frequently in the street. Not just on a Saturday night as the pubs were emptying. So many young people walked down the street holding mobile phones to the side of their heads, completely oblivious to the fact that their conversation was far from private. To be honest, if Laura were asked to say whether she would object more to hearing details of someone's latest surgical operation than to details of someone's husband's infidelity, she might have said spare me both, but cut the cursing. Laura was nevertheless, and inevitably, getting used to youngsters punctuating their calls with swearing, but she took umbrage at its cropping up within the home.

She took the paper, laid it on the kitchen table and restored the damaged column. The article was short.

Council to rename Beggars Way

Roselake Town Council agreed last Monday a request by residents of Beggars Way to rename their leafy road Cypress Avenue.

Laura was puzzled. 'What does this mean?' she asked.

'Presumably what it bloody well says,' Graham said, his decibel level only reducing slightly. 'The buggers want to change the bloody name.'

Laura couldn't see this was worth risking a stroke for and told Graham exactly that.

'I'm not going to have a flipping stroke, I'm just flaming angry. How can they do that? It's not on. It's outrageous.'

At least Graham's swearing had toned down a notch, if not in quantity then in degree of obscenity, Laura was pleased to note.

'But what's so wrong about changing the name?'

'Wrong? It's bloody obvious, you silly woman. This has been Beggars Way for centuries.'

Laura pondered her response. It might not be politic, she decided, to raise the point that when they first saw their property in the estate agent's window, Graham's reaction had been "Beggar's Way? Who'd want to live in a road with a name like that?". Nor did Laura want to escalate Graham's verbal abuse of her beyond use of the word "silly".

Instead she used some invention. 'But it might be nice to change address for once and not have to spend weeks packing and unpacking all our furniture and belongings. You know how hard that was the last time. Nearly killed us. And Cypress Avenue is quite a nice name. Rings some sort of bell but I can't place it. We could send out change of address cards to all our friends and get letters congratulating us and telling us all their news. Like another Christmas but more personal, and none of those unimaginative robin pictures.'

Graham was neither amused nor mollified. Nor was he to be drawn into a conversation about social interaction with old friends. 'Beggar's Way it is and Beggar's Way it will stay, if I have anything to do with it. And talking of that, just who are these bloody residents who asked for the name change? Not me for a start.'

'Nor I,' Laura was forced to concede.

'Well then. It's an outrage.'

'Well you can't do anything tonight. Why don't you go down to the Council offices tomorrow morning and ask what it's all about?'

Graham fanned his face with an untorn part of the paper. 'I suppose. You don't think the Gazette offices would be open now?'

'No. Watch Midsomer Murders or something and forget it until tomorrow.'

'I bet I've seen it before ten times.'

'I'm sure you have. But I checked tonight's episode. It's one with that actress you're fond of, what's her name, the one with the big chest.'

Laura knew how to hit Graham's weak spot. She had no idea whether the actress in question was in tonight's decades-old episode, but since she seemed to appear in roughly half the episodes you watched of that or any other similar vintage series it was a fair bet Laura's ruse wouldn't be discovered.

Graham made an attempt, but was too agitated to watch television for long. He went to bed early and had a sleepless night.

It was very true that the short stretch of highway Beggars Way had been so named for a long time. Old maps located its beginning at the gate of the ancient chapel of St Cecilia and indicated its course eastwards towards the modern Roselake centre. I say modern, Roselake had changed little, at least in pattern after the Regency period. But for a fire or two over the centuries since then, and the incursion of modern chain stores like Boots, W H Smiths, and more recently the Costa, Wetherspoons and Boston Tea Party brigade, it would still have been recognisable to a time traveller from the 18th century. Roselake could have retained a High Street to be envied up and down the country. However, now, to the blinkered eye of the shop-seeking or in-and-out passing visitor its visual impact based on ground-floor shop frontages was just like any another town up and down the length of modern Britain. But Roselake still had a hint of history here and there discernable to those who had looked up a town guide book - the old coaching inns, the churches, the museum and old schoolhouse, the toll gates.

Brittany has menhirs and dolmens associated with fertility rites. India has ancient wells for barren women to take a dip in. Roselake has St Cecilia's Chapel. In the town's history and legend St Cecilia's takes a prominent role. Although modest in size, it was not modest in reputation, especially in the 14th century when the legend arose that any Roselake woman who was desiring motherhood but had so far been denied, should spend one night within the chapel and her wishes would be fulfilled. The legend persisted and was incorporated into the town's seal, which shows an obviously pregnant woman hand in hand with a more ambiguous male figure whose attire has caused some debate, but whose long skirts today would point in a particular direction, that of a churchman. In the oldest extant version of the seal he appears tonsured, and holding something in his free hand. Conjecture has been that this was a musical instrument, maybe a flute or similar, as befitting a reference to St Cecilia's patronage of music. However to avoid rude speculation the object was removed in versions of the seal remaining from about 1830 onwards.

At the time the legend of the gift of pregnancy arose, it was recorded that the priest of St Cecilia's was a certain Father Crispian. Some doubt exists in the church records of how someone so young came to be appointed to his position. One scholar in the following century asserted that Crispian had discovered the peccadillo of his abbot superior, John of Dunkeswell, on which through fear of exposure of said peccadillo Crispian was banished to Roselake. The scholars did not publish openly until recently the suspicion that the nubile young women of Roselake had their wishes fulfilled by the proactive efforts of the young and virile Father Crispian during their night in the chapel, and speculation is that he ensured they had the promised vision by supplying them with a potion which made them receptive but not recollective of his activity on their behalf.

Today St Cecilia's is deconsecrated and remains unused except as a wedding venue, a joint venture between the church, which still owns the premises, and the Roselake Carvery, which provides the reception facilities including a pre-honeymoon suite to encourage the young marrieds to re-enact the union of Crispian and the childless wife, if they need any such encouragement.

The Carvery also most importantly provides car parking. Beggars Way was long ago sealed off at the chapel end to allow pedestrian only access, and make Beggars Way the quiet cul-de-sac it now is. A main road now runs past the chapel from the town towards Exeter.

Leading down to the chapel, on the northern side of Beggars Way, is a mixture of buildings, a ruined workhouse cottage near the chapel, a couple of Edwardian houses, a 1930s pair of houses at the eastern end, and in between these a number of roomy bungalows built in the 1950s and 60s.

On the opposite side of the road there are no houses for the majority of the stretch, instead the road is flanked by a green bank fronted by trees of modest size, but adequately sheltering the road from view of the council estate to the south. At the eastern end of Beggars Way, in the 1990s, a small development was allowed to occupy the site of an old school premises, which were demolished. Fronting onto Beggars Way, the houses had garaging and parking to the rear, so had no significant impact on the existing houses over the road, but nevertheless a divide had been created by the construction of this new mini-estate of modern, characterless, terraced properties.

When Roselake town clerk Hilary Jessop arrived to open up the council offices on Thursday morning she did not expect to find someone pacing back and forth waiting for her. She arrived as always on the dot of 9.25 a.m. to give herself time to unlock the office and collect the post from the mailbox before opening the doors to the public at 9.30 as advertised. Normally no visitors arrived before ten o'clock, since most were elderly and waited to use their free bus passes before venturing out. Hilary therefore usually had plenty of time to open the post and plan her morning before being interrupted by interlopers. She resented opening up her space to the hoi polloi, she viewed the offices, and indeed the council, as her preserve.

Hilary had performed the duties of town clerk for three years. The previous incumbent, a pedantic and mean-minded individual, had kept the councillors on the leash and under the lash by inflicting on them his apparent superior knowledge of local government law. In reality this was seriously flawed, but the town councillors did not know that. There are few qualities needed to fulfil the duties of a town councillor. Intellect and knowledge of legalities are not amongst these. So a town clerk has an immediate advantage, especially if he has ruled the roost for at least a decade.

Uncharitably, but not unfairly, it has to be said that Hilary Jessop could also be a pedantic and mean-minded creature, and in that sense she was a natural successor to Jeremy Jennings. She had little knowledge of town council procedures and legalities when she applied for the job, but had demonstrable advantages over the other applicants. She was female, and obviously intelligent. Key was the first of these qualities. The chairman of the selection committee, undergoing a time of challenge in his married life, took a fancy to her. But perhaps, even if this had been not a deciding factor, the same decision would have been arrived at as there were no other able applicants. Hilary was appointed to the post, shipped off on a training course and came back with attitude. She was a quick learner. She used what she had imbibed on her course to persuade the council that they had been doing things wrong for years and that she would now be the sole arbiter of procedure, would go through with a new broom, revising standing orders and issuing council guidance. Three years on, her position was now unassailable.

The councillors were now under her control. Unfortunately from her point of view, the public were not. But usually they trickled in to her office in such small numbers that she didn't have to face a peasants' uprising. This morning's early visitor looked controllable, as Hilary read a certain anxiety, rather than a propensity for aggression, on his face. She opened the office door and made to close it in Graham's face. Graham was not happy. It was hard whether his little squeal was the start of an "Excuse me" or "Just a". But Hilary got the message. She turned and pointed to her watch. The clock was still a couple of minutes short of half-past.

Graham fumed but had no choice. He stood and waited. Minutes ticked by as Hilary made herself a cup of tea, a deliberate ploy to assert her bailiwick and her supremacy.

Five minutes late, Hilary opened up the door and smiled at Graham, beckoning him in. However duplicitous she might be, no-one could say that Hilary did not know how to smile, fleetingly maybe, but effectively. Graham, who had been working himself up into a fever planning how he would deliberately point to his watch when the door opened, found himself instantly disarmed. He followed Hilary through the entrance lobby, which had a couple of chairs and all the personality and appeal of a dentist's waiting room, to the small reception office, furnished only with an enquiry desk. Hilary retired behind her desk counter and dropped its hinged section to separate herself from her visitor. Behind her a second door led to her own office domain.

'Now, how can I help you, Mr…?'

Hilary's tone was harsher than Graham had expected. She had an extremely pleasant oval face under neat well-cut short auburn hair, and Graham had already experienced her ability to turn on charm. But her tone was now surprisingly authoritarian, accentuated by a stern glance over her spectacles which she wore perched on the end of a rather dainty nose. They would have seemed at high risk of falling to the floor had they not been held by a gold chain which hung rather attractively at the sides of Hilary's slender neck. She wore a plain white blouse over a grey skirt. Both were well-filled. Graham's confidence was unsettled as his manliness was stirred.

17

'Ferguson. Graham Ferguson,' he replied nervously. 'It's about this.'

Graham pulled the Gazette clipping out of his jacket pocket and placed it on the counter.

'Well, it appears to be a rather mauled snippet from a newspaper. Your point being?'

Graham's minutes waiting outside the council door had not improved his mood, he had tried to control himself, but this rather insulting speech by Hilary was enough to resurrect Graham's anger.

'It's an outrage. You are not going to change the name of Beggars Way. You council people think you can get away with anything just because you got a few voters to elect you in. Well I'm telling you it won't wash!'

Hilary measured her response. Her desire was to tell Graham exactly what she thought of him and where to go, but that wasn't going to happen. The smile had worked before, she tried it again. The fact, as already commented on, that she was not unpleasant to the eye, at least to that of a man of advancing years, worked in her favour, as she knew it would.

'Mr Ferguson, can I first of all say I am just the town clerk. I don't make the decisions, I just record them. It's really rather unfair of you to blame me.' Hilary carefully avoided the truth that she was elected by no-one, except the mayor, in case that inflamed Graham's rant.

Graham backed down. Hilary gave that smile again and wobbled her chest under the pretext of raising herself to her full height. He was now vanquished.

'I'm sorry, I, I, really don't know that much about politics.'

'Don't mention politics to the town council, Mr Ferguson, I'm sure all the councillors would say that they are there with the sole intention of looking after the interests of the community, not to indulge in politicking and pursuing party interests.'

Graham refocused. He was starting to feel he was being patronised. He had been patronised before, as some people are whose physical presence is not entirely prepossessing or assertive. He recognised the signs.

'So please explain to me about this article.' Graham pointed to the news clipping, trying to put a note of authority into his voice.

'Can I ask you what your interest is in the matter?'

'I live in Beggars Way and this is the first I've heard of any plan to change the name.'

Hilary paid closer attention to the text of the article. A warning bell sounded in Hilary's brain. As I said she was not unintelligent. She had the first inkling that this was a matter that deserved careful handling.

'Well the article is a little inaccurate. This matter arose at last week's council meeting and the councillors made their decision. The council did not agree to change the name. We, that is they, received a letter from what we, I mean they, took as representatives of the residents of Beggars Way asking for a name change. The council simply decided they had no objection in principle.'

'So they agreed the change.'

Hilary winced, but gave it a second shot. 'No, let me try to explain further. The ability to change the name falls not within the remit of the Town Council but of the District Council. The District Council will take the Town Council's views into account as their primary direction in the matter. There are sundry other enquiries they must make before they take a decision.'

'So it's not cut and dried?'

'By no means. As I have just explained.'

'But the Town Council has decided?'

'Only as a preliminary assessment.'

'So this article's wrong?'

'I'd not say it is wrong, just that it is not entirely accurate.'

'So. What do we, the real residents of Beggars Way, have to do to stop this?'

'But we had a letter from residents, as I told you.'

'I would like to see that. Can you show me a copy?'

'Have you any proof of residence, and your interest in this matter?'

'No, and I'm sure I don't need it. I may not know about politics, and I don't have a law degree, but I do have the internet. I looked up the Freedom of Information Act before I came.'

For the first time Hilary saw Graham as an adversary not to be dismissed lightly. He was, of course, absolutely right, even though he was fibbing on this occasion. Someone had told him about the Freedom of Information Act during a pub discussion of whether they could find out why the District Council had allowed a cull of the seagulls in Rosemouth, despite a public outcry. It is doubtful, however, whether such a request would have revealed that just days before the Council's decision, the leader's wife had had her chihuahua puppy killed in a gull attack.

Hilary decided not to test Graham's knowledge of the law. But she still wanted to make a point.

'You can have a photocopy. It will cost you 50p.'

'50p for a photocopy? That's extortionate.' Graham blustered.

'I don't make the rules,' Hilary lied.

Graham fumbled in his pockets. He had no change. He withdrew his wallet from his trouser pocket and extracted a note.

'I'm not sure I have change for that,' Hilary said.

Graham's exasperation level was rising. He fumbled in his trouser pocket and came up with a pound coin.

'Nor that,' Hilary said unhelpfully.

'Well give me two blooming copies then,' Graham blurted.

Owing to the arrival of three more enquirers at the office, fresh off the occasional town bus, Graham was directed into the lobby to sit and read the letter the Town Council had received. It was dated two weeks ago, and was short and to the point.

Dear Sir/Madam

We, the undersigned residents of Beggars Way, request that the council renames our road Cypress Avenue, which is far more suitable for its leafy environs.

'Leafy bloody environs?' Graham swore to himself. What on earth was that supposed to mean? The signatories all lived on the south side of Beggars Way, the terraced housing. They hadn't even managed to keep grass leaves growing on their arid lawn handkerchiefs, probably still poisoned from construction activity.

Moss Lane might be more appropriate, Graham thought, his sense of humour waking up.

Graham stood in the queue for a further interview with Hilary. He listened to a woman complaining about the amount of dog poo that accumulated in the drive of her home and heard Hilary stressing that this was a District Council matter. The lady, Mrs Hacker, said she would see about that and warned Hilary to expect a letter from her solicitor if she slipped on a stray dog turd or her child contracted toxocariasis and went blind. Hilary mentally scoured her brain and, remembering that the Town Council had insurance against a variety of possible claims, smiled sweetly and said she would await a legal envelope, but Mrs Hacker was far better advised to consult Mrs Sweeney at the District Council if she wanted any action.

Graham listened to a man complaining that someone kept parking in his disabled parking space and heard Hilary explain this was a County Council matter. The man limped off without further remonstrance.

Graham then overheard a complaint about rats in the back garden and, again the complainant, a Mrs Griffiths, was informed this was a District Council matter. Deirdre Griffiths argued that rodents paid little attention, even assuming they were literate, had access to the internet, and were politically aware, to council responsibility demarcation boundaries. This was the Town Council who - supposedly - served the Roselake residents, and she wanted it sorted out pretty damn quick. She had a young kitten but was not prepared to wait for Gilbert's maturity and anyway he had been neutered and might never become a rat catcher. Graham smiled at all this but was warned off by a piercing glance from Hilary, who continued to advise Mrs Griffiths that she should take her complaint elsewhere.

Graham began to wonder if the Town Council served any purpose at all. The short answer was in reality it had little responsibility or authority, but its existence served to persuade the Roselake electorate that local democracy was well and thriving.

Graham reached the front of the queue. Admittedly it had not been very long, and had been handled quickly by Hilary's no-nonsense approach. With no-one to overhear, Graham pointed out vociferously the deficiencies in the letter the council had received, as he saw them. Hilary used her sweet smile again but sensed it had lost its charm when Graham's moustache failed to raise itself at the sides. She reiterated to Graham that the matter of renaming streets or roads was an issue for the District, but was forced to admit that if Graham made a persuasive argument to the Town Council opposing the name change and made it by tomorrow in writing with some support from other Beggars Way residents, this could feature on next Monday's council agenda.

Graham left with his own agenda fixed in his mind. He had formulated a plan.

CHAPTER 2

Graham did not go straight home, but dropped in at number four. His friend Lawrence was the best person to speak to about the state of affairs. Lawrence Stone was home, but did not invite Graham in. He was in the middle of the latest spat with his wife Patricia. It had not yet reached frying-pan throwing level but had escalated and was rapidly nearing that point when interrupted by the doorbell. Lawrence's face looked drawn, but then in contrast to Graham's rounded features he always looked pale and on the haggard side of thin and troubled. Lawrence grabbed his jacket from the hall coat stand, shouted roughly 'Got to go out', presumably for Pat's benefit, and grabbing the startled Graham by the arm said, 'Thanks, my friend, let's go to the Carvery, I owe you a drink.' Graham got the message. But he looked at his watch with concern. It was barely half past ten. No way was it yet sun over the yardarm time. But he needed to talk to Lawrence, and intuited that Lawrence did not want to go to Graham's and have Laura start asking questions about Pat's well-being, and why Graham and Lawrence could not have had refreshment and chitchat at number four.

The Carvery provided the nearest bar to Beggars Way. Other than that advantage it had none. To men of Graham and Lawrence's generation the music was diabolical and too loud, the service over-familiar (Graham winced whenever he heard "What can I get you guys?"), and the beer would only satisfy the palate of a youngster wanting to lose his ale-supping virginity. Graham had just ambled back from town and his left knee was aching. If they were not to drink at the Carvery, it was a trek out to the Broadwood estate to the Haymaker's, which was an improvement on the Carvery, as it at least served a decent beer, even if the décor was designed and remained still after thirty years to the tastes of the 1980s incomers. It would have been an even longer trek into town to the Mill or the Anchor, both traditional pubs on the west side of town which employed jovial staff and served real ale.

Lawrence and Graham established themselves in a corner, pushing the Carvery's mock medieval menu aside, and planting their pints and double scotches on the table. This must have been quite a dingdong, for Lawrence to splash out on double chasers, Graham thought.

'Funny, isn't it?' Lawrence said.

'What is?' Graham was puzzled. Graham had a sense of humour, somewhat eccentric, and dry perhaps to some people's taste, possibly due to the fact that as a boy he had been what used to be called reserved or shy, and spent too much time sitting on his own, reading. Probably today such behaviour would be called introverted bordering on the anti-social and calling for some remedial psychiatric attention. But he had muddled through, as most people would, without such intervention, and had given up reading Kafka and Dostoyevsky decades ago. As proof of his rehabilitation he often incurred Laura's displeasure by viewing old Carry On films, which he claimed raised the use of pun and double-entendre to the level of art. Laura had her own view on that. She believed personal intimate relations and talk about them belonged in the bedroom, not on a screen in the lounge. And some bodily functions deserved no mention at all anywhere.

'Marriage, eh.' Lawrence didn't elaborate but downed his double scotch without touching his beer. He grinned.

Graham didn't see what was amusing about marriage. Challenging, demanding, sometimes. Welcome, warm and reassuring often. Amusing, rarely. But he was anxious to raise the subject of the renaming of the road, not have Lawrence start pontificating about wedlock in general or the deficiencies of Lawrence's own matrimonial arrangements or spousal choice.

'I suppose.'

Silence followed. Graham thought the best opportunity for him to bring his preferred subject of conversation up was when he returned with another large scotch for Lawrence. Which he did. This enabled him to broach the subject directly.

'You know they want to rename Beggars Way "Cypress Avenue"?' Graham said, after slamming the new glass down on the table to announce his arrival back in Lawrence's company.

Lawrence looked blank. 'What?'

'Those newcomers over the road want to change the name of our lane to Cypress Avenue.'

'What, Beggars Way?'

'Unless you have a blooming mansion somewhere else, right. They've only gone and written to the town council and presented it as though it was a done thing, like we all want it.'

'That's nonsense. I'm happy as it is. I suppose. Never thought about it.'

'Me too. Happy with the name I mean. So what are we going to do about it? Did you see yesterday's Gazette? Talked of it as a fait accompli. Roselake Town Council has agreed. Well I went in this morning and it's BS. Take a look at this.'

Graham pulled out of his jacket pocket a copy of the letter to the town council. Lawrence read it.

'It's those Grant people, the ones with the kid who leaves his bloody windows open playing all that loud throbbing music with the speakers pointing in our direction, and the Barkers who are as common as muck, and the Jacksons who don't even give you time of day.'

'I know all that, Lawrence. It's all down there in writing, who signed. Now the point is, what are we going to do about it?'

'What can we do?' Lawrence was eyeing the interior of his glass with a look that said he was concentrating more on the imminent prospect of its becoming an alcohol-free zone rather than on the subject of his friend's concern.

'I was in the council offices this morning. All we have to do is get some signatures on a rival letter to say we don't want to change the name, get it in to the council by tomorrow, and the whole issue will be reopened.'

Lawrence downed the remainder of his second double scotch and with an "I'll get you another" lurched towards the bar. When he came back to the table he asked 'Why don't we want the name changed, exactly?' Graham's eyes lifted to the ceiling and he proceeded to tell Lawrence how this would be a very grave blasphemy. How it would overturn centuries of Roselake history.

'And how those jumped-up bastards over the road would get the better of us,' Lawrence added.

'Exactly,' Graham agreed.

Lawrence tilted his whisky down his throat and raised his hand in arm-wrestling fashion. Graham felt impelled to take his grasp. Lawrence didn't want to fight, he wanted to make a declaration. 'All for one, one for all.'

After another couple of drinks Lawrence and Graham had an agreed scheme. Despite their units of alcohol consumption, it was a fair and moderate one. They returned to Graham's, number fourteen. Lawrence was not sure what reception he would have from Pat if he went home. If she were feeling repentant or forgiving she might be cooking him lunch, and if he didn't return it would not go down well. But if Pat were intractable and still on the boil she would be brewing up an argument to last the rest of the day. On balance Lawrence thought best to repair to Graham's, let Graham write the letter they proposed, and while waiting enjoy a cup of Laura's coffee.

Graham fumbled with his keys and Laura came to the door. She sniffed the air, said 'What the hell are you two doing getting drunk at this time of day?' and returned to whatever she had been doing in the kitchen.

Graham followed her through and asked if there was any chance of a coffee. The answer was an emphatic and unapologetic negative. Graham asked didn't Laura want to know how he got on at the Council earlier. Laura did not. She told him she was going out shopping, he could tell her later when she was back and he had sobered up.

'Told you,' Lawrence said, when the door had slammed.

'Told me what?'

'Funny, marriage.'

An hour later Graham had managed not only to keep Lawrence happy with a supply of strong coffee, but had produced a final draft of a letter to the Town Council. The scheme was to tout it round the northern side houses canvassing signatures this evening. On the assumption that nobody had yet caught on to the fact there was a plot to rename the road, that might take some time, as explanations would be necessary.

The letter was addressed to the town clerk. Slightly embarrassingly, in his agitation this morning, Graham had forgotten Hilary Jessop's name, but was saved by that nice Mr Google who provided the web site address of Roselake Town Council and all its contact details. Unfortunately Hilary's marital status was not specified (she was unmarried, but definitely not a dried-up spinster, as we shall be made aware of shortly) so Graham had to use Ms, which he hated.

The letter read

Dear Ms Jessop

Thank you for providing this morning the information regarding an application the Council received requesting a change of name of Beggars Way.

We, the undersigned residents of Beggars Way, confirm that we oppose any such change, and request that the Council reconsiders its approval in principle, and instead recommends refusal of the application.

Yours sincerely

'That should do it,' Graham said, passing the final version to Lawrence.

'I should bloody well hope so,' Lawrence moaned. Do you realise how long you've been sitting at that machine? And how many drafts it took? How much ink you've wasted? At least you'll have enough waste paper for setting your fire all next winter.'

Graham didn't take offence. He was fully aware that his fingers had experienced a degree of difficulty following the instructions of his brain, and that his brain had experienced a few judgement wobbles during the preparation of the letter, despite the sobering effects of espresso. The spellchecker had corrected "refusle", but had reserved judgement over "principle" or "principal", which left Lawrence and Graham to debate that final outcome. 'I'll print an extra few copies,' Graham said. 'If anyone's out we can leave them and ask them to sign and bring round tonight or first thing tomorrow.'

'How are you going to tell them if they're out?'

'Good point, I'll write another note to drop through the letterbox with the letter.'

Lawrence sighed. 'If you think I'm waiting another geological era for you to type another letter you're mistaken. I'd better go home and face the music. Just print me three or four copies of the letter for me to take now. I'll start about six o'clock tonight. If you manage to write a line or two by then for a while you were out note, drop it round before then. I'll do numbers two to twelve on our side of the road, you do the rest. I'll see you in the morning. Or earlier, if I need a bed for the night.'

Lawrence did not, after all, need to beg a night's lodging from his neighbours. It's true Pat was prone to attacks of temper. You might have said it came with her redhead genes, unless you knew that her hair colour, whilst carefully maintained to avoid any suspicion otherwise, was not the one God had given her or planned for her from birth. Fortunately for Lawrence, Pat was volatile but forgiving. She was easily moved to forget her tantrums, and Lawrence's homecoming was a welcomed one. So welcome was he in fact that he totally ignored his duty to go out collecting signatures.

At the same time as Lawrence and Pat were making up in the traditional time-honoured way, Hilary was engaged in a similar activity. Not that she had fallen out with anyone, but it was a bit of a habitual practice and duty, if a moderately pleasurable one. She had just taken a delivery of wine, and was entertaining the deliverer. For preference she would have enjoyed different company, but she was in the predicament of having developed in the past a taste for fine wine. This was during her one and only cohabiting relationship, with an affluent partner whose pocket had educated her. She had subsequently lost the taste for her partner, and simultaneously for cohabiting, but not her taste for wine. In London she had maintained a relatively high-level job, or at least well-paying, which meant after going solo her wine enjoyment suffered no interruption.

Unfortunately, three years later, her circumstances had changed. The unsatisfactory outcome of an office relationship deprived her of both reputation and employment. Her redundancy money, although somewhat over-generous, in order to reduce the chances of further embarrassment for her boss whose personal assistant had provided more than secretarial and administrative support, was not going to last forever, and personal budget cuts had to be made. After much paperwork study, and failing to find new employment she thought worthy of her, Hilary decided she had no alternative but to leave London in order to minimise her outgoings. For weeks she weighed the pros and cons of various parts of the country. The North was a desolate land, so she had read in the paper recently, according to a southern Lord somebody or other. Wales she had found cold, grey and bleak. Scotland had its quota of ubiquitous midges. She was not fond of water, which ruled out East Anglia.

Hilary's thoughts therefore turned to the South-West. Warm she was told, due to it being in receipt of the benefits of the Gulf Stream. No-one warned her that it also brought a rainy and damp climate. Hilary liked the idea not of owning a nice Devon thatched cottage - she was far too sensitive about insects which she was sure infested straw rooves - but of living amongst them, they were so picturesque, she thought. Roselake had a fair number of pretty cottages to be admired on walks out, and reasonably-priced more modern accommodation. It was on a train line with direct link to Waterloo, which gave Hilary a quick escape route back to civilisation if she needed it. Roselake was decided on. She found an inexpensive house in the town centre to rent, and her move worked out well for her.

Hilary was slightly discomfited to find that certain commodities were no cheaper in Roselake than they had been in London. She realised she was unlikely to satisfy her urges for the wines she craved, whose prices were hiked by subsequent budgets and a catalogue of alleged production problems blamed on climate change.

Hilary accustomed herself to the inevitability of a reduction in the standards which her nose and palate would have preferred. Although she knew she would miss the tingle of excitement she had experienced when bidding at Christies fine wine auctions, and indulging in London society chatter about this year's new find, after arrival in Roselake Hilary was ready to drink her remaining stock and throw herself on the mercy of the town's purveyors of what she expected to be mediocre wines, if her occasional investigation of London supermarket wine shelves had been any yardstick. To her surprise, she had found a High Street shop which was a cut above the off-licence chains and supermarkets she had been used to turning her nose up at. For some weeks she had rejected the shop because of its off-putting name, but she was pleasantly surprised when she finally entered "Roselake Bin Ends". It offered good well-selected wines at sensible prices. Another plus, it provided her with a range of new taste experiences, even if she could not afford the wines on the higher shelves and racks, which she still lusted after. The shop, which had a constantly shifting stock, was run by two brothers, who had bought the business two years ago as a going concern from Marcus Webber, who said he wanted to retire. After the sale was completed, Marcus promptly opened a new shop in Rosemouth and resumed profitable trading with a bonus of a nice sum stashed away towards his genuine retirement, which he figured was still some years away.

This didn't, however, affect the Roselake wine shop which was rebranded and revitalised by the Parsons brothers. Malcolm assumed the pose of resident wine buff and friend to all, while his brother Oscar travelled around the country, and indeed occasionally on the continent, constantly finding new deals. It was said by some that quite often shop stock had fallen off lorries. This was certainly in many cases literally true. Frequently, stock appeared on the shelves and in the bins with wine-stained labels, unbroken bottles legally acquired after road accidents. It was also true that Oscar was indeed more of a wheeler-dealer and ambulance-chaser in search of the vinous equivalent of road kill than an upright businessman, although he did have genuine master sommelier qualifications behind him. But the customers were content to enjoy bargains, no accusations were ever made in public against Oscar, and even if they had been, complaints would have not have gone very far. Oscar ensured that the local police had a regular opportunity to sample the shop's wares.

Whilst Hilary had more of a personal affinity with Malcolm, with whom she enjoyed reminiscing about her previous wine tasting existence, it was Oscar who, being the more practical of the brothers, and it must be said the friskier of the two both in mind and body, offered a solution to Hilary's frustration at not being able to afford her desired wine treats.

Once a week Oscar would come round in the evening to deliver a few bottles or a box of wine, and Hilary would offer compensation for his generosity. Oscar was robustly attractive, with a manly jaw and manly rest of him, and Hilary did not find reciprocating Oscar's munificence an imposition.

Had she possessed a more romantic imagination and inclination, or been in a less mercenary frame of mind this evening, Hilary would have preferred to be in the arms of her more regular lover, Brian Sanderson. Brian was currently Mayor of Roselake, and had served in the same office three times in the past. The post was annually-appointed through election by the town council members, but it was understood that two years in a row would be the maximum before allowing another councillor to don the ermine-dressed robe and tricorn hat, and wear the gold plated chain and enamelled badge of office. But even when not mayor, Brian effectively ruled the roost on Roselake Town Council. No-one was elected mayor or deputy mayor without being made to feel under an obligation to him. He had a forceful personality, was generous to his friends, and cut the legs from under his enemies.

Until very recently, which in Devon time means about ten years ago, he had served on the District Council, and held influential posts within the ruling party, hoping to rise eventually to become leader. Unfortunately he was too prone to serving himself by abusing his position as Chairman of the Planning Committee rather than serving his electoral constituents, and when a particularly reprehensible breach of council and planning rules became public knowledge it was reported to the Local Government Ombudsman. Brian found himself on the slippery slope. He bluffed and blustered for a while, but eventually his continued presence in prominent council office became too much of an embarrassment for his party, and too much in particular for the then leader of the council to stomach. Brian was forced to resign. He then compensated by setting out to rule Roselake by moulding the Town Council to his purposes. However, in his business activities, which included property development and consultancy, he continued to use his district council experience and contacts with officers and councillors. In brief, he advised developers proposing dubious schemes as to who was the best person on the council to cultivate friendship with or bribe.

It was Brian who had taken a fancy to Hilary when she applied for the job of town clerk. After her appointment, Brian made it crystal clear why she had achieved this, and down to whose sole influence she had gained the post, and he was pleasantly surprised to find that his sexual advances were not unwelcome. Although his marriage to his wife Sylvia had since recovered from its lowest depths, there had never been any question thereafter of Brian and Hilary's relationship being discontinued. Brian assumed that the financial assistance he gave Hilary occasionally, especially when she helped him with one of his business deals, paid for the expensive bottles of wine he sometimes saw and occasionally shared when he visited her at her home. Brian of course did not know about Oscar, nor the fact that Hilary was salting Brian's cash away to put aside for a rainy day when her face lost its youth, her breasts drooped, her bottom sagged and she developed varicose veins.

Brian found it extremely useful to have not only an undemanding and willing bedfellow but a town clerk who was always guaranteed to be batting for his team. Although his town council role was more useful in maintaining his public status than directly lucrative, Brian did take some personal pleasure in being able to manipulate lesser beings, as he considered the rest of the councillors to be. Hilary proved a loyal assistant in helping to bend councillors' opinions in the direction Brian desired. From her point of view Hilary was happy to run the town council office, taking regular salary rises, and she took private pleasure in being the right hand woman of a man of some local influence, even if Roselake was not the City of London.

This evening the man of influence was involved in delicate negotiations over a contract for the construction of a new town centre community complex. The delicacy of the matter involved how the payments that Brian would receive for his involvement would be hidden from public scrutiny.

For many years now, even decades, Roselake's population had been growing, with new housing estates springing up as the demand for retirement homes from incomers from the south-east was fed by a council in league with local developers. Individual councillors, developers, builders and other parties to the construction supply chain had all benefited from the enthusiastic housing expansion policy. Roselake's population had nearly doubled in the last thirty years. Unfortunately the town centre had not changed to accommodate the needs of the increased population, and the new estates were built with no community or entertainment facilities to relieve the pressure on the centre.

A growing divide had developed between the incomers, whose vision of a rural town retirement idyll fell flat when they realised there was nothing for them to do in town once the shops had closed, and the older indigenous Roselakeians, who liked the town the way it was - or the way they remembered it - as it had been in their youth. The incomers also found that in this part of the country you remained just that for perhaps two or three decades before becoming grudgingly accepted as a local resident and feeling able to contribute to town politics. The younger, more mobile, estate-dwellers largely ignored old Roselake, and worked and fed their leisure and shopping needs in Exeter.

The Town Council was therefore for many years dominated by the old Roselake community, as it always had been. As individuals aged they became more conservative and crusty in their attitudes and spending habits. Retirements from the council, other than forced by the intervention of the man with the scythe, were rare. The atrophying councillors saw nothing wrong with the crumbling St Andrews Church hall, which was the only publicly managed hall in the town. They saw nothing wrong with activity groups having to beg for accommodation in cold and leaky Scouts' halls and other private premises, or the local operatic society having to perform outside the town. They saw nothing wrong with having themselves to meet in a hundred years or more aged school converted to a haven where the elderly could enjoy their tea and biscuits, as long as they weren't dependent on a wheelchair – Victorian architects did not build disabled access into their thinking. And the more crotchety old guard thought, what was hardship? These whingeing folk hadn't been through a World War. They didn't know how lucky they were.

If the councillors ever commented on the lack of entertainment facilities, it was only to reminisce and glorify bygone years when the High Street still had character, or to recall the day in 1960 when the Roselake Gaumont cinema burnt down, never to be rebuilt or replaced.

This last incident was less remembered for the loss of a public facility, than for the scandal which surrounded it. The word "arson" was never broadcast in public, but spoken sotto voce in the tap rooms of public houses.

Everyone knew that Harry Ruddock, the owner of the Gaumont, was finding times hard. The cinema's heydays were long gone. Harry spent little money purchasing the top releases. He tried a series of "foreign film" screenings, thinking foreign language films were far more risqué than Hollywood, in the hope of attracting the dirty mac brigade. But attendances soon fell off when the poor projection meant subtitles were difficult to read and there was not as much naked bust and buttock as expected.

As a final stab at success, Harry reverted to booking Hollywood's latest. Psycho was going the rounds and packing houses everywhere, or so the distributor said. Harry booked the film for a week's run. But after two days the audience dropped off to the usual half-dozen snogging teenagers. His wife Betty asked why Harry was surprised, when cinemagoers could travel to Exeter or Rosemouth and watch films in comfortable seats, in a theatre which didn't smell of damp and mould.

After the Friday night showing, early in the morning, the Fire Brigade turned out to put out a blaze at the Gaumont. The fact that it took some time between the 999 call being made and the fire engine arriving was much commented on subsequently. The discussions ranged from questioning what the volunteer firefighters had been doing in bed that night that they were so loath to leave, to the suggestion that Harry had a hand in ensuring a late arrival. Certainly by the time the Brigade reached the scene they had little chance of rescuing the building. They turned their hoses on the next door buildings to save them. The Gaumont was destroyed and gutted. Fire station chief Joe Palmer did not receive a commendation for bravery, what he did receive was an amount of speculation, when a month or two later he and his wife went on an expensive Mediterranean cruise.

With no report of any suspicion that the fire was due to other than a smouldering cigarette or similar cause, the insurance company paid out. Harry sold the site for redevelopment, left his wife and eloped with the usherette Penny Gilmour. She was a local butcher's daughter, and it had been rumoured even before the fire that she was expert in playing hide the sausage with Harry.

The lack of leisure facilities was brought up at the Town Council formally once, when they were forced by public complaints to wonder why there were so many youths sitting on doorsteps in the High Street drinking cans of lager and urinating in public. The councillors invited the police community liaison officer to their next meeting to discuss the problems, only to hear of police manpower and funding shortages. Councillors complained that funds should and must be made available, but at the police suggestion that the Council should themselves pay for video surveillance cameras the issue was quietly shelved. The local youth continued littering the High Street, and, due to help from a hacker who developed the skill of monitoring automatically the police airwaves, always avoided a visit by the local community officer, who could duly log no undesirables encountered. No statistics equals no problem. The police knew well about the radio monitoring, and used it to their advantage in manipulating their performance reports.

In view of Council inertia on the question of town facilities, it was left to local residents to start a campaign to rectify the situation. A group was formed to promote the building of a new community complex in the town. This project had been running for the best part of twenty years now. Their argument was unassailable, but they were not people with clout, either political or financial.

Opponents of the scheme formed their own group. They had a powerful and simple argument. It would cost too much. This argument won over not only the ageing population who survived by the skin of their teeth on pensions of declining worth, but incomers who had partly been attracted to the area by the prospect of low outgoings. There was, however, a deeper objection to the project amongst council members, rarely expressed except in private, of course. Any idea of a facility organised by the community, who would take the credit, rather than run by the elected representatives on the town council, was anathema.

For two decades there had been deadlock. The breaking of the stalemate was down to Brian. Some of the old guard opponents of the community complex scheme passed on to a better place, and Brian's control of the council increased. He saw the opportunity for himself to not only be seen as the mover and shaker, and to gain the credit for building the new complex, maybe even get a statue of himself built, but more importantly to enable his architect and construction firm friends to get their fingers in the pie. Not to mention siphoning off a good share for himself. Within a year Brian had a proposal drawn up. He had secured base funding in principle from the District Council, and negotiated a Public Works Board loan.

The scheme still faced stiff opposition. Nevertheless Brian was negotiating his cut tonight in confidence that it would go ahead. Hopefully pretty damn soon.

CHAPTER 3

Unlike Brian, a natural optimist, Graham was not feeling confident about anything. Lawrence had not called and was not answering his phone. Graham had only achieved limited success in pressing his neighbours to write their signatures on his letter to the council. It had taken him half an hour even to get Laura to sign, which she did eventually only in the hope of an easier life. It wasn't that Laura was totally unwilling, just that she had her mind on mixing flour, sugar, butter and eggs in a careful attempt to make a sponge cake of better quality than her last three attempts, when Graham had burst into the kitchen rather undiplomatically and with bad timing.

Mr Brown at number sixteen had been out. His wife was attractive in rather an old-fashioned china-doll way, but her vacant eyes indicated her brains were perhaps not as well arranged as her facial features. Graham had to explain several times what the problem was and what he wanted to do about it. After nearly three-quarters of an hour discussion, and a visit lengthened by Amy Brown's offer of a cup of tea which Graham considered unneighbourly and impolitic to refuse, just when Graham was getting his pen out for Amy to sign she said she'd better discuss it with her husband Tim when he got home. Tim and Graham, although next-door neighbours, were only on polite speaking terms. Tim had never entirely forgiven Graham for failing to consult him before erecting some new fencing with the aim of keeping the Brown's terrier Alfred out of Graham's garden and stopping the animal defecating on his flowerbeds and lawn. Graham pointed out that the fence was not only necessary but Graham's sole responsibility according to his house deeds. Tim, however, thought the fence unattractive and took what he considered unfounded allegations of his pet's offences as a personal slight. Although Alfred had now departed to wherever dogs go when they die, Tim had refused to fully bury the hatchet. His lack of green fingers meant his attempts to grow climbers his side of the divider to hide Graham's fence from view always failed, and this was a constant reminder of his grievance.

The rest of Graham's evening visits followed a two-pronged pattern. Longer than expected discussion, or frustration on the doorstep with no response to his knocking or bell pushing. The only short visit was to number twenty-two, where the young Taylor couple could not wait to sign and get Graham out the door, for reasons he could not imagine, although he thought he had detected an interesting herbal smell whilst on the doorstep and Mrs Taylor appeared rather dishevelled. The Harwoods at number eighteen were out, as were the Groves at twenty. At The Gables Mrs Kennedy, a widow, needed the best part of half an hour before she signed. Graham now knew every detail of the problems of Mrs Kennedy's distant family, spread from Australia to Canada to Basildon, and about her cat Toby's wayward dietary habits and consequent medical problems. At Glendale Cottage Graham met an attractive young woman he had not come across before. She said she had just moved in. Graham was too distracted by her physical charms to question why he had been unaware of the fact that he had a new neighbour. Not having asked the right questions on introduction, he ended up spending twenty minutes with the woman before he realised she was the owners' daughter house-sitting and was no use to him for his signature purposes. Nor would her parents be, as they were on an extended holiday visiting relatives in Seattle. Or so Lisa Thornton told Graham.

The real story – whether Lisa knew it or not she was not going to relay this to Graham - was that her parents had in fact separated and were currently undergoing an acrimonious divorce. Acrimonious or not, if you are looking for the spark that ignited the divorce to be a scandalous tale of adultery, wife-beating or any such gross misdemeanour you won't find it in the breakdown of the marriage between Iris and Jack Thornton.

Being of somewhat liberal politics, the couple's daily national reading alternated between the Independent and the Guardian, until the Independent stable let the i tabloid out for a public run. The Thornton's financial cup was not overflowing, and their attention span for news reading these days was limited, so the opportunity to economise as well as having a need-to-know summary read was seized on. The bonus was the puzzles page. Iris was a keen fan of the Killer Sudoku, and Jack was happy filling in the idoku. Demarcation lines were agreed. The word puzzles and ordinary sudokus were left to whoever was experiencing high boredom factor on any particular day.

An amicable agreement turned to disaster when one afternoon Iris had to accompany her ageing father to a hospital appointment. Jack waited, and as tea-time came and went and the clock ticked by, Jack filled in the idoku.

An hour later there was still no message from Iris, no sign of her return. Jack had moved on to fill in the medium and hard normal Sudokus by the time the phone rang. Iris said her father had to stay in hospital overnight, no cause for alarm, just tests, but she would be late home. No she didn't want to eat anything, she expected she would be late and just want her bed.

Jack was a little concerned about Iris, and her father. Figuring Iris would not be needing puzzles later, and tomorrow there would be a new i, he brushed his own worries away by filling in the Killer Sudoku.

This was a grave error. The next day Iris was enraged to find that while she had been half the night reassuring her father, Jack had been so insensitive as to steal her Killer. Jack protested in vain he didn't think she would mind and would understand he needed something to take his mind off her father's problems. Iris told him the marital rules had been broken, and started wondering how many others had been broken. And she knew very well what Jack had been getting up to all those years ago with Dinah Saxon. Jack was outraged at this suggestion. Mostly because he had never got up to anything with Dinah, although not for want of trying. He could list Sheila, Harriet and Una amongst his infidelities, but that's not the point. It always wounds more to be accused of something you haven't done rather than something you have. He blustered and fumed, and made the mistake of hurling similar accusations at Iris. Women, as is their wont, tend to respond to these things differently from men, and in this case Iris had indeed been a guilty party. Counter accusations flew. The row escalated and other issues bubbled to the surface after being hidden for years, in one case up to thirty years. Iris and Jack decided their rift had grown so deep that life together was no longer compatible with a rosy future. They slept in different rooms and stewed. The next morning, despite day-after qualms they were both too stubborn to go back on their divorce vows, and the rift became permanent. As they could not agree on who would leave home and who would stay whilst separation was in motion, they both left. The last Lisa knew of Iris she was on a luxury cruise, having successfully raided the couple's joint Halifax account. Jack, being left with only the crumbs in their shared Westminster account, was last heard of on a ferry crossing to the Isle of Wight.

So, partly due to this sad little everyday tale of marital cleaving, all Graham had to show for his evening's work was a mere five signatures. David Grant had managed twelve signatures on his letter. This was not looking promising. Graham had another restless night.

The next morning Graham couldn't wait to find out what Lawrence had achieved. And he hadn't even got Lawrence's signature on his letter, for heaven's sake. He went round to Lawrence's house. Pat answered the door and gave Graham a broad smile. She said Lawrence had had to go out, he'd be back at lunchtime. Graham asked if Lawrence had left for him the signatures he had collected last night. Pat replied he hadn't been out last night. Graham asked why not? Lawrence had made a promise. Pat laughed. Graham asked what was funny. Pat's thought had turned to the meaning of being on a promise, but she just shrugged and said she didn't know. What was it about anyway? Graham explained they needed signatures on a letter and asked for Pat's. Pat said yeah sure but asked what it was all about. Graham said trust me, just sign. Pat said ooh I don't know about that, and Graham mentally threw his hands up in despair. Graham was too gentlemanly to take it out on Pat, but inside he was fuming. He returned home. Laura had to bear the brunt of his anger, as wives often do. She told Graham he'd just have to make the best of a bad job and take what he had down to the council offices.

Hilary had told Graham that he should deliver his letter Friday early so that she could prepare the agenda, but she hadn't been specific about a time deadline. Graham considered trying to raise more signatures this morning, but in view of how time-consuming this had been last night thought better not. So again nine-thirty saw him waiting on the council doorstep for Hilary.

'Is that it?' Hilary asked, when Graham presented the letter and signatures.

'I really didn't have much time to get any more,' Graham replied, a little downcast.

'Any more what?' Hilary asked with a slightly exasperated tone of voice.

'Signatures. People were out, and I only had…'

'I wasn't talking about signatures, Mr, er, Ferguson, was it? I had expected a rather longer submission, as you seemed so perturbed about the affair.'

'I said what needed saying and that's it,' Graham said, his hackles slightly rising. He had spent over an hour and a half on the letter and he thought he was the best judge. 'And anyway the original request you had from those Grant people wasn't exactly the length of War and Peace, was it?'

War and Peace was frequently quoted by Graham in conversation. Mainly because he knew one thing about the book and one thing only. It was a long one. He had tried to read it once, many years ago, in his teens. He never got beyond the first twenty pages. It wasn't that he didn't have the intellectual ability or desire to continue, it was a stamina issue. Inserting a bookmark and seeing it had travelled so short a way, and had so far to go, destroyed his enthusiasm. He had turned instead to the The Ginger Man, which had the advantages of being far shorter and more sexually stimulating for a young man.

Hilary's forehead creased at Graham's remark.

'Fair comment, maybe, Mr Ferguson. But, if you are asking the council to go back on a decision they took last week, I was thinking maybe a longer explanation of how this situation has arisen might have been appropriate.'

'Don't ask me how this situation "arose". You know more than I do. First I heard about it was in the Gazette, as I told you yesterday. All I know is that we don't want the name changed, and that's an end to it. And anyway, didn't you tell me the Council had only expressed an initial opinion, and decision-making is not in your hands?'

'I'll remind you Mr Ferguson, that I am only the Council's clerk, not a member of the Council. But yes, you remember correctly. So far we have just sent a letter to the District on the matter. Nothing definite.'

Graham mentally queried, not for the first time, the "we", but kept his growing mistrust of Hilary to himself.

'Perhaps I could see a copy of that letter,' Graham said. He gave a broad confident smile to hide the fact he was becoming a little frustrated. His grin exposed a piece of sausage that had become a temporary feature of his dental display.

'Of course,' Hilary said, looking away and changing tack. 'Would you like a copy to take away?'

'Yes please.'

Hilary disappeared into the office and after the sound of a filing cabinet drawer being opened and closed, she returned with the letter to the District Council. Graham wondered why he had not heard the whirr of the photocopier.

'I expect that will be 50p,' he said, fumbling in his pocket.

'Not this time,' Hilary said. 'I printed off a batch for the council meeting agenda. There are a couple of spares.'

'Oh. Thank you,' said Graham, disarmed.

'You're welcome.'

Graham glanced quickly at the letter. It simply stated that the Town Council had received the enclosed letter and had no objection in principle to the proposal to rename Beggars Way.

'Is that it?' Graham asked.

'Is what…Ah I see,' Hilary smiled. 'Touché.'

Graham left the council offices on better terms with Hilary than he had expected. She promised not only to include Graham's letter on the agenda for Monday night's meeting, but said that if Graham had more signatures to add to support his letter, those would be brought to the council's attention as long as he delivered them to the office by closing time on Monday. In fact it was her strong recommendation that he did just that, since as things stood Mr Grant's faction appeared to be pointing towards becoming the necessary majority of residents the name-change procedure demanded.

Hilary was not flooded with visitors that morning, and had adequate time to type up the agenda for the meeting. The agendas would go out this afternoon. In Hilary's mind the Beggars Way issue was decided. Beggars Way it was, and Beggars Way it would remain. This opinion was due not so much to consideration of the case, but to the fact that she had changed from being dismissive of Graham to actually quite liking the little man. She had certainly taken a dislike to David Grant when, the week before, he strode into her office and handed her his group's letter. His attitude was demanding rather than requesting, far less supplication, and Hilary, had she been forced to put her impression into words, might have said he was an arrogant cocky little bollocksy know-all. Most of all, she would not forgive him for deceiving her into believing he represented all the residents of Beggars Way. It had caused her to show negligence. She should have checked the electoral register herself before presenting Grant's letter to her council.

Worse, in addition to writing the formal letter from the Town Council to the District on the subject, she had this week made informal telephone calls to the relevant officer, Sue Eastwood, at the District Council and given her what she now knew to be misleading information. Ms Eastwood sounded very young, and very gossipy. She was standing in for her superior Eve Coombes, who was currently nearing the end of her maternity leave, well-deserved, particularly as she had produced twins.

Hilary would have at some stage to make the position clearer to Ms Eastwood, and that would be embarrassing. Moreover this would be a severe blow to Hilary's pride. For the moment Hilary decided to keep quiet and wait until after next Monday's meeting. The only fact which might help her completely losing face with Sue Eastwood was that Sue had never dealt with a request to rename a street and had seemed a little vague when asked about the procedural detail. Sue had obviously mugged up from some manual and didn't have a complete grasp.

Hilary did not yet have a plan as to how to scupper Grant's proposal, but then she hadn't realised she would need one, and how such an apparently trivial issue would come to generate such discord. However she was caused to recall her conversation with Sue Eastwood, and she distinctly remembered Sue saying that the residents would have to pay for the name change, a fixed cost for the requestors plus a cost of around thirty-five pounds per household. Hilary thought Graham should know this, as it would undoubtedly sway people to his way of thinking, maybe even provide the killer argument in his favour. She hadn't recorded Graham's telephone number, and it wasn't on his letter, so Hilary typed a quick note to go off to him first class in today's post.

Monday's town council meeting began in the traditional way, with prayers. However there was a change to the norm. It was usual for the vicar of St Andrews, Gloria Paynton, to attend, say a few words of prayer and scoot off to prepare for whatever her evening's commitments were, or in the absence of duties, to enjoy a glass of wine. But Gloria was indisposed, having slipped on a discarded beer can in Church Lane, and damaged her hip. Her curate, John Phillips, was away on a long weekend, and had not yet returned, although he had been expected back at lunchtime.

Late morning he had called Gloria to say he had been detained due to a transport difficulty. Which was true. In a way. He had arranged his weekend outing with a friend - as yet unmet – with whom he had been in contact through the internet, by the name of Pam Cochran. Pam and he shared a common interest in archaeology, it seemed, and after they had seen each other's comments on a web discussion about whether the supposition that as a norm twenty percent of a menhir is buried was correct, they decided through personal message correspondence to explore some of Cornwall's prehistoric past.

Pam lived in Dorchester, and had offered to provide the transport. She called at Roselake in her little Renault to pick John up. They started getting along fine. John had taken the relationship on trust as being a platonic one. Pam, however, had different expectations, and was pleased to find John was more physically attractive than his web picture suggested. Although John's eyes strayed, as a man's might, his loins sent his brain no message to counter his chaste preconceptions. The truth is, it would have taken an extremely able photographer, not to say a magician, to show Pam in an attractive light. Nevertheless things went well between them until they arrived at their destination, a country hotel well situated for rambling amongst the Stone Age village remains and stone circle fragments they had come to explore.

Pam had been surprised to discover that John was a curate, she had not asked about his work in their web exchanges. So when John, who had booked the accommodation, asked at the hotel reception for two rooms Pam was disappointed, but then assumed wrongly that John had made the arrangement for appearance's sake. She gave John a knowing glance and assumed the lack of a wink or similar response was due to caution in front of the receptionist.

Pam and John had, as you may have gathered, assembled different objectives for the weekend. Pam assumed that any walking amongst ancient monuments would be secondary to the pleasure of sharing a bed. John remained in ignorance of this, and stayed focussed solely on the potential pleasures of fresh air and historical interest.

That evening, after dinner, Pam bade John goodnight with a knowing smile, went to her room and prepared herself for an expected knock on her bedroom door. It did not come, and Pam fell asleep, already tired by the afternoon's walk she and John had taken. In the morning she felt guilty, and wondered if John was angry at her for failing to answer his tap on her door. But John made no reference to the night's events or lack of them, and when Pam said she had been a bit tired after the walk yesterday John made a remark to the effect that they would take it easy this morning to store some energy for the rest of the day. At which Pam's spirits perked up due to misinterpretation.

Following an afternoon which had offered no respite from walking activity, and a good dinner, accompanied by a bottle of wine which Pam hoped would make John lose his curate's inhibitions, the two repaired to their separate bedrooms.

Pam lay awake waiting, but nothing happened. She decided to take matters into her own hands and crept out on the landing to John's door. The door seemed locked. Pam knocked timidly at first, louder when she had no reply. Eventually the key turned. A dishevelled John was not too careful in his use of words when he asked what Pam was doing knocking on his door at this time of night when he was asleep.

Finally Pam got the message. She returned to her room and set her alarm for early. She left the hotel at seven, informing the desk clerk that she didn't want breakfast, she had received an urgent call and had to return to London (why did she say London she asked herself later, but then London always sounds as though important things go on there rather than anywhere else in the country). She told the receptionist that Mr Phillips, who of course had arranged the booking, would pay the bill. She went out to the car park, got in her Renault, and drove home to Dorchester.

John awoke to find Pat gone, with no explanation. He was not only very puzzled, but also naturally very disconcerted to realise he would have to make his own arrangements for returning to Roselake, not the easiest thing having being abandoned in the middle of a moor, with public transport being of the once-a-week variety, and a curate's salary not extending to expensive taxi rides, not to mention having to foot Pam's share of the hotel bill.

So, in a nutshell, Gloria had been left facing a dilemma this morning. She could let the town council meeting go ahead without invoking God's help in aiding the quality of the debate and decision-making, which frankly was rather an appalling thought given how even with God's assistance the council often made such a dog's dinner of things. Alternatively she could find a substitute. Gloria was a realist and recognised the possibility of prayer from another denomination's priest or pastor just conceivably being effective. Or at least better than nothing. She prayed for the Lord's guidance and he pointed to her address book.

She tried the Methodist church, but the minister was away. There was no reply from the Baptist preacher. Since Gloria had a low opinion of the Plymouth Brethren and the local Community Church. she had no alternative but to call Father Patrick Mullins at the Catholic Church of the Holy Ghost. This she did, with some reluctance, but her finger found its way to the numbers on the keypad in the correct sequence. It wasn't that Gloria and Patrick were on unfriendly terms, but a division between the Roman Catholics and the Anglicans of Roselake had set in during the reign of Father Patrick's predecessor, Father Peter, whose behaviour was not exemplary and had left a bitter taste in the mouth of those who knew, or thought they knew, some of the details. Gloria was disappointed to find that some members of her own congregation were not averse to propagating rumour, in a rather malicious way, she thought. Fortunately a major embarrassing police inquiry into paedophilia was averted when Father Peter was removed and replaced by Father Patrick. The attendances at the Holy Ghost Church, which had been in decline over recent months, started picking up again with the new incumbency, and the reasons for Father Peter's transfer to greener pastures, or as it happened being put out to pasture with no pastoral role, were never discussed.

Seeing the opportunity as another step forward for his Church, Father Patrick leapt at the chance to address the Town Council. He asked Gloria what brought about this hint of reconciliation. Gloria said it was to further the initiative of the national Ecumenical Week. Father Patrick asked but wasn't that last week, and Gloria had to gloss over her error. However, Father Patrick gladly accepted the duty, and Gloria gave him a quick briefing. She immediately rang the town clerk. Hilary had once told Gloria something or other to excuse her lack of involvement in St Andrews affairs, and said 'Of course I'm a Catholic myself.' Gloria had not known if this was

48

gospel truth, but surely Hilary would have to be receptive to the idea of Father Patrick attending to say prayers. If not, Gloria would pointedly remind Hilary of what she had said previously.

As it happened, Hilary was telling something close to the truth. She was a lapsed Catholic. She had received her education in a convent school, and that was enough for a lifetime. Not that the school was blighted by scandal. Hilary just found it boring. She wanted more fun out of life than the nuns appeared to have. The older nuns seemed happy in their existence, but in her six years she had seen a young nun, whose face was unlined, fresh and smiling when she joined the convent, become old before her time. Hilary wanted one type of forbidden fruit in particular, and the conflict between this desire and what she was taught caused her lapse from the faith. Sometimes she regretted her departure from the school. If there had been one pleasure in her convent school years it was confession. Sometimes she told fibs in the confessional to tease the priest. That had all been rather fun. Whenever she thought about the issue more seriously, she still missed the comfort of receiving absolution. Few people knew about her lapses any more. And a lapse unshared is a thing of little satisfaction.

Shortly before seven p.m. on this Monday Father Patrick came along to the council offices to introduce himself, and was greeted by Hilary and the mayor. Father Patrick had brought with him, he announced, a little gift for the town council from his church in celebration of the event and would like to offer it in public before he said prayers. The mayor looked at Hilary. It was going to rock the boat enough to have a Roman Catholic priest saying prayers without it seeming he had been wholly embraced into the affections of the Council. Hilary stepped in and took the gift-wrapped present from Father Patrick's hands and said thank you so much, it would enjoy pride of place in the mayor's office. Unfortunately it was a very busy schedule this evening and it was better to announce the gift formally at a later date. Father Patrick had no option but to smile and accept the rebuttal graciously. Hilary led him into the council chamber, aka the Senior Citizens' Centre, where the council members were now assembling. She showed him to a chair on the left of the mayor's, and then positioned herself on the mayor's right. As the mayor entered, the appearance of his chain of office commanded the assembly to rise, which fortunately caused enough chair scraping and shuffling of feet to mask the comment by one of the grumpiest of the senior councillors, Donald Ridgeway, who had suddenly woken up to the fact that 'It's the bloody papist'.

The mayor took his seat. Hilary, Father Patrick and the councillors sat down again.

Brian announced that in the furtherance of Ecumenical Week it had been decided that tonight's prayers should be said by Father Patrick, and he was sure that the council would welcome this initiative.

'My arse,' Councillor Ridgeway muttered.

Father Patrick stood up again, his own seat hardly having had time to warm the chair. Gloria had instructed Father Patrick to be short and succinct in his offering of prayer, and Father Patrick contented himself with asking the Dear Lord to bless this council, and its deliberations, may the councillors be imbued with wisdom, charity and quality of judgement befitting their status in the local community and the hopes and aspirations of the people of the town.

Father Patrick sat down again, along with half the councillors, those who had felt obliged to stand during the blessing. He made no sign of leaving. In fact he was rather interested to see how God responded to his prayer.

Brian looked at Hilary, who crossed behind Brian's chair to whisper in Father Patrick's ear. The priest got the message, stood up, made the sign of the cross, drawing another 'Bloody papist', this time more audibly from Councillor Ridgeway. A couple of the other councillors chuckled into their hands. Father Patrick appeared not to notice. In fact he had an acute sense of hearing, but had acquired a thick skin. He was shepherded away by Hilary, who on returning to her seat nodded to the mayor. Brian declared the meeting formally open and called it to order.

The matter of pre-meeting prayers had caused quite a stir in the Council a year ago. There were moves afoot nationally to make prayers during meetings unlawful. Roselake Town Council had always opened their meetings with prayers as far back as anyone could remember, and the raising of the question whether the practice should be abandoned had generated strong feeling, especially from the older and long-standing members of the council. They denounced the National Secular Society, instigator of a legal challenge to the holding of prayers, as anarchists who wanted to destroy the fabric of society. Despite Hilary's warning that they might be placing themselves against the law of the land, the respecters of tradition insisted the Council should not change its ways. The younger members of the Council were vocal in announcing their own opinions, the majority holding that saying prayers was an outdated practice that had no place in a modern secular society. The Green councillor, Judy Harker, had particularly strong views on the matter, but kept quiet as she was never inclined to be outspoken on controversial issues. Her strategy for green progress was to be nice to everybody, and organise a monthly litter-pick, of course.

The only councillor to speak strongly against the tide of conservative opinion was Frank Parton. Frank was the council's anorak, a pedant of the first order. Which had led to no love being lost between him and Hilary Jessop, whose pedantry was equal to his own. But whereas Hilary assumed her pedantry as a tool to manipulate, Frank had no option. Pedantry was an uncontrollable aspect of his nature. He did not realise what a crushing bore he was, and how his being a stickler for pointing out details of history, legal arguments and council procedures which other councillors were unaware of alienated his fellow councillors. All but one that is, Jane Owen. It was not because she and Frank shared membership of the same political party, rather that she thought him rather a handsome and imposing figure (although his figure had in truth gone to pot long ago - Frank was no spring chicken), and she had occasional dreams of romantic involvement with him. Frank had no such dreams, he was a confirmed bachelor. There was a time when he had pursued, but never netted, a spouse, mainly because of his insufferably boring personality. His thoughts had later turned to acceptance and embrace of celibacy, an admirable state of body to contain an unpolluted academic mind.

On the matter of prayers, he managed, as always, to hide his own view on the matter simply by pointing out the absurdity of the situation. He pointed out how illogical the law would be if it continued to impose worship in schools whilst at the same time banning it from public life in council meetings. After he had delivered a convoluted speech to this effect, the mayor asked him if he was proposing a motion. Frank said no. To a chorus of "hear, hear"s, Donald Ridgeway asked the mayor why Frank had been wasting all their time for so long then, and proposed no change of procedure. Hilary intervened and, reminding councillors of the legal prospects, suggested a compromise, to retain prayers but to include them before the formal opening of the meeting rather than risk flouting the law by holding them as part of the official meeting agenda. The mayor saw the sense of this and asked Councillor Ridgeway to amend his proposal accordingly. Donald Ridgeway did so, but not without adding a few grumpy remarks about atheists ruining a Christian country. There things remained until today.

CHAPTER 4

Unaware of any history of discord on the matter of prayer, Graham sat waiting for the start of business. Hilary had said of course he'd be welcome in the public gallery, which consisted of a couple of dozen creaky wooden chairs set out in three rows. Graham had got there early. Expecting more members of the public to arrive, and being oft-times shy of nature, he sat in the back row, so that he would not feature prominently amongst the crowd and obtrude in the councillors' view. In this he was disappointed, as no other citizens turned up. Unless you count an elderly lady, who entered the room, tapped Graham on the shoulder and asked where the tea and biscuits were. She had expected to find the Senior Citizens' Centre in operation rather than the town council. Disabused of this belief she shuffled off disappointed and muttering to herself.

Perhaps we should count as a member of the public Anna Shales, who had been sent by her boss Carla Davis to report on the evening's activities. Brian was due to make a new proposal for the community complex which Carla foresaw as potentially controversial and newsworthy. Anna plonked herself down on the far seat in the back row on the opposite side of the aisle to Graham, surreptitiously pulled out her mp3 recorder, and, to prove she was a genuine member of the press, ostentatiously removed from her handbag a pen and notepad.

To be fair to Hilary, if Graham had thought the council meetings were packed houses, it was not Hilary's fault. She had warned Graham that there was no large public audience expected. Graham had asked about public participation in the council meeting and Hilary had said he was welcome to attend as an observer. She had not volunteered the information that members of the public could, according to the adopted meeting rules, register to speak for three minutes to any item on the agenda. Democracy should only extend as far as audience attendance in Hilary's view. If the public wanted to speak at meetings they should have put up for election. And those who had been elected didn't want to spend half their meeting time listening to public grouses. Of course if a member of the hoi polloi enquired about specifics, Hilary would dutifully read them their rights, but she never volunteered information and effectively managed to discourage would-be speakers. On this occasion she would have deterred Graham from any attempt to speak by pointing out that the matter of the renaming of Beggars Way was under clerk's correspondence. Since the agenda didn't list that correspondence in detail, the item was not technically on the agenda and Hilary would have felt within her rights to deny Graham.

Not that Graham would have been in a position to argue his case very well today. He was feeling out-of-sorts. He had experienced a disappointing weekend attempting to collect more support for the retention of the name Beggars Way, despite being newly-armed with the information that changing the street name would cost the residents money.

Lawrence had ducked out of the canvassing, claiming a groin injury. Graham knew Lawrence played no sport, and was not a keen gardener, so could only guess how Lawrence had picked up a strain, assuming he was not fibbing. Graham did not ask. He shrugged his shoulders and was resigned to the fact that it was left to him to do the door-knocking on the other half of the north side of Beggars Way.

Whilst the response, where he got any, was not antagonistic, it was lukewarm, and Graham had managed a final total of thirteen signatures for his letter, half of what he had hoped for. And only one more than the number on David Grant's letter. Although Graham was encouraged by Hilary's declaration that Grant had to achieve a two-thirds majority of all the residents when it came to the crunch, Graham had narrowly failed to achieve his side's third of the total householders. He had convinced Tim and Amy Brown, and had signatures from Jack and Sally Taylor at number twenty-two, Carl Wetherby at number eight, his next-door neighbour Terry

Jenkins at number twelve, Mrs Kennedy, the Harwoods, plus Lawrence and Pat.

It was with more than a little trepidation that Graham sat waiting for the matter to, hopefully, be resolved in his favour.

'One matter arises from clerk's correspondence relating to the last meeting, and is one I recommend the Council needs to consider and take a decision on this evening,' Hilary announced, in her plummiest authoritative tone, demanding attention, if not obedience.

'It transpires that the request to rename Beggars Way as Cypress Avenue has opposition from some residents. This was not apparent to the council when it made its agreement in principle to the change. I have received a letter signed by thirteen residents of Beggars Way stating that they oppose any alteration of the street name. They are requesting that the council reverse its earlier decision to support the name change.'

Two hands were raised to request to speak. The mayor signalled to Councillor Hunt, who rose from his seat, as convention demanded. He looked to his left and right, for effect.

'Mr Mayor, why were we not better informed at the last meeting? I was given the impression that the whole of the road supported the change. If this is not the case, I would like to know why we were not properly advised.'

As you will gather, no love was lost between Derek Hunt and Hilary Jessop, the target of his attack.

Derek was rather an anachronism. He was a Labour party member of the old guard, who often talked about his Marxist ideals. However, he was quick to endorse New Labour when he had a sniff of the idea that a popular perception of a change of party direction might increase prospects of local electoral success. But the prospects remained at nil. Derek's district council election leaflet with a picture of a smiling Tony Blair on the front had been met with amazement and sniggers and comments that it was a complete surprise that Tony was standing in the local ward. After this rebuff and his coming bottom of the district poll for the fifth time Derek retreated into consolidating his position on the town council. He had some accountancy experience and his knowledge of council financial matters was more than the rest of the councillors' put together. Which was not saying a lot. Derided as a Labour Party hack, he curried favour by adopting a skinflint attitude as chairman of the finance committee, which went down well with all. Whether the constant refusal to even drip feed finance into matters of local social concern tallied with his avowed communist leanings, few commented on this hypocrisy, particularly as the only adverse comment as to the practicalities would have come from his local political party, of which he was in fact the sole active member.

The mayor turned to Hilary, who cast Derek a shrivelling look and replied 'I think members will recall that I simply read out verbatim a letter received from a number of residents of Beggars Way and apart from advising on the District Council's policy on street-naming changes it was left to members of the council to debate the issue. I don't remember Councillor Hunt making any request for further information at the time.'

'I think that answers that, Councillor,' Brian said. 'Yes, Councillor Harding.'

Derek Hunt sat, muttering to himself.

'Mr Mayor,' Edward Harding said, 'I, too, recall the last meeting and have read the minutes. These simply state we have no objection. We were told that this is an issue for the District Council to decide, and the District Council has been advised of our position. I fail to see why we should embarrass ourselves by further involvement. As the clerk explained, the District Council will have to perform its own canvas of residents, so I suggest we leave things as they are and I propose no further action.'

A couple of assenting grunts followed Harding's speech. Councillor Harding was new on the council, part of the last election intake, but Brian saw him as a potential thorn in his side. Harding was a businessman, and had some intelligence and common sense. He also had some principles. This did not bode well. He had so far not come into conflict with Brian, but it would surely happen.

'Thank you, Councillor Harding,' Brian said, ignoring the fact that Harding had attempted to propose a motion. 'Councillor Parton, you wished to speak.'

Frank Parton rose to his feet. 'Yes indeed, Mr Mayor. As members will be aware I was unfortunately not present at the last meeting.'

'Fortunately, you mean,' Don Ridgeway muttered, just loud enough for his neighbour Ken Baker to hear and chuckle at. Neither of them had any time for Frank's pedantry and his habit of rabbiting on at length until reined in by the chair.

Frank Parton continued. 'Whilst I have no wish to disagree therefore with what Councillor Harding has said, there is one issue I think might have been overlooked. Namely, that as I recall, there are no cypress trees in Beggars Way. This brings me to question whether the proposed name Cypress Avenue is appropriate.

'I think it is particularly important for us to consider very carefully any change to a name which has historical significance. I am sure many of us are aware that Beggars Way has a long history stretching back over centuries. In fact I would oppose any name change on those grounds alone.'

'Here we go,' said Don Ridgeway, turning to Ken Baker. 'Another bloody lecture.'

Frank Parton, who had paused on catching Don Ridgeway's comment, was not to be deflected.

'The origins of the name Beggars Way trace back to around 1530, according to the nineteenth century historian Nicolas Thaddeus Blakeley. According to Blakeley's research, the lane was so named because of…'

Frank was interrupted by a 'Point of order' cry from Derek Hunt.

'Which is?' Brian asked.

'Bloody irrelevance and time wasting. We know the history. We know it's an old name. Let's move on.'

'I tend to agree with you,' Brian said. 'Councillor Parton, I'm sure what you have to say is very educational, but this isn't a schoolroom. Can you come to the point very quickly please?'

'Mr Mayor, I object, I think it is very important that councillors understand that we can not just discard Roselake's glorious history without a full appreciation and due consideration. I think it is important, indeed vital, that we understand its richness and relevance to today.'

'May I ask,' Brian interrupted, 'what relevance the name has to today, when I think we have not seen any beggars there for who knows how long. If you want to see beggars you can go to the High Street and count the buskers and Big Issue sellers. Surely you are not proposing we change the name of the High Street to Mendicants Highway?'

Brian's putdown drew some polite laughter.

'Mr Mayor, that is false logic. A false analogy, if I may say so, is no substitute for a reasoned case. I refuse to bow to what is known in popular philosophy as a straw man argument. By that I mean...'

Frank was interrupted by a chorus of groans from his fellow councillors and a hammer of the gavel from Brian.

'Councillor Parton, you are trying our patience. Move on.'

'What I am suggesting is that by understanding the richness of our heritage we can inform ourselves better as to whether we should continue tradition or depart from it respectfully.'

'Councillor Parton, I think you have made your point. More than once. If you have a proposal to make, please make it. Otherwise sit down.'

'Mr Mayor, if I may speak.'

Judy Harker had no particular opinion on the name change, but as the Green Party member on the council, she found it imperative to speak whenever trees were mentioned.

Brian nodded, and Frank Parton sat.

'Mr Mayor, I think Councillor Parton has a valid point but may be mistaken. I remember canvassing in Beggars Way, before I was elected a member of this council, with a substantial proportion of the votes, as members may recall, and I seem to remember seeing cypress trees there.'

Brian rightly doubted whether Judy Harker would be able to tell the difference between a cypress and a plastic Christmas tree, but refrained from saying so and called Charles Threlfall to speak.

Councillor Threlfall was a retired teacher and shared with Councillor Parton a certain propensity for pursuing the irrelevant and hypothetical on the grounds that logic held sway.

'Mr Mayor. Whether there is a cypress or two in Beggars Way is beside the point, as you yourself suggested eloquently a few moments ago. We only have to consider other Roselake road and street names to see plenty which are totally misleading and irrelevant to today. Are there any badgers in Badgers Walk, to give just one example?'

Threlfall paused, smirking at his rhetorical question.

'No, because the builders gassed the setts when they were clearing the site,' Councillor Harker was heard to comment.

Brian, fully aware that Threlfall was only following the furrow he himself had already ploughed, allowed Threlfall to continue. A bit of flattery is a useful debating tool.

'Are there any airline pilots living in Aviators Way?' Threlfall continued, undaunted, 'Beavers on the Beaver Estate?'

This drew a snigger from Peter Galway, who was perhaps more attuned to modern youth and its slang than Threlfall, whose forehead creased in puzzlement for a moment before he continued.

'And as you yourself so aptly put it, Mr Mayor, are there any beggars in Beggars Way? No Mr Mayor, and it is totally irrelevant whether there are any cypresses there either. I move no action to be taken.'

'I second that,' said Councillor Baker, waking up for a moment after being nudged accidently by Don Ridgeway, who had leant in his direction in order to withdraw his hand from his pocket and raise it to speak. Unfortunately the nudge conveyed the wrong message and Don was further frustrated in failing to catch the mayor's eye. He lost interest in the proceedings.

'It's been proposed and seconded that we take no further action,' Brian said. 'Yes,' he said wearily, after Councillor Galway raised his hand. Peter Galway had been co-opted onto the council rather than being elected, which made him a lesser being in some councillors' eyes, but they had to tolerate his utterances as, being something in the Scout movement, he had in the past staked some claim to representing Roselake's youth and their opinions, of which he had, looking round at his bewhiskered colleagues, little fear of rebuttal. Whilst not in the same league as Brian in using the Council as a springboard to further his business ambitions, Peter Galway's main motivation in joining the Council had been to further his interest as proprietor of the Greendale Garden Centre, one of the two horticultural nurseries on the periphery of Roselake. Indeed the contacts he had made, not to mention the gift of an expensive ten-foot Chusan Palm to Brian, had resulted in some lucrative orders from the County and District purchasing departments.

'Mr Mayor, as members will know I have some expertise in such matters.' Although his experience regarding cypresses was largely confined to selling the universally hated Leylandii, Galway had some tenuous justification for his comment.

'If there is disagreement on the matter, as seems the case, I propose we establish the facts. How can we take a sensible decision in the absence of the correct information? I propose an amendment to the motion, that we convene a working group to have a site inspection and determine whether there are indeed cypresses on Beggars Way, and report back before any further decision is taken.'

'I second that,' chirped up Judy Harker.

'Point of order Mr Mayor,' Threlfall said, and Brian with a barely concealed sigh asked him to speak up.

'The motion is to take no action. How can it be an amendment to take some action? It's out of order. It's negating the motion. I move we vote on my motion as proposed and duly seconded.'

Brian felt obliged to ask Hilary her opinion. Especially as she had kicked him in the shin. She gave her judgement.

'In my opinion, if Councillor Galway is suggesting that a site inspection is arranged to ascertain further facts, and those facts are brought back to the council, that is not negating the motion as it may still result in the council deciding to take no further action. I suggest that Councillor Threlfall accepts an amendment to the text of his motion to agree a site inspection and if the site inspection shows there are cypresses on Beggars Way then the council's previous position stands.'

'What?' Councillor Ridgeway asked, 'I didn't follow a word of that.'

'It must be perfectly clear to the rest of us, Councillor,' Brian said, somewhat disingenuously. 'The motion now before us is that we have a site inspection and if there are indeed cypresses then we allow our previous advice to the District Council to stand. Are you prepared to move, Councillor Threlfall?'

'Can the site inspection also check on the number of beggars?' Councillor Harker threw in, with a smirk. The mayor threw Harker a look of annoyance and was undeterred.

'I repeat, Councillor Threlfall, do you move?'

Threlfall shuffled in his seat. He recognised failure. In any event what he had intended was to move on to the next item on the agenda as quickly as possible and all his intervention had achieved was to undermine that. 'Yes, Mr Mayor.'

'Do you have a seconder?'

Ridgeway nudged Baker again. 'That was you.'

Baker said 'What?' but his further contribution was not required as Judy Harker waved her hand in the air violently as if to say 'me me me'.

'Yes Mr Mayor,' was actually how she expressed it.

'Good,' Brian said. 'Can I make a further suggestion that the report of the working party is brought back to next week's Planning Committee meeting and they are given delegated authority to take a decision?'

Hilary kicked him again but he ignored her.

'If you're proposing, I'm seconding, Mr Mayor,' Judy said.

'We can leave it to Ms Jessop to formalise the wording, I am sure. All agreed?'

The voting was unanimous before Hilary had the chance to turn Brian's shin purple.

'Can we determine the make-up of the committee and fix a date please?' Hilary asked, resigned to the fact that things were not going as she had hoped.

'I suggest the councillors who expressed particular interest in this, namely councillors Parton, Galway and Harker,' Brian said 'All agreed?'

The voting was unanimous.

'Mr Mayor, can I suggest Friday morning?' Judy Harker said. 'I have commitments for much of the rest of the week, including the cleanup West Walk, the opening of the ....'

'Yes, yes, we don't need to hear your full list of diary engagements, Councillor Harker. You'll be telling us when you go for a hair appointment next. Councillors Parton, Galway, Friday morning 10 a.m. suit?'

Frank Parton and Pete Galway nodded. Judy Harker fumed. She knew a dig at her personal appearance when she heard it, not to mention a sexist remark. She was not young, had never been particularly admired for her looks, but in her youth she had often been complimented on her crowning glory. Unfortunately over the last couple of decades her hair had gone its own way, which departed from the way she would have desired, and the way that would have enabled it to continue receiving compliments. It had not aged gracefully. At least it could be said it had kept pace with her face.

'Next item on the agenda then,' Brian said. 'Roselake's entry in the Britain in Bloom competition.'

Graham was in a quandary. Were there any cypresses in the banks of Beggars Way? Did the odd tree in a garden count, whether front or rear, as opposed to along the southern roadside bank? What did a cypress look like anyway? He stood up and exited quietly by the rear door, destined to spend the rest of the evening on the internet googling cypress trees and how to identify them, and having done so wait impatiently for tomorrow's daylight to allow an on-site investigation.

At the end of the council meeting Hilary and Brian saw the last councillors out, locked the outside door and returned, just the two of them, to the mayor's office for their regular after-meeting de-briefing session. This consisted less of council business than other more physical activities.

Brian grabbed Hilary's behind and said 'Now what was all that kicking me under the table for, eh?'

'I thought you should have been firmer,' Hilary said, pressing herself towards him with a smile, leaving Brian to interpret her remark as he wished.

Brian didn't bite. 'What do you mean, firmer?'

'I don't think you should have let the planning committee make a decision. They might make the wrong one.'

'And that would be?'

'This name-changing nonsense has to stop.'

'Ah I see. Why is that, exactly?'

'Because I have taken a dislike to the man who proposed the change, and a liking to the man who leads the opposition.'

'Ah,' said Brian. 'Not too much of a liking I hope?'

'Don't be silly. He's old and unprepossessing. Physically, I mean. Short and stout.'

'Ok then. You win.'

'No name change, agreed?'

Brian squeezed Hilary's backside. He knew which side his bread was buttered. 'Agreed.'

'I wonder what that gift from Father Patrick is,' Hilary said, looking away from Brian and gazing at the discreetly gift-wrapped package which Father Patrick had brought.

'Let's open it and find out, shall we?' Brian asked.

'Ooh yes let's,' Hilary replied. 'I so enjoy opening presents.'

The wrapping paper was peeled off to reveal a cardboard box with oriental script. But the picture on the box was plain to interpret. A figure of Christ.

Hilary opened the box and its contents were revealed. It was some sort of electrical tableau of JC in beatific pose with outstretched and raised hands. The centrepiece was framed by a rounded arch in the form of a flowery pergola festooned with lights. A wire led to a surprisingly British three-pin plug.

Hilary and Brian looked at each other, a frown on Brian's forehead.

'Shall we plug it in?' Hilary asked.

'OK,' Brian replied, intrigued.

Hilary placed the figure on the sideboard at the back of the office below the wooden board with gilded letters detailing the town's former mayors.

Switched on, the light display consisted of alternating red, blue and green Christmas decoration sized lights which with a stretch of visual imagination indicated a clockwise rotating display, which was rather appealing, if not reaching the dizzy heights of the Blackpool illuminations.

'I rather like it,' Hilary said. Brian said nothing, indicating his own view.

'Maybe it looks better with the lights out,' Hilary said, and moved over towards the doorway, turning off the office ceiling strip light.

'There's that to be said for it, I suppose,' Brian said reluctantly.

'Come on Brian,' Hilary said, sidling over to the mayor and sliding her fingers under his suit jacket collar. 'Doesn't it turn you on a bit, the idea of someone watching us?'

Brian hardly thought a plastic religious effigy was a "someone", but was coming round to the idea that if it was good for Hilary it was good for him. He gulped.

'I suppose.'

'Then let's do it,' Hilary said. She bent over the mayor's desk and hitched up her skirt.

CHAPTER 5

Graham's internet searching revealed only that he had little aptitude for recognising one tree from another. Of course he remembered from his childhood days what an oak leaf looked like, or a maple, but evergreens were so much harder to distinguish between than deciduous trees. He could get the hang of the fact that cypresses had short stubby leaves, and these were different from the long needled pines, but even his confidence in this conclusion faded when he found a Swamp Cypress and realised he was unable to distinguish that from a Common Yew or indeed a Cow's Tail Pine. It occupied his mind for a while as to whether he was likely to find a Swamp Cypress in Devon, as he read it was a species common in the south-east of the United States, but since Columbus first fetched up thereabouts over five hundred years ago, maybe it had had a chance to emigrate. Graham had recently watched a BBC documentary about British botanists who had scoured the world to bring back alien species for cultivation in Britain. Perhaps they had shipped Swamp Cypresses back home. Graham realised he had in any event been googling mainly American web sites, and perhaps that was unhelpful. He yawned, and gave up for the night.

His internet efforts proved themselves to be as uninformative as he had feared when, shortly after daybreak, he went out to see if he could spot any cypresses on the bank. He thought he recognised one or two trees that definitely were not cypresses, he knew an oak when he saw it and a chestnut tree, but the others all looked depressingly similar to each other in the light of day and real life trees didn't fit their web page picture stereotyping.

Although he was still cross at Lawrence for being so uncooperative, there was not an insuperable rift created, and anyway Graham was desperate for help and called at Lawrence's house. Lawrence came to the door, wiped a bit of egg from his lips and asked Graham what he was doing coming round so early. He was in the middle of breakfast. Lawrence did not demand an immediate answer and he said to come in anyway. He asked if Graham wanted a coffee. Pat made an awful Nescafé or worse. Graham had tried her coffee twice and both times wished large aspidistras were still in fashion as houseplants. Graham's knowledge of aspidistras was on a par with his knowledge of cypresses, but he'd once seen someone pour an unwanted cupful of something into a large plant pot, during an Agatha Christie murder mystery film. He didn't know whether the aspidistra survived the poison attack, but being something of a TV murder mystery buff Graham remembered Gracie Fields had played the first US TV Miss Marple. The connection with one of her songs - one of her greatest hits, we would say today - had also stuck in his mind. Graham begged a tea, unaware of another literary link with George Orwell. Graham was not an avid reader, unlike Laura. If it hadn't been translated into a film or TV series, Graham didn't recognise a book, and rarely knew the paper origins of a screen detective, with a few exceptions such as Miss Marple and Hercule Poirot.

While Lawrence chomped away on the rest of his bacon and egg, Graham related the relevant events of last night's council meeting, and asked Lawrence if he could identify a cypress when he saw one, because he bloody well couldn't. Lawrence said him neither, he never knew one bush from another. Graham said they're trees not bushes. There you go then, Lawrence said. There followed a discussion about what exactly was the difference between a tree and a bush, but since neither of them really knew what they were talking about, the matter remained unresolved apart from a feeble last comment and agreement that size matters.

Lawrence wiped his chin and came up with a suggestion. Why didn't they go to the library and get some books. Books about British trees. Surely that would be better than trying to print fuzzy pictures from the internet of trees from America or India.

Graham thought this a good plan.

Despite the best efforts of the highly proactive Roselake librarian Barbara Middleton, the town's library was no longer extremely well-endowed with books, since much money had been spent -

wasted some might say - in recent years on rarely-hired CDs and videos. Needless to say this was not allowed for by an increase in budget, so it had sapped the book lending service's purchasing power. The latest cuts meant that priority was now given to providing internet access at a number of workstations in the library.

Barbara queried why the County felt the urge to switch budget and support an information medium which was now clearly doing very well under its own steam. In answer, the County changed the lending rules to encourage more reading of books the library did stock. No longer would a library member be limited to borrowing six books at a time for three weeks, but could take twelve books at a time for six weeks. Barbara could not see how six divided by three gave an average reading period per book any different from twelve divided by six, and wondered how borrowers hoarding unread books at home was going to increase the library's effectiveness, but kept this concern to herself, since her comments on policy had already fallen on hostile ears and Barbara was reminded pointedly that a staff budget review was currently in progress. She knew not to push the issue further. She had already caused some upset, and when she received a new distribution of books including ten copies of a number one bestseller rather than the variety of progressive titles that central purchasing knew she wanted, she saw this as a deliberate ploy to annoy her. She did not rise to the bait.

But despite the continuing regressive nature of the library service, the fact that the library shelves were not as full and varied as Barbara would have liked, and indeed despite minor staff cuts and opening hour reductions, Roselake had fared better than most local libraries because of Barbara's efforts. The County Council knew this full well, and any threats from the centre to her personal standing were only shots across her bows. Barbara held the record for the number of times an individual had received the honour of County Librarian of the Year, and there would have been an uproar in Roselake if she got the sack, or there was even the whiff of such a threat. Barbara had initiated a community outreach service which was second to none in the county. It was a mystery why she remained a widow, as she still had an attractive appearance as well as a caring nature, supplemented by an intelligent mind. Few people, however, thought of these things. Barbara had become simply a Roselake institution. Time and again Barbara's sister had tried to persuade her to outreach on her own behalf and acquire a social life, but Barbara was happy in what she was doing, her son and daughter-in-law were about to make her a grandmother, and Barbara thought that enough prospective non-bibliothecal excitement in her life.

For reasons suggested earlier, Barbara and Graham were strangers, although she would have recognised Laura. But of course when Graham explained his predicament to Barbara, she was only too glad to offer him her help. She found two books which according to her computer answered Graham's needs precisely and should be in branch stock. She pointed him to the appropriate shelves.

Graham, despite searching three times, only found one of the two. "Identifying Garden And Native Trees". The title "Tree Recognition For Beginners" was not to be found. Although Graham had balked at Barbara's mention of that title, she had assured him that it had many useful pictures and was not as patronising as the title suggested. And certainly not as insulting or as childishly and humorously titled as the "For Dummies" series.

He left Lawrence searching the shelves in case the book had suffered misfiling, and went back to Barbara to ask for help. Barbara's reaction to the misfiling idea was rather frosty, but her assistant Cathy Leeds overheard the conversation and told Barbara and Graham that a few minutes ago she had had a similar enquiry. Graham glanced towards the door and thought the woman scuttling away seemed familiar. It was in fact Judy Harker, but as her behind had been perched on a council chamber chair the last time Graham saw her he was unable to recognise it as it disappeared and hence unable to recognise her. Her hair, as we have said, was rather forgettable. Barbara looked up the records for the title again and confirmed the item had just been borrowed.

'This'll have to do,' Graham told Lawrence, as he checked out the copy of "Identifying Garden And Native Trees". 'Let's go and do our own site inspection. Proper this time. With the book.'

'Fancy a drink on the way?' Lawrence asked.

Graham thought for a second or two. It was still early in the day for him, and he was anxious to get this tree thing settled. But re-establishing the bond between them seemed a good idea.

'Yes, give us a chance to sit down and check out the book first,' Graham replied. 'But it's your shout. You messed up mega over the weekend.'

'Dear me, Graham, you surprise me, that's rather a modern colloquial expression for you,' Lawrence said with a grin.

Graham and Lawrence were fortunate in one sense, in that the borrowed book from the library gave them, so they believed, just the information they wanted. A straightforward field guide to species identification. The negative conclusion of their foray into the field, or rather onto the roadside verge, was that Graham and Lawrence agreed they had found two cypresses in the bank. Tucked among the larches and junipers were a pair of trees Graham and Lawrence identified as Cupressus Macrocarpus. A Monterey Cypress. Unfortunately they had not turned over to the next page, where they might have found an alternative suggestion, but the disappointment of the identification stopped them in their tracks. They both groaned. Actually Graham groaned, while a triple-worded blasphemy escaped Lawrence's lips.

'That's it then, we're screwed,' said Graham.

'Not yet,' replied Lawrence, tapping the side of his nose with his finger.

Graham woke in the night due to a struggle with a bad dream. A dentist was drilling painfully into his right upper jaw. The noise stopped. He started slipping away again and the dream reimposed itself. Graham was not sure now it was a dream. The noise seemed real, but then dream manifestations always do until you reach upwards towards wakefulness. Graham reached the necessary level of awareness, prompted by the need to make a visit to the ensuite, but before relieving himself he went to the window and parted the curtains. There was nothing to see and the noise had stopped. He performed the needful and returned to bed. Laura had not awoken.

Graham thought he heard a car in the road but dismissed it and went back to sleep.

The next evening Graham waited drumming his fingers impatiently for the Midweek Gazette's arrival. He was itching to find out whether there was any more news of the Beggars Way affair. When the paper arrived he found on page six a short article, written by Anna Shales although the column went without by-line credit. It stated that in response to a letter from residents opposing the name change, the Council had reviewed the situation and appointed a small committee to attend a site inspection on Friday morning to investigate whether the road was lined with cypresses and the renaming proposal would be justified.

Actually that is to rather over-formalise the article's content. Such an account does not well explain why it sent Graham's blood pressure soaring, not only because he felt himself ridiculed, but because his belief that newspapers always produced accurate accounts of events was offended. So to present the fuller picture - the article appeared thus –

Are residents barking up the wrong tree?

A row erupted at Monday's Roselake Town Council meeting when councillors learned that not all residents of Beggars Way were in favour of the Council's move to rechristen the road Cypress Avenue. A missive from local householder Graham Ferguson making scathing comments on the plan was read out to council members.

Tempers frayed during the ensuing debate as councillors came into acrimonious conflict over whether the town's historical tradition would be subverted. Councillor Frank Parton was incensed when his purple prose speech was interrupted by cries of "irrelevant' and "time wasting".

Mayor Brian Sanderson restored order with skilful aplomb, and to restore harmony to the meeting advocated that a site inspection be convened to verify whether there were indeed cypress trees located in Beggars Way. The mayor's suggestion was passed nem con. The inspection will take on Friday morning at ten o'clock.

From this we can deduce three things. Firstly that Anna was trying to spread her wings as a fledgling reporter, and was arriving at an undeserved and inappropriate overconfidence in her journalistic and linguistic skills. The recent gift to her on her birthday of a synonym app had made a contribution to the article's wording. Secondly we can deduce that she was developing something of an affection for Brian. Thirdly we can assume that by passing for publication such a report her boss Carla Davis was having a particularly bad hair day. Carla had been suffering not only from the severe after-effects of the previous night's drunken excesses. The effects on her judgement caused by her headache were exacerbated by a bout of depression, partly alcohol-induced and partly caused by the fact that she had just experienced rejection by her sex partner of three weeks, with whom she had been hopeful of constructing a more lasting relationship. Carla only recognised her failure of supervision of her work junior the next day, when the Gazette's owner Philip Davenport called her to ask what the eff she was thinking of publishing an article so critical of the Roselake Town Council. In order to defend herself, Carla had to defend Anna, and assured Philip that the article was no more nor less than the truth (as she said this Carla crossed her fingers and crossed herself three times) and that the Gazette was hardly likely to be criticised for this, especially as the Mayor had received a generous compliment. Philip was mollified to the extent that he did not threaten any sackings, as he usually did when he was seriously displeased. The conversation ended and Carla was prompted to say 'Thank you God' and raise her eyes upwards in the hope that God was watching and appreciative of her recognition of his good works. Her inclination was to ring through to the main newsroom and ask to see Anna in her office straight away. But the situation was a little ticklish, since Carla could hardly come down like a metric tonne of bricks on Anna and her article without having some excuse for her own culpability. She decided to wait. After the paper had appeared on the streets she would tell Anna she had received a complaint that the report was inaccurate, and warn her to be more careful in future, to moderate her reporting, and remind her that she was a local reporter, not a poncey art critic. Another day or two increased the likelihood that Anna would have wiped her mp3 recorder of the account of the meeting which would have enabled her to counter Carla's complainant. Of course Carla had no idea of the veracity of the account. I hope we have provided sufficient information on the matter for our readers to make their own judgement.

Whilst it would be an exaggeration to say Graham's reading of the Gazette article provoked an apoplectic fit, neither would it be accurate to say that it invoked catatonia.

After a brief exchange with Laura, whose response to Graham's upset over the article was that she was busy and he could talk about it later, Graham showed his displeasure by exiting the house and slamming the door. He went round to number four. He asked Lawrence if he had read the Gazette and what did he think. Lawrence said no, he had better things to do with his time at this hour, hint hint. Like eating his dinner, he expounded, when Graham frowned in unenlightenment. Nevertheless Lawrence invited Graham in and asked what was eating him.

Graham sat in the Stones' dining room as Lawrence resumed his position at table and returned to the attack on his chicken leg. After a quick and not overly-friendly smile at Graham, Pat did the same. Pat did not, in Graham's mind, do herself any favours by her eating technique, but then although he was innocent of any real accusation of sexism he had a natural male attitude, and that extended to a woman's heaving breast having a different effect on a man's libido from that of chomping with open mouth at table.

As Lawrence and Pat ate, Graham read to them the Gazette article. Lawrence couldn't see what the fuss was about.

'It names me,' Graham complained, 'and says I made a scathing attack. You read the letter. You know that's not right.'

'But point is, does it matter?'

'They'd no right plastering my name across the page, for a start.'

'There's many a politician who'd pay good money to have their name plastered across a page in the paper.'

'Well I'm not a bloody politician.'

'Political activist, then,' Lawrence said with a grin.

'Objecting to a name change is politics now is it?'

'If politics is about stirring people up then yes.'

'Just who have I stirred up?'

'Yourself, mate.' Lawrence chuckled at his little joke.

'You're a bit of a prat sometimes, Lawrence,' Graham opined.

Pat's mouth rounded in an unvoiced 'ooh', and glanced at Lawrence with a smirk which Lawrence could have considered endorsement of Graham's statement on an "isn't that what I've been saying for years" basis. Alternatively Pat could have been mocking Graham. Lawrence decided that choice was too much of a conundrum and said nothing.

'Anyway,' Graham continued, ignoring Pat's comment on his attitude, which seemed crystal clear to him, 'the letter we sent, I mean I sent, since you couldn't be arsed to do your side of the signature collecting, just said we opposed the change. If that's "scathing" I'm a bloody Dutchman.'

'Language, Graham,' Pat interjected with another smile. 'Who'd have thought it of you, meneer.' She winked at Lawrence. This time Lawrence was pleased at confirmation Pat was on his team, and was pleasantly reminded of a glorious weekend in Amsterdam he and Pat had enjoyed in their youth.

'All right,' Lawrence told Graham, 'I tell you what. I promise I'll get those extra signatures by tomorrow. OK?'

Graham was still not happy. 'It'll take more than signatures with those bloody, sorry Pat, blooming trees there.'

'Have you checked them out today? Whether they are blooming?' Lawrence asked with a sly smile.

'No, why should I? We both agreed they were bloody, sorry Pat, cypresses, so that's an end to it. We're sunk.'

'You go and take another look tomorrow,' Lawrence suggested, ignoring the fact his punning had missed its mark by a mile, and with a wink to Pat. 'Check out if they are really cypresses.'

'You mean you've changed your mind? They're not cypresses?'

Lawrence patted the side of his nose with his forefinger. 'Just check them out again.' Pat was in on the joke and nodded wisely.

As it happens there was one other reader of the Gazette article at home that evening who was well stirred up by it, and by Graham's activities. David Grant was severely annoyed, and let it out in a burst of expletives. Fortunately he was able to do this without fear of criticism, since his wife Connie was able to turn her tongue round a few choice phrases herself when prompted. His son Arnold was out, but since Arnie had received an ASBO three years ago for an offence to which his swearing was a minor contribution, if he had been at home he would be unlikely to have tut-tutted his father. Fortunately, although David had been unable to stave off the ASBO, he had had words with the magistrate with whom he shared lodge membership, and Arnie received the minimum ASBO term, which meant in theory he was soon free to rejoin his mates in their public mooning and urination without incurring the full weight of the law.

After his short-lived but heartfelt outburst, David picked up his smartphone and called his next door neighbour, Josh Barker.

'What's up, Dave?' Josh asked.

'Have you seen tonight's Gazette?'

'No, what am I missing?'

'That bloody Ferguson over the road has been sticking his oar in at the council. He says residents don't want it to be called Cypress Avenue.'

'And what does the Gazette say about it?'

Despite the fact that Josh was sitting a few feet away from his own copy of the Gazette, and the fact that Dave had only a two metre walk from his front door to Josh's, it never occurred to either of them that they had options for communication and social interaction other than digital. For the next few minutes Dave read out the Gazette story into his smartphone, punctuating his account with the occasional acerbic comment.

'So what we gonna do?' Josh asked, cutting to the chase.

'We need to check out that bank. See if there are any cypresses.'

'Are there?'

'Buggered if I know. Do you?'

'Nope. I can't tell one tree from another. Hang on, I've got an Observer's book of trees somewhere that came to me in my Dad's things after he died.'

'Any good?'

'Dunno, never looked at it.'

'Well sod that. I'll bring my phone.'

'You got an app on trees? You turning into a loony left green tree-hugger?' Josh asked with a snigger.

Dave ignored the irrelevance. Dave tolerated Josh as a next door neighbour, and someone who was useful occasionally, rather than embracing him as a friend. He had a lower-class mentality, as Dave saw it. Dave himself, had in his own view moved way up the ladder. He had, it was true, been born in a northern terraced back-to-back a year before it was razed by the slum clearances of the early nineteen-seventies. Now he had what he considered a respectable professional standing as an independent financial adviser, and had achieved in his own eyes a high level within local society. This did not have universal recognition. Sheila Jackson, at number five, regarded him as no more than a cheap insurance salesman, which was actually a fair description of his work. Sheila's opinion didn't count in Dave's eyes, he knew this was formed when she found him leering at her chest one time. She herself was no better than she ought to be in his opinion. He'd heard stories about goings-on whilst her husband, something in refrigeration, attended business conventions. What really ticked Sheila off was that after she had clearly excited his interest, Dave refused her advances. Dave knew one of her supposed previous "admirers", who had at one time suffered an unfortunate infectious disease which was difficult to cure.

'No, but we can google,' Dave said, just a hint of exasperation in his voice.

'Too late now, it's dark.'

Dave thought that was bleeding well unblindingly obvious but held back from saying so. 'Tomorrow morning, I mean. The paper says we have time until Friday morning.'

'To do what?'

'Make sure they find some cypresses, of course.'

Daylight found Dave and Josh down the road matching what they found on the bank with the pictures in Josh's Observer Book of Trees. Their first and earlier attempt using an app on Dave's phone had proved useless, and a smirking Josh had returned home to pick up his book, pleased to have notched one up against his neighbour. Josh was fully aware that Dave tolerated him as a second-class captain's mate rather than embracing him as an equal. Josh didn't mind. When they had a few drinks together down the pub Dave was generous with his cash after a few beers, and subsidised the move to spirits.

Even with the schoolboys' bible of yesteryear in their hands, they still couldn't fathom out whether there were any cypresses in the bank. Their guess was not. Suspicions about foul play were aroused when Josh commented that it was a bit queer there were wood shavings and small pieces of tree bark lying around in a rather unoccupied part of the bank. Further grubbing around revealed two fresh stumps which had been covered with a small mound of soil. Dave and Josh twigged what had happened at the same time and glanced at each other with bulbs of enlightenment in their eyes.

'The bastards,' Dave exploded. 'They've cut the buggers down. I'm not bloody well standing for that!'

Dave arranged to meet Josh at lunchtime. Josh worked in a builders' yard and had access to a lorry. Ideal for transporting cypress trees, Dave suggested, with a wink.

Before his appointment with Josh, during a break in his diary commitments, Dave walked up South Street to the council offices. Hilary Jessop took a moment to recognise him. Her face hardened.

'What can I do for you?' she asked.

'You'll remember I brought a letter in a week or two back about changing the name of Beggars Way.'

'Actually no, Mr, er…'

'Grant. David Grant. You don't remember?'

'I remember the letter. You can't expect me necessarily to remember every face that I see in these offices.'

Dave got the message and moved on. He hadn't come with the intention of picking a fight. 'I saw an article in the Gazette yesterday. Said there was to be a meeting about trees in Beggars Way.'

'That's right.'

'So if there are cypresses there that's OK and the council will change the name, is that it?'

'Not exactly,' Hilary said wearily, hoping not to have to repeat the account of who did what.

'So what then?'

'If there are cypresses, the council might be persuaded to go along with the name change.'

'And if not?'

'That's really up to the council, not for me to say, Mr Grant.'

'But they might be reluctant to agree, right?'

'Possibly.'

'And you've had a Mr Ferguson saying he doesn't want the name changed.'

'That's true. And not only Mr Ferguson. It seems you don't have a consensus Mr Grant. It looks likely that Beggars Way will stay Beggars Way.'

'What do you mean?'

'A consensus is a ...'

'I know bloody well what a consensus is, thank you very much.'

'I will thank you not to swear at me. There is a zero tolerance policy against abuse of staff in this office.'

'I bet you need it if you're always so flaming arrogant and patronising.' Dave scowled, his voice harsh.

Hilary's face was flushing with anger.

'That's quite enough, Mr Grant. Any more of that and I'll have you removed.'

'Who by? That decrepit lot of senior citizens next door?'

True, gone were the days when the Roselake police station was manned and Hilary could have availed herself of the presence of a uniformed officer within a matter of minutes.

It was unfair of Dave to assume that all visitors to the Senior Citizens' Centre were decrepit wrinklies. One or two could certainly be found who needed more than a little assistance in getting their wheels through the street door, which was not designed for wheelchair access, and due to lack of funding from the District Council was still in breach of government recommendations and Disability Rights Commission guidelines. But there was of course the slightly more mobile older section of the ageing community, who visited solely for tea, biscuits, company and a chat, and there was another younger group, who normally came to the centre during the last hour or two of the daily open sessions, who formed in Hilary's terms the post-Saga group. Having spent some ten years or so as customers of that company in hope of social interaction, holidays in the sun and romance on cruise ships, they still had some physical vigour even though they had got used to being called pensioners. In other words the centre acted as an over-sixties singles meeting place. Friendships and more intense relationships, long or short, were made by widows and widowers, and even elderly spinsters who decided at last that they had been missing out on some of life's pleasures. Relationships were discreet, but that did not stop tongues wagging. One Cyril Harding was rumoured to have bedded twenty-three of the female visitors to the centre over the last four years. However, even Cyril, although still physically active in a certain respect, was hardly able to be called upon as available for active service as a bouncer.

Hilary was forced to admit to herself her bluff had been called. She wondered if she could get away with the lie that the office was protected by a district-wide public buildings security system, but decided the absence of a video camera and a large alarm button on the wall would call any such claim into doubt and prolong the conversation, which had already gone on long enough in her view.

'This interview is finished Mr Grant.'

'No it isn't. What do you mean, Beggars Way will stay Beggars Way?'

'I mean unless you have a good majority of the residents, two-thirds, in favour of a change you won't find the District Council agreeing with your request. Is that simple enough for you to understand?'

Dave, who could throw an insult as well as anybody, decided this was not the time. He turned round and walked to the door. 'I'll get my majority, Mrs…'

'Ms,' Hilary replied coldly to his back. 'Jessop.'

Dave left the offices determined. Hilary picked up the phone. She was now equally or even more determined. She would scupper Grant's plans, without relying on Brian.

Josh picked Dave up at one-thirty as arranged. Dave would not have chosen to be seen sitting in a small builder's truck, nor did he like the idea of his work suit being covered by dust. He swept the passenger seat as best he could and Josh drove out of town to the Baytree Garden Centre. Dave had made an exploratory telephone enquiry and had been assured that the nursery was well-stocked with cypresses.

At reception he found the young woman who had answered his call, and asked her where he could find the cypresses.

'Those are trees, right?' the girl answered. Dave asked for her superior, after a short exchange reminding the girl she had earlier told him they were in stock, and receiving the answer that that was true, the computer said. Didn't mean she knew what they were, exactly.

The owner of the centre was more helpful, and led Dave and Josh round the back of the greenhouse sales area to the open-air nursery.

'What sort of cypress are you looking for?' Peter Galway asked.

'What sort have you got?' Dave parried.

'Oh, various types. How many are you looking for? A stretch of hedge?'

'Just two.'

'Ah, decorative, for the garden.'

'Right.'

'How far apart will you be planting them?'

Dave held his hands out in an approximation of the distance between the two stumps they had found.

'In that case can I recommend a tall slim cypress? The Tuscan cypress would be ideal. We've got various sizes between one and a half and three metres. Over here,' Peter pointed and led Dave and Josh to a row of trees of varying sizes in large tubs.

'Those would do fine. How much for something like that,' Dave asked, pointing, 'two or three metres are they?'

'Two metres, a hundred and thirty-five quid. Three metres'll cost you two fifty.'

Dave swallowed. 'That's a lot.'

'We've got a three for the price of two offer.'

Dave looked at Josh. Josh shook his head. Josh had no intention of paying out of his own pocket anyway, but didn't want his friend paying so much he hadn't enough left over to buy a round or two.

'No, that's too pricey. What else have you got? Something a bit cheaper,' Dave suggested.

Peter sighed. Another cheapskate. He led them over to the Leylandii.

'This might be what you're looking for. Two and a half metres, give or take now, grow faster than Jack's beanstalk, I'll let you have two for eighty, OK?' Peter said.

'Seventy?'

'Seventy five?'

'Done.'

Dave let Peter and Josh load the trees into the truck. He declined the offer of purchasing a book on post-planting aftercare. The trees only had to stay alive until Friday lunchtime.

During the drive back to Beggars Way it was made clear to Dave that Josh was unwilling to share the cost of the trees. It was Dave's idea, he insisted. Dave did not argue to the point of falling out with Josh. The plan was to store the trees in Dave's garage until the early hours of the morning. Then Dave would need Josh's help with carrying and digging. They discussed the planting exercise. Josh, knowing he was likely to bear the load of the manual work, expressed reservations about getting the trees out of their pots and sunk in a big enough hole to get them standing upright. Dave proposed the solution. They would bury them in their pots. That would require less spadework. When the trees had done their job, they could be dug up and Dave would have two new additions to his back garden. Josh said fine. Did he have to wear a balaclava or a ski mask tonight? Which would make the better fashion statement? Dave told him not to be an idiot, and just to turn up at half past twelve tonight. Face paint camouflage would be fine.

It had been very considerate and helpful to minor miscreants for the County Council to have decided (supposedly on climate change grounds but in reality for reasons of budget) to turn off the street lighting at twelve-thirty in the morning. Whether energy cost savings were outbalanced by the public costs of petty vandalism is not known. But the night-time blackout enabled Dave and Josh to carry out their planting activities without detection, and by Friday morning two cypresses were standing proud where only a day or two earlier two junipers had grown, and given their lives in vain, misidentified innocent victims. Of friendly fire, we might say, in modern parlance covering unfortunate results of often callous carelessness.

CHAPTER 6

The following morning, the Council's site inspection committee duly assembled at ten o'clock in Beggars Way. The three councillors, together with Hilary to keep a record, strode up and down the bank lining the south side of the road. The group stopped in front of the two recent additions.

'Those are cypresses all right, those two,' Councillor Parton declared.

Hilary grimaced. She had been hoping for a different result. Yesterday's meeting with David Grant had only confirmed her impression of him as a nasty little man whose plan she would thwart. But Hilary now had a fall-back position, so she was not unduly perturbed.

Judy Harker was puzzled. She did not remember seeing the trees as they appeared now when she had walked Beggars Way on Wednesday with her library book, carrying out her own surreptitious pre-inspection visit. She had not identified any trees as cypresses. Had she been wrong? She waited for Peter Galway's opinion. She did not want to embarrass herself, nor admit her only knowledge came from her borrowed copy of "Tree Recognition For Beginners".

Peter, of course, had not been recognised by Dave and Josh as a councillor during their visit to his nursery yesterday. Nor had he recognised them, however his suspicions were now aroused and indeed confirmed by seeing the two Leylandii which had been standing in his nursery until yesterday, and which looked identical (only an experienced nurseryman would be able to explain how) to the two he had parted with the day before. On the pretence of investigating further, he reached down to one of the trees and deftly removed a Baytree Garden Centre price label that had been inadvertently left attached to a lower branch during the night planting.

This posed a slight problem for Peter. Did he declare his knowledge of what had gone on? Did that mean he should declare a financial interest and say nothing? Or declare the interest after identifying the new intruders? Not being an expert on council rules, and not wanting to fall victim of Hilary's acerbic comments, Peter was in a quandary. He was more expert in helping scouts tie complicated knots than untangling knotty procedural problems. The deciding factor was that Dave's seventy-five pounds had not actually gone through the till. He decided to keep his reunion with his stock to himself, and only muttered, 'Yes, those are cypresses' in answer to Frank Parton's declaration.

'Yes I agree,' said Judy hastily. 'They certainly are.'

'That's that then,' Hilary said, closing her ring binder and returning her pen to her jacket pocket. 'Crystal clear. I'll see you on Monday, councillors.' She pursed her lips.

On Monday evening, shortly before seven, Dave crossed South Street from the short stay car park to the town council offices. Dave had failed in his attempt to persuade Josh to attend the council planning committee meeting with him. Josh was booked for a darts match at the Seven Stars in Rosebridge and would not be swayed. Josh was by no means short of brain cells. Although he had never actually tried the experience, he knew intuitively that a night out at the town council was just one step above watching Andy Warhol's Empire as the most boring experience ever. Not that he had ever seen that film, just as Graham had never read War and Peace. Indeed he hadn't even seen the first five minutes. But Josh had heard about the torpor-inducing film once. It had been the answer in a pub quiz to a decider question between Josh's team and rivals, and Josh's team had lost the annual championship. Some things you never forget.

But in truth it wasn't the darts match that promoted his stubbornness in declining Dave's invitation to the committee meeting. On the last occasion Josh's team representing the Roselake Grapes had visited the Seven Stars for a match, they had lost rather embarrassingly. Josh had never scored consistently well from the oche but after the match he had much more success in scoring with the Seven Stars barmaid, with whom he had spent a very agreeable half hour after she finished work for the night. He was therefore looking forward with considerable anticipation to tonight's return match.

So Dave entered the Senior Citizens' Centre alone. He was soaking wet, after only a short hundred metres dash from the car park. He had not foreseen the cloudburst that started when he was half-way into town, and he had no raincoat or umbrella. He pushed the centre door open with water dripping down his forehead and onto, and bouncing off, his nose.

Dave was therefore in no mood to wave cheerily at his new enemies Graham Ferguson and Lawrence Stone, who were the only occupants of the public seating. He gave a curt nod, the friendliness of which was undermined by a scarcely concealed snarl.

Graham and Lawrence responded in similar formal fashion, but without the curling of the lip. Graham tried a smile which expressed disapproval of its recipient at the same time. Both Graham and Lawrence were feeling smugly confident that the removal of the cypresses, as they thought them to be, had scuppered Dave's plans. Prompted by Lawrence's heavy hints, Graham had revisited the roadside bank on Wednesday and found the result of timber-felling activities. Being of a rather law-abiding disposition, he was not sure how strongly he should tackle Lawrence on the matter. In the event, he turned a blind eye, acceding to conspiracy membership, after his remonstrations met with the reply from Lawrence that he had not chopped the trees down. Graham remembered that Lawrence's nephew worked for a tree surgeon company, so accepted Lawrence's word as being technically true, his conscience was clear, and he chided Lawrence no more.

Dave crossed the floor behind Graham and Lawrence and sat over on the far right of the front row of wooden chairs. His first choice creaked and Dave moved to a safer perch. No reporter was present. The local newspaper hacks did not often attend full council meetings, far less planning committee meetings. Whether someone wanted to build a garden shed at the rear of a house on the Beaver estate was of little interest to the majority of Roselake's residents. In any event the council only made recommendations, which the District Council totally ignored in the majority of cases when they met subsequently to make the final decisions.

On this occasion, although Anna Shales had a minor interest in the Beggars Way question, she decided her evening was better spent elsewhere. It might have been of interest to see whether the committee recommended taking action on the unlawful erection of a satellite dish in the High Street's conservation area above the kebab shop, more out of a desire to see whether racial intolerance was becoming rampant on the council, but as with the outcome of the Beggars Way decision she could phone Hilary tomorrow for an update. She was not interested in whether the committee approved an application for a dormer window on a house in Gladstone Avenue, or any other similarly unexciting items on the evening's agenda.

At one minute to seven the door opened again and in, together with a gust of rain, came a rather wet Derek Hunt. He was perhaps also a little sozzled, considering the way he meandered over to take his place at the committee table, to join the waiting councillors and the clerk.

Hilary looked at her watch and, reaching over to the committee chairman, Paul Hart, suggested the meeting commence. Hart drew the meeting to order.

Paul was an affable sort of chap, a retired businessman with rather malleable but definitely right-wing political opinions. Brian Sanderson found it useful to have a stooge sitting as chairman of the planning committee. As we have said, Brian still had his finger in various planning pies that it would not be politic to advertise that he had helped to bake himself. Although he remained a planning committee member, to keep an eye on his protégé, Brian took a back seat, and absented himself on the occasions his interest would have been too obvious. Paul had been ever-grateful to Brian since Brian had hushed up the potential scandal about Paul's misguided personal habits. Politicians with an MP's status could get away unpunished with lies about their use of rent boys and coke, but town council hopefuls were easy pickings for the town's gossips if their peccadilloes extended beyond financial self-interest, bribery and corruption, which were comparatively acceptable.

Paul beamed as he tapped his gavel on its wooden stand. Graham and Lawrence halted their conversation, which had been full of whispered condemnation of Dave Grant's personality.

'First item on the agenda,' Paul announced, 'is the report from the site inspection committee on the Beggars Way naming question. Councillor Parton, would you please enlighten us? And in one sentence please, we don't want to be here all night.'

As you may gather, Paul Hart and Frank Parton were old sparring partners.

'Excuse me, Chairman,' Hilary butted in. 'I have received a new communication from the District Council which may negate the outcome of the inspection, which was, in fact, the recording of the presence of two sickly cypress trees.'

Frank rose to protest at the suggestion that the trees in question were in ill-health, but Paul flagged him down. Peter Galway was miffed at the denigration of his produce, but kept a straight face and hid his own irritation.

'Carry on, Ms Jessop.'

'I have, as I said, had communication regarding the progress of the name change application. And it is now clear that there is a prior claim on the name Cypress for a Roselake street name. Cypress Avenue, or Cypress anything is no longer a possible choice as it is a name already dedicated to a new street on the Badger estate. Post Office rules would seemingly bar us from introducing two new similarly named addresses. It would be too confusing.'

Frank Parton rose, asking to speak. 'Mr Chairman, this is outrageous. Is Ms Jessop now telling us we were wasting our time last Friday? Why were we not told about this earlier? Why did some of us take valuable time off work to perform our civic duties? Time which cost me money, ate into my personal leisure time by having to use that to make up for lost business hours? I demand an answer.'

Paul turned to Hilary. 'Ms Jessop?'

Hilary was by now well-practised in fending off Frank's mock outrages.

'Mr Chairman, naturally I would not have wasted Councillor Parton's time knowingly, nor that of the other councillors, whose time was I am sure equally valuable to them. If Councillor Parton is accusing me of doing that then I would request he withdraw the suggestion.'

Frank was still on his feet and regarded that as giving him authority to continue. 'I withdraw nothing. I demand an answer. When did the clerk find out about this?'

Hilary tried her sweet smile. 'Mr Chairman, this information came to me only today. I have had no opportunity to convey this to anyone before now.'

'I think, Councillor Parton, you should accept that with good grace,' Paul said. 'For once,' he couldn't help himself adding.

'That still isn't an adequate answer,' Frank persisted. 'We always make recommendations on street naming. How come names we suggested were changed, if that is what happened, on the Badger estate, without this council's approval?'

Hilary smiled her patronising sweet smile once more. 'Councillors may remember that we were indeed consulted regarding preference for names to be used for the estate. We declined to comment because although the estate has Roselake addresses and postcodes as far as the Post Office is concerned, some of the streets themselves in question lie outside the St Marks parish boundary and are in the Hettisham parish council area. This council decided to leave the issue to Hettisham council to decide, and not confuse the issue by two councils independently suggesting names when that situation could give rise to conflicts or duplication. As Councillor Parton might now recall.'

'I remember no such thing,' Frank interjected.

'That's unfortunate,' Hilary responded, making a show of looking at her notes. 'And a little surprising, even if an oversight and an unusual lapse. I checked my notes and the council minutes for the thirteenth of April and it was in fact Councillor Parton who moved the motion to leave the issue to Hettisham.'

Frank sat down, his colour rising in annoyance at defeat. Hilary placed her notes back on the table before her, a smug smile on her face. Not because of causing Councillor Parton's discomfiture, but because the exchange had drawn attention away from her account of events, which was totally false and deceptive.

Following Dave Grant's visit to the council offices on Thursday morning, Hilary had decided whatever arboreal content was found by the inspection working party the next morning, she would stall Dave's plans. She had made a telephone call to Sue Eastwood at the District Council, enquiring about progress on the naming of the new streets on the Badger estate. Sue rather reluctantly admitted that she had not given this matter full attention. Before she went on leave months ago her boss Eve had received a reply from Hettisham Parish Council which was rather unhelpful. The parish had no firm suggestions, but had suggested maybe the District could, together with the developer, come up with some pleasant rustic names. The matter had dragged on ever since. It was a mystery to Hilary why the council should want to perpetuate a reminder of the rural area the estate would destroy, but it suited her purpose admirably. Sue had not yet taken action, the developer Cosgrove Estates had responded by suggesting that its sales potential was best served by traditional street naming rather than the modern propensity in other parts of the country for embracing New Age names like Meditation Avenue, Yoga Lane, Karma Way or Mindfulness Close, nor did Cosgrove want to introduce names suggestive of the influence of ethnic minority groups. Cosgrove didn't provide a full list of traditional names but suggested those based on trees, like Chestnut Avenue, or on herbs - for example Rosemary Walk - might be appropriate, and said that Cosgrove would be guided by the District Council provided these suggested guidelines were followed.

From her investigation of the documentation file and email trail, Sue had concluded that Cosgrove had got the hump because an earlier communication from Eve had rejected a number of Cosgrove's first suggestions for the simple reason that they were already in use in Roselake, and Cosgrove had not done their homework. Eve's communication had not been as tactful as it might have been in pointing that out. Cosgrove's reply had been even less tactful, saying in brief that if Eve rejected Cedar Avenue because Cedar was already in use in the town, maybe Eve could suggest some other trees or whatever she chose.

Sue was grateful for Hilary's offer of assistance in saving her the trouble of looking up Roselake's street name atlas, and for her offer of help in deciding on a list to offer Cosgrove to replace the rejected names. She was grateful too for Hilary's offer of meeting that lunchtime to sort the matter out over a bottle of prosecco. After two glasses Sue was ready to include Cypress Avenue in the list of the Badger Estate's new nominated street names as a replacement already deemed agreed by Cosgrove for Cedar. Sue agreed to pre-date that list, and to send Hilary an email dated Monday morning to advise her that the Cypress designation was already allocated.

Paul Hart declared the committee should move on to the next item as no action was now required. Frank argued the toss, but Hilary laid the law down. The only power delegated to the committee by council was to determine whether there were cypresses along Beggars Way. The outcome of that question was now pointless in deciding whether to continue supporting that particular name change, and the committee should not discuss the matter further nor consider alternatives. Paul declared the matter closed and moved on to discussion of an unauthorised satellite dish in the town's conservation area.

Dave Grant walked out in disgust. Graham and Lawrence took their leave confused but in better spirits. Lawrence asked Graham if that meant they had won. Graham said maybe they had won a battle but the war was not over. They went to the Lamb and Flag across the road, intending to wait a while until the rain cleared. Over a beer they puzzled why the clerk had told the committee the inspection working party had found two sickly cypresses. Two stumps, the trunks hacked off just an inch or two above the ground could hardly be described as an ailing tree, just as the Monty Python dead parrot could hardly be described as resting. A conclusion was reached to go and do their own further inspection, but that decision was overturned on the appeal of staying in the

Lamb and Flag for another couple of beers. An hour later, as Graham and Lawrence left the pub, if they had looked back at the council offices they would have seen through a chink in the curtains a flickering display of red, blue and green lights which signalled another post-meeting reunion of the mayor and the town clerk.

Dave's mind wasn't on his driving on the way home. He thought he may have hit a cat, or maybe a dog, after he saw a moving blur in the middle of the road, causing him to swerve violently. He might have sensed a bump, but he hadn't stopped to check for roadkill. Dave didn't find any bloodstains on the front of the car when he parked it in the garage, so he shrugged the incident off. It didn't enhance his mood though, as his wife Connie saw immediately he entered the house.

'Zulu, babe?' she asked. 'And I'll bring you some scotch.'

Dave nodded. Whenever he came home in a foul mood Connie knew to leave him alone in the lounge with his favourite DVD and a drink. Dave had watched Zulu maybe thirty times. Connie couldn't see the attraction herself. It wasn't like she thought of Dave as a racist. But maybe, she always reasoned, watching a film like that and seeing bodies piling up, black or white, was a better way of sublimating Dave's aggression than his going out getting drunk and screwing other women, a prospect Connie would not look forward to again. In her mind the marriage had already used all but one of its nine lives, calculated on the basis that Connie only knew the half of it.

Dave's annoyance did indeed subside after Zulu and an adequate quantity of Tesco Special Reserve, but – maybe due to overconsumption of the Tesco Special Reserve – he still had a restless night. The disappointment over the suggested new name for Beggars Way was not an overwhelming setback, and Dave had already put in plans which hopefully would bear fruit the next day. Dave hadn't enjoyed the look Hilary Jessop had given him when she glanced his way as the committee took its decision, a look of condescension and spiteful triumph. That had irked. And the battle with Ferguson and Stone was now personal, after the tree felling incident. Dave knew exactly who was to blame.

The next morning Dave sat in his South Street office drumming his fingers. He'd asked his receptionist Sandra if she knew what time the Midweek Echo was distributed around the supermarkets on Tuesday mornings. Sandra said she didn't know. Dave had sent her out for a couple of copies at nine-fifteen, but Sandra had returned empty-handed.

Dave had a visitor to the office scheduled for ten. At nine forty-five he asked Sandra if she would go and look again for the Echo. Sandra told Dave if he was that anxious to get a copy he should go himself. It wasn't part of her job description. This was a pointed reference. She had only recently started working for Dave, and relations between them had not yet settled down, due largely to Dave's trying it on just a couple of days after Sandra had started her employment. Sandra was not amused and had told Dave so in very clear terms, including the declaration that bonking the boss was not in the job description as per the newspaper advertisement and any attempt to dismiss her because of her refusal to oblige would result in some rather unwanted publicity. Dave had backed off, and Sandra had told him she would continue working for him on the understanding he was very much on probation. That suited Dave fine as Sandra proved competent. His male pride didn't suffer unduly as he didn't fancy her all that much anyway. She had a rather square face on the pleasant side of plain, and had a body that was reasonably shapely, but which looked better from the front than it did from the rear. Sandra knew all this quite well. Which had one positive side-effect. She never had to ask 'Does my bum look big in this?'. But Sandra was a realist and was happy with herself, especially as she knew she had sufficient charms to net admirers – she had never been short-changed in that department.

She would have quite liked to tell Dave to push off in clearer and ruder terms, but she recognised that leaving two jobs in a short space of time would not have looked impressive on her CV. The last departure, brought about by a similar occurrence, namely over-ambitious advances by her short-lived boss Max Welch, had been passed off as due to a family bereavement of her employer, which had caused him to cut back on his business expansion plans. Max had been happy to write a letter of recommendation to that effect, as he had come under some pressure from Sandra, who had stated her willingness to inform Max's wife of the goings on in his office. Sandra had done her homework, and over a few G&Ts the secretary she had replaced was willing to talk about her office affair with Max in detail. More detail than Sandra actually wanted to know, but this provided ample ammunition. Max's wife Shirley had an unforgiving nature and Max, faced with a touch of blackmail, chose the easy route out and wrote Sandra a glowing reference.

Terminating a new job within days was hardly a career choice, and the pay was good, the job seemed undemanding, so Sandra made her peace with Dave, with certain conditions. These were that he would not grope, would not leer and would not treat her as a dogsbody gofer. This was the card she played today.

So Dave was forced to slide out of his chair and rush off down to the High Street to check out the arrival of the Echo. He returned out of luck, still no sign of the paper.

The potential new clients who were due at ten were late, and Dave sat waiting impatiently. And within a minute or two of the arrival of the couple, who were in their early sixties, Dave determined they were time wasters. They were after freebie advice. He gave them a standard brief speech on their investment choices, handed them some literature and asked if they needed help making their wills.

Shortly before eleven, Dave went down the road again to check out the supermarket, and again to see whether the paper had arrived. This time he had success. A Budgen sales assistant was placing a pile of Echos in a wire newspaper stand outside the store entrance. Dave snapped up the top copy, almost before the girl could retrieve her hand, and flicked through the paper. He grinned when he came to page five. There was the article he was hoping for, headlined "Iffy names knock £000s off house prices".

Dave grabbed another half-dozen copies from the rack and returned to his office for a serious read. The salesgirl gave him the finger behind his back.

Iffy names knock £000s off house prices

Living in a road with an unfortunate name can knock thousands off the value of your home, according to a leading Roselake estate agent.

Edward Cowley, of Cowley and Birt Estate Agents, was commenting on a hot issue being debated by Roselake Town Council, whether to allow Beggars Way to change its name. Residents feel the current name is demeaning to the neighbourhood.

But now Mr Cowley says not only are homeowners justified in wanting a change to a more salubrious name, but living in a road with an undesirable label can knock tens of thousands off house values.

'A national survey recently found that if you live in a street with a risqué name your house could be worth up to 22% less than a similar property in a sensibly-named street just a stone's throw away,' says Mr Cowley. 'Beggars Way may not be the worst name imaginable, perhaps, but I have twenty-odd years experience in the local property market and I can say a less than perfect name does keep house values down.'

Roselake Town Council meets again next Monday to consider whether to grant the residents' request.

'Perfect,' Dave said to himself, a smug grin on his face. His expenditure of time and money on his fellow lodge member Eddie Cowley on Saturday had paid off. Eddie, over a meal at the new Thai and Japanese restaurant in the High Street, had agreed to put his name to a press release, after Dave had placed a draft in front of him and suggested this would be good publicity for Eddie's business as well as for Dave's plans to achieve the name change. Whatever the smug older residents across the road thought of the historical value of preserving the old name, they would soon change their minds when the threat of losing value on their homes raised its head. Of course any loss had already been incurred, but the reality of the situation was a side issue. Money and greed overcome all scruples and common sense.

Dave fed Eddie with the results of his internet research. A valuation company had indeed produced a report suggesting that inappropriate names were bad for house values. In truth they were not just mildly inappropriate but downright rude, like "Crotch End" and "Cock Street". Top of the list of the UK's rudest names was apparently "Minge Lane", with "Slag Way" and the curious "Fanny Hands Lane" runners-up. In comparison with these naughties, Beggars Way seemed entirely inoffensive, as Eddie pointed out. But after another bottle of saké Eddie agreed to Dave's suggestion, with an amendment which adequately expressed his reservation without ruining Dave's message. For his part Dave received a cast-iron guarantee of publishing in the local papers, as Eddie was a significant contributor to both the Gazette and Echo's advertising revenue.

As Dave was smirking at his success, Graham and Lawrence were sitting in the Carvery enjoying a pint. Possibly enjoying is an exaggeration, as they were drinking more to quench their anger than to enjoy the brew. They had just discovered the replacement trees in the bank. After recovering from a bout of indignation, they agreed this demanded holding a council of war.

'You don't think we're wrong, do you?' Graham asked.

'Of course we're not wrong, it was that bastard Grant and his mates. Who else could it be?'

'I suppose,' said Graham, not being able to come up with any alternative suggestion.

'The cheek of them. And not even bothering to take the bleeding things out of their pots!'

'Why d'you think they did that?'

'Blowed if I know. But makes it easier for us, doesn't it?'

'To do what?'

'Remove 'em of course.'

'But it's too late, the council's already seen them.'

'Who cares about the council? We pinch them, that'll put Grant's nose out of joint. We could probably get a few bob for them, too. My nephew Phil could shift them for us. Or you could plant them in your garden, if you want them.'

'I'm not sure I'd be comfortable with the evidence of a crime permanently rooted in my garden.'

'Crime? What crime?'

'I think it's called theft.'

'Theft? Who from?'

'Well the council I suppose. They own the bank, don't they?'

'Public land. We're members of the public aren't we? You can't steal from yourself.'

'Bollocks. It's council property.'

Lawrence was as always undismayed by presentation of facts.

'But if someone left a couple of plants in your drive, without your knowledge, may I add, then next day they were gone, would the person who took them be stealing from you?'

Graham pondered this as he emptied his glass.

'You've got me there. I suppose not.'

'Well then,' Lawrence said with a grin of triumph. 'Fancy another pint?'

Graham stalled by looking at his watch, which really had nothing to do with whether he wanted another beer. He was still unhappy about the idea of removing the cypresses from the bank, but he had become an implicit accomplice in the original crime of sawing down the two junipers and knew Lawrence well enough to see that that would be the next argument he would bring up if he continued his objection.

'Yes please, but let's switch to Witches' Frogspit. That Otter's Pisswater tasted as bad as its name.'

The Carvery had a habit of trying new local brewery guest ales from time to time. Some of their experiments worked out better than others.

'Agreed. Can't have 'em under the Trade Descriptions Act though, I suppose,' Lawrence said as he picked up their glasses and lumbered off to the bar.

Graham and Lawrence couldn't think of any new plan to thwart Dave Grant, nor any stratagem to regain the upper hand before the next council meeting, and they were as yet unaware that today's

Echo article would tip the balance seriously in Dave Grant's favour. They enjoyed the Frogspit and had another. Plus chasers.

Graham found out the truth of the matter that evening. As he was enjoying his post-dinner nap, longer and deeper than usual because of the Frogspit, he half-heard the metallic springsnap of the letterbox.

'It's for you,' Laura announced, as she placed the envelope, together with the usual coffee, on Graham's side-table by his chair.

'Who from?' Graham asked.

'You'll find out if you wake up and open it,' Laura said, and walked off to the kitchen. She had not quite forgiven Graham for coming home from the Carvery having had rather too much to drink.

A quarter of an hour later she returned and asked if Graham had finished his coffee. She was a little concerned about his colour, which was slightly paler than usual. Normally his chameleon abilities swung from pink to the red side of the spectrum, so he was showing more shock than anger.

'What do you make of this?' he said, pushing the letter towards Laura.

She read it, her lips moving as she did so, as it was short, and she wanted to make sure Graham understood she was reading it properly.

'No idea,' she said, and scurried off to the kitchen again with Graham's empty coffee cup.

Graham stirred himself and followed her.

'No come on, seriously, what's this about?'

'What it says, presumably, Tim and Amy want to withdraw their names from your petition, or whatever it is.'

'But they can't!' Graham's complexion was reddening now.

'Their decision, I imagine,' said Laura, closing the dishwasher door and pressing the program buttons.

'But why?'

'Like they say, something in the paper.'

'But what?'

Laura was losing patience. 'How would I know? We never read the Echo.'

'I'm going round there now to sort it out.'

'No you're not. You promised you'd help me wind some wool for my knitting morning tomorrow.'

'But this is important!'

'So's my knitting morning. To me. But not to you it seems. Typical!'

Graham knew when he was beaten. He needed some paracetamol, and he was not up to arguing. He looked at his hands, stretched his arms out, put his fingers together with thumbs outstretched and prepared himself mentally for the inevitable. Laura smiled, bent over and kissed him on the head.

'I'll get my hanks of wool,' she said.

CHAPTER 7

The next morning Graham passed on a full cooked breakfast, his stomach still couldn't come to terms with the fact that, for reasons unknown, his next door neighbour had stabbed him in the back. He was determined to have it out with Tim as soon as he could. Laura suggested he should take some yoghurt to calm his innards down. And told him it was far too early to go round bothering people.

Graham reluctantly agreed. But as it happened the answer to his question came from a phone call the Fergusons received twenty minutes later.

'What can Mr Taylor be needing to talk to you about at eight thirty in the morning?' was Laura's question, as she passed the phone to Graham.

The good news was that Graham found out why he was losing support on the Beggars Way issue. The bad news, which upset him deeply, was that Jack and Sally Taylor also wanted to withdraw their names from Graham's petition to the Council.

Graham no longer needed to quiz Tim Brown. He stormed off down the High Street to acquire a copy of the Echo. Laura sighed as Graham slammed the door, and wondered where this was leading. She just hoped Graham had taken his blood pressure pill this morning. She didn't dwell on that for long, she had the clearing up to do and then receive her knitting club guests.

Budgens had not yet placed the Echo in the stand outside their door. Graham stood in the doorway waiting. A young lad skateboarding on the pavement outside scraped to a halt, banged open the glass door and bumped into Graham. He told Graham to get out of the effing way and made derogatory remarks about Graham's age and family heritage. Graham told the lad to sod off and that he was a nasty little something even more stinging in his mind than "bastard". A tall lad came through the door, obviously a chum of the skateboarder, and took up the argument. He made unpleasant insinuations. Namely whether Graham enjoyed abusing little boys. He stood in front of Graham, towering over him, and told him if he had a problem he might like to take it up with him. Graham was incensed enough to pick a tin of tomato chunks off a nearby shelf and, holding it up in the face of the older lad, told him unless he wanted a face like the contents of this can he should sod off effing quick. The tall lad sensed Graham's determination. His bravado disappeared and he did as requested. The skateboarder ran after him.

A middle-aged woman tried to squeeze past Graham in the aisle, a sheaf of Echos in her arms.

'Any problem, sir?' she asked.

'None,' said Graham. Apart from the fact that his heart was racing madly. The woman wore a badge that told him her name was Sylvia.

'That's good,' Sylvia said. As she shuffled past him to take the bundle of Echos outside, she whispered 'Good for you. About time these young hooligans were brought down a peg or two.'

Graham followed Sylvia out of the door, waited until she had placed the Echos in their stand, and picked one up. Sylvia and Graham smiled a brief goodbye as Sylvia went back to woman her till. He started flicking through the pages of the paper to find the article Jack Taylor had told him about.

But Graham, although mollified somewhat by Sylvia's comment, which helped also decrease his mounting blood pressure in realisation of what trouble he might have got himself into, was not in the right frame of mind to stand and read the Echo article. He went home.

His arrival caused some embarrassment. He had forgotten that Laura had her knitting friends round, and his tirade on bursting into the lounge was more suitable for the ears of a tolerant partner than for half a dozen relative strangers. Laura put her knitting aside and shooed Graham out. She wasn't going to tell Graham what she thought of his entrance speech right now, as her visitors were no doubt straining their ears, but her look persuaded Graham that he had made a serious faux pas.

'I'll go and see if Lawrence is in,' he said sheepishly.

'What a good idea,' Laura said, kindly in the circumstances.

Laura rejoined her knitting circle. Needles clacked.

'They're all the same, aren't they,' Andrea Robinson commented, after a minute's uneasy silence.

'Who are?' asked Harriet Wilkins.

'Men,' Andrea replied. 'You'll find out, Sheila,' she added. Sheila offered a fleeting unenthusiastic smile. Sheila Waring was the only unmarried member of the group, but since she had reached her mid-thirties without attracting any serious admirers it was entirely possible she would remain a spinster and never find out that men are not the saints her friends thought she might imagine them to be. Having been the youngest in a family including three older brothers, Sheila in fact, had she ever thought deeply on the matter, would have felt grateful that the opposite sex now largely ignored her.

'I suppose it's this name change business,' Jenny Harwood offered Laura in sympathy. 'Easy to understand how it could upset some people.'

Laura thought Jenny lingered too long and placed too much emphasis on the word "some".

'By the way,' Jenny continued, 'John wants to talk to Graham about that. I know we signed, but after that thing in the paper about it costing us thousands if we don't change the name I'm not sure.'

'That's rubbish,' Laura offered, her hackles having been roused.

'Well that's as may be, but John says we can't ignore it.'

'Excuse me, I'm not up-to-date on this one?' queried Harriet. Jenny was the only one of the knitting group who lived close by, the others were not necessarily vitally interested in the future of Beggars Way, nor did they necessarily read the free press.

'Some people over the road want to change the name from Beggars Way to something fresh. They think the name is a bit of a blight. Graham is quite het up about it, wants it to stay the same.'

'Oh,' said Harriet, and lost interest.

'It came up at the Parish Women's Group meeting the other day,' Katherine Leach remarked. Katherine was a newcomer to the town. She was not particularly religious, but had included the PWG in her sights when she set out on a programme of infiltrating a number of Roselake's social groups, which she selected by reference to the Library's list. She had recently moved down from Holmer Green near High Wycombe, where she was well known as one of the village's most able gossip and rumour mongers, and it was her desire to maintain this habit, more than anything else, that prompted her social involvements.

'Informally, of course,' Kate, as she insisted she be known to her "friends", continued. 'Over tea and biscuits. Of course we had all read about it in the papers. But Betty Hetherington became quite worked up about it, insisting that the centuries-old names must be preserved, to conserve the town's heritage. Jackie Parkinson took the opposite view and the discussion became quite agitated.'

'I can't see how it's important enough to make a big fuss about, myself,' Andrea said.

'Well Betty and Jackie did. Like I say, the argument became quite heated. Gloria had to step in, cool things down and change the subject.'

'Gloria?' Harriet queried.

'The vicar,' Kate replied.

'Oh,' Harriet said, and lost interest again. She examined her knitting and was annoyed to find she had dropped a stitch.

'Well, no doubt you moved on to discuss more important matters,' Laura said, wanting to shift the topic herself.

'Only if you consider red underwear an important topic,' Kate said, pausing to invite further inquiry. None came, so she continued anyway. 'Amongst the items donated for the next jumble sale there was an assortment of ladies underwear, of a rather saucy nature.'

'For the jumble sale?' Jean Lacie asked, 'I wouldn't fancy wearing second hand underwear, thank you very much. Yuck.'

'It wasn't second-hand, actually,' Kate corrected her. 'It was all brand new, still in plastic wrapping. Lots of frilly, lacy stuff, and some which the word skimpy just doesn't adequately describe. And the most vulgar red bra and panties you have seen in your life. We couldn't imagine who would be brave enough to come to the jumble sale and buy these things. And who would even have the cheek, if I can put it that way, to wear them, even in the privacy of their own home.'

'Raises the question who had the nerve to donate the goods,' Laura said, perceptively.

'Ah, well, that's easy,' Kate said. 'It was redundant stock after the sex shop in South Street closed down. Poor Mr Perkins lost his shirt in that venture.'

'And some other clothing, obviously,' Andrea said with a cheeky grin.

'I never saw anyone go in there all the time it was open,' Harriet commented.

'Who would dare, in Roselake?' Jean asked. 'Did Mr Perkins have any, er, different items in his surplus stock he donated for the jumble sale? Not that I am interested in that sort of thing myself, of course.'

A couple of the women sniggered. One can only imagine what sort of items they had in mind to cause such amusement.

'Heaven only knows,' Kate replied. 'Or at least heaven's ambassador, Gloria Paynton. She took the Perkins delivery.'

'Maybe she kept some choice items back for her own use,' Andrea suggested, with a laugh.

'I am sure Gloria is way above that sort of thing,' Kate said. 'Mind you, when we were talking about what sort of woman would wear red underwear, Gloria said she personally saw nothing wrong with it. And, what's more, she let it slip out that she even knew a man who wore red underwear.'

'How on earth would a vicar know a thing like that?' Jenny asked.

'A good question indeed,' said Kate with a wink.

'You're not suggesting she has a man-friend she's hiding from the town?'

'Not necessarily, but I can suggest who has,' Kate said. 'It came out at the Women's Institute last week. You know that woman who's town clerk, looks all prim and proper and doesn't even look at you in the street when she passes you?'

'You mean Hilary Jessop?'

Kate nodded. 'Her neighbour, Rose Newby, says that every week she has a case of wine delivered, and the delivery takes a long time, if you know what I mean.'

'No!'

'Regular as clockwork.'

'Who's the man?'

'Rose doesn't know. But the fact that there's only one wine shop in Roselake now must narrow the field down.'

'Well, I've come to the end of a row. I think I'll make the tea now,' Laura said, standing. She went off to the kitchen, rather weary of all the gossip. Before Kate appeared on the scene the conversation had been of a higher tone, books people had read, whether Alexander McCall Smith's Ladies Detective Agency series had lost its way, that sort of thing. Laura really hoped Kate would get tired of knitting. She was demonstrably hopeless at it. But the immediate problem was whether Kate would be relaying Graham's indelicate outburst to the whole of Roselake.

Meanwhile, Graham and Lawrence were in the Carvery again, indulging in a beer, and conversation rather above the level of red knickers, reversing the norm of knitting circle versus pub discussions. They took turns to read the Echo article and tut-tut. Consensus emerged that the article was bollocks, but extremely damaging to the cause, as, Graham pointed out, had already been proved by four defections.

'What are we going to do?' Lawrence asked.

'What can we do?' was Graham's unhelpful rejoinder.

'Buy another pint and mull over the options?' Lawrence suggested.

Graham, who normally would not have risked another so early in the day, but was still suffering from the effect of his confrontation with aggressive adolescents and his embarrassment at home, nodded approval. Lawrence went to the bar.

'I think we should tell the paper what we think,' was Lawrence's suggestion when he returned to their table.

Graham groaned. He had just remembered that the Midweek Gazette was due out today. He had enough nous to realise the Echo had not just found the story through its own initiative, but that it had been given them by Grant. In which case he had for sure given the same story to the Gazette, and today's issue would be carrying the same report. He passed this revelation to Lawrence.

'And if we've lost four signatures already, when it's out in the Gazette we'll lose more,' was Lawrence's pessimistic comment. 'Pat for one.'

'What?' Graham blurted, 'Surely Pat is on our team?'

'Not where money is concerned,' Lawrence admitted. 'She whinges often enough already about me not keeping her in the manner to which she would aspire.'

'Which is?'

'A shopping card with a higher credit limit,' Lawrence said.

'You're joking, I hope.'

'Only a small exaggeration, my friend. A whiff of our house losing thousands of pounds and she'll be another defection.'

'But didn't you tell her it would cost everybody thirty or forty pounds each for the name to be changed?'

'No, I forgot to mention it, but that's small beer compared with thousands. It's less than Pat spends on having her hair done regular. In any event, once she catches on to this newspaper report she'll nag and nag and make my life a misery.'

'In any case we have to put a stop to this. We'll have to put out our own press release, redress the balance, like.'

'But just you and me can't put out a press release. Doesn't it have to be official, like?'

'OK so we'll call ourselves the Beggars Way Residents Association.'

'What, just us two?'

'We could ask others to join. Later.'

'I'm not joining any bloody committee. Sitting and talking for hours and getting nowhere.' Lawrence snorted.

'OK we'll go to the press just you and me..'

'So now we're house valuation experts?'

'No, but I know someone who is. John Arden of Arden's, on the High Street. We bought our house through him.'

'And why should he help?'

'I don't know, but no harm in asking.'

'But we couldn't get a story in the papers before next week anyway. Might be too late.'

'Doesn't stop us getting a second opinion and circulating it around the neighbours.'

'Fair plan, Graham, but what about the Taylors and Browns wanting to remove their signatures from our petition? Shouldn't you tell the Council?'

Graham frowned. That hadn't occurred to him. 'Let's wait and see if there's any more fall–out. Anyway, if we get John Arden to sign a letter saying in his professional opinion there is no problem with Beggars Way affecting our house values, we can get them to retract their retraction.'

'If he won't do it, maybe Quentin Fairbrace would.'

'Who?'

'The agent Pat and I bought number four through.'

'Is he an expert?'

'No, but he's well-connected. Carries clout. Plus he owes me one.' Lawrence tapped his nose to invite Graham not to ask.

'OK, Placed the name now. I've seen his ads in the Gazette. But he only has a half page. Arden's got two if not three.'

'Doesn't matter if we only want a letter, not a press release, he just needs to sign with a set of initials after his name.'

'Like what?'

'I don't know, but Quentin's well-heeled enough to have some association membership or qualifications, that's all you need in that business.'

'Qualifications?'

'No, money for membership fees.'

'I still think we should try John Arden first.'

'OK, drink up and let's do that.'

The good news was that Graham and Lawrence found John Arden sat at his office desk. The bad news was that he refused to help.

Being an estate agent, he said no with an ingratiating smile, but it was a "no" nevertheless. His excuse was that he did not have a strong opinion either way about whether the name Beggars Way was a plus or minus factor as a selling point. The reality was that he was currently under consideration for entry to the Masons. He knew full well that he would be scuppering his chances if he went head-to-head in the press against Ed Cowley, for the simple reason that Eddie was his proposer. John and Eddie had recently drawn a truce over stealing each other's leads and other dirty tricks which had blighted their rivalry. As part of the truce agreement Eddie would introduce John into the Masons, and John would not publicise Eddie's drug habit.

So for a disappointed and disgruntled Graham and Lawrence it was on to their next port of call, the Fairbrace agency. Unfortunately, Quentin was not in the office. His assistant said he would be back in half an hour, if they cared to return. They cared. Lawrence suggested they wait in the nearby London Inn. Graham's opinion was that he had drunk enough beer for the morning, but agreed Lawrence's suggestion of a coffee laced with brandy.

Graham didn't take to Quentin. Smarmy toffish git, was his unspoken comment. Quentin's window was filled in the main with rural properties with a few acres of land rather than Roselake town houses, and a pair of wellies in the corner of the office behind Quentin's desk suggested that many of his viewings were carried out in muddy fields rather than on clean carpets.

Nevertheless, Quentin listened with interest to Lawrence explaining the predicament. Quentin had no reservations about contradicting Eddie Cowley's version of property matters. Common little oik, would have been his description of Eddie had he been asked. Quentin was old Devon family, gentry. He rarely had Roselake property, where the turnover money was, with low sale value but high saleability on his books. The rare appearances in his portfolio were on the occasions when his country farming friends had an ageing relative die in the town house they had been shipped off to after they had become too old to tend cows, drive tractors or castrate lively young rams, and needed close access to the town's medical services.

Quentin had little interest in the topic matter of whether the name Beggars Way affected house prices, but he was still in debt to Lawrence for his agreement not to shop him after a hit-and-run accident Lawrence had been a witness to. Indeed Lawrence had been inside Quentin's Range Rover at the time. This arrangement had been negotiated after Quentin's promise to either reduce the price of the property Lawrence eventually bought, or to share part of the agency commission. Since the only casualty of the hit-and-run was a car, and Lawrence was sure the owner would be able to claim on his own insurance, Lawrence had no scruples about accepting the deal. The financial agreement came to nothing after Quentin failed to persuade the owner of number four to negotiate, so Lawrence felt justified in maintaining that Quentin still owed him.

After Quentin's agreement to become involved in the affair, attempts to draft a letter by committee failed. Quentin delegated the job to Kylie, his assistant, to whom he explained the situation. A letter was duly drafted, amended and finally agreed, and Kylie ran off a couple of dozen copies. Quentin signed them individually. This quite exhausted Quentin, and he suggested the three of them repair to the London to regain strength. Lawrence was willing, but Graham put his foot down and said no, he needed to go home, address envelopes, and deliver the letters. Lawrence did not offer his help, so Graham left Quentin and Lawrence to decide between a quick one at the London or whether Quentin should buy Lawrence lunch.

Graham's return home was not as badly received as he had feared. Laura's welcome was a relatively mildly-delivered rebuke about being surprised Graham had the cheek to come home expecting lunch, after the exhibition he'd put on in front of her friends this morning. But she then got a pie out of the oven and said no more on the morning's events. Or anything else.

After his conversationless lunch Graham retired to his study, stuffed envelopes with Quentin's letter and addressed them to the neighbours. He included all the houses in the road, with the exception of David Grant's.

Graham was quite pleased with the letter. It read -

Dear Resident

You may have seen in the press a report that as a houseowner living in Beggars Way your property value may be adversely affected by the road's name.

I would like to reassure you that in our professional opinion this is not the case. On the contrary, our many clients hailing from London and the South-East would see a traditional and historic name as a major plus factor, possibly enhancing your property's desirability.

Should you ever wish to place your house on the market, we can assure you of obtaining the best possible price, as well as a level of service second to none.

With best regards

There's only one way to fight BS, thought Graham, and that's with equal BS. Despite Lawrence's earlier misgivings, he took an executive decision and typed up a press release, purportedly from the newly formed Beggars Way Residents Association, committed to preserving the road's name and heritage, to send as a cover for Quentin's letter. He walked to the mailbox to post copies to the Echo and Gazette, then went round the houses to deliver the envelopes to his neighbours in what he hoped was a pre-emptive strike in advance of the Midweek Gazette's arrival through the letter boxes this evening.

When the copy of the Gazette arrived at number fourteen, Graham rushed to the door and grabbed it. Laura, almost physically pushed out of the way by Graham in his dash for the paper, kept her peace. She had had enough of Graham for the day and was not, given the mood he was in, wanting to start an argument. Nor was she wanting to discuss the issue of the naming of the road, which was now a nagging thorn in her side, generating so many minor arguments recently. It was becoming an obsession with Graham. In her darkest moments Laura wished her mother were alive so she could raise the threat of going to stay with her until Graham sorted himself out. Not that Laura thought uncharitably of her mother whatever her mood. She had enjoyed an idyllic childhood, had loved her parents dearly, and there wasn't a week, or hardly a day, went by that she didn't have a pleasant thought and memory of them which would cause a smile to break out on her face.

On first reading of the article in the Gazette, Graham's face reddened and his blood pressure shot up. After the fifth reading he came to realise it was not as disastrous as he had feared. The Gazette had been a little more diligent in following up on Dave's press release, due, as it happened, to Carla Davis upgrading the whole issue's importance rating.

Beggars Way - are residents thousands of pounds out of pocket?

Street names with negative connotations could knock thousands off house prices, a Roselake estate agent claims.

Edward Cowley, of Cowley and Birt Estate Agents, threw his hat into the debate on whether Roselake Town should change the name of Beggars Way.

'A national survey found that if you live in a street with a risqué name your house could be worth up to 22% less than a similar property in a sensibly-named street just a stone's throw away,' says Mr Cowley.

Mr Cowley refused to be pressed on by just how much he thought Beggars Way homeowners might have had their houses devalued.

When contacted by the Gazette, Beggars Way resident David Grant was adamant that if the name were not changed it would cost residents thousands of pounds.

Exeter estate agents Smythe and Sons were unconvinced.

'I am sure that a vulgar name, referring to certain parts of the body for example, could affect a property value, but Beggars Way seems pretty inoffensive to me,' said director Derek Smythe.

The Town Council is due to debate the issue again next Monday. The Gazette will continue to keep its readers informed, as we do on all important local issues.

Over the road, Dave was less happy as he read today's edition of the Gazette. Not to put too fine a point on it, he was well pissed off.

'Look at this crap,' he said to Connie, pushing the paper in her direction across the kitchen table.

'Not now, babe, I'm cooking.' she replied. 'Just tell me.'

'The Gazette's screwed it up. It's come out all wrong.'

Dave was even more disgruntled when Josh phoned him and asked wasn't that letter from the agency a crock of shit.

'What letter?' Dave asked.

'The letter came through the door today.'

'I didn't get any letter.'

'Well I did.'

'Well I bloody well didn't, like I said. What are you on about?'

'This letter we got. About Beggars Way property values.'

'We're going round in frigging circles, here, mate, spell it out for me.'

Something clicked in Josh's brain. 'Ah OK, you haven't seen this. I just assumed it had gone round all the residents.'

'Well it obviously bloody didn't.'

'I think you need to see it.'

'So bring it round.'

Josh was growing tired of being bossed around by Dave.

'Can't right now. Dinner's nearly ready. Why don't you come over in an hour or so.'

'Jeeze, Josh, this is important.'

'So's my dinner. If I don't eat it when it's ready Ellie will go mental.'

'I've got to go out in twenty minutes.'

'So get your arse round here and pick it up.'

Dave picked up the letter. He was still seething as he went off to his Masons meeting. Connie left for her hen party. Their son was left alone in the house.

Not quite alone. To make the most of his parents' absence, Arnie invited his new girlfriend Jessica round. Jessica lived over the road, which was how they had got together. Jessica was the daughter of James and Jenny Harwood at number eighteen, so she and Arnie had been aware of each other since the Grants moved in. Arnie hadn't taken much interest in her at first, thinking her on the plain side, with rather frizzy hair, but his interest perked up when he realised Jessica was becoming careless about closing her bedroom curtains when she went to bed at night. With the aid of a pair of binoculars he realised there was sizeable potential advantage for him in building up their acquaintance. And inviting her to his room.

'I saw a film the other day,' Jessica said, 'and this guy smeared his girlfriend's nipples with honey and then licked it off.'

'What film, Jess?' Arnie asked.

'I dunno.'

'Who was in it?'

'Dunno.'

'OK so?'

'I just thought, maybe…'

'What?'

'Maybe we should try it.'

Arnie's pants were already down. He was ready for more serious action. He hadn't expected this intervention.

'Sure. Sometime.'

'Like now?' Jessica crossed her legs.

'I'm not sure there's any honey.'

'Why don't you go find out?'

Arnie gave in to the inevitable. He drew his pants up and went to the kitchen. He checked the larder. No result. Fridge. Same. He had done his best.

'Nope. No honey.'

'Maybe we could try something else. What about peanut butter?'

Arnie groaned. He resumed his search. This time he found a half-full jar. He took it back up to his bedroom.

'There you go,' he said.

Jessica pulled a face. 'Sun Pat Crunchy? I don't want my boobs all scratched to bits thank you very much. Just forget it. Get your mum to put some honey on her shopping list.'

'I don't think she does shopping lists. I think she just takes the car down to the supermarket and buys everything in stock.'

'Except honey.'

'Maybe.'

'Maybe she used up the last jar getting your dad to...'

Arnie pulled a face and put his hand over Jessica's mouth. He was still of an age when the idea of any sexy goings-on between his parents was unthinkable to him.

'I tell you what she does a list of,' he said to change the subject. 'The only thing. The wine she wants delivered next time round.'

'She has wine deliveries?' Jessica said, rather unintelligently.

'That's what I just said, isn't it?'

'Where from?'

'Where from what?'

'Where does she have the wine delivered from?'

'I dunno. Off licence, supermarket, whatever.'

'My mum and dad get Tesco wine. Says so on the label. Haven't you ever noticed what sort of wine your mum drinks?'

'No. Anyway, what's it matter?'

Arnie's mind had turned back to getting on with the business in hand, and was unzipping his fly. What sort of booze his parents consumed was not foremost in his mind right now.

Jessica wondered whether to tell Arnie the story she had overheard her mum relaying in the kitchen tonight, what this woman had said at the knitting circle. About wine delivery not being the only service offered by the wine shop man. Maybe she and Arnie could have a giggle about whether or not Arnie's mum was also the receiver of his favours. She decided to keep quiet, at least for now. Not because she had twigged that Arnie might actually get quite upset by the idea of his mum having an adulterous relationship, more that what Arnie was revealing as he removed his trousers was turning her own mind back as to the main purpose of her visit, and the need to conclude business well before the expected return of Dave or Connie.

The next morning Graham was ready to start canvassing the neighbours for their reaction to the Quentin Fairbrace letter, but stopped at his gateway when he saw a small group of people at the end of the road. Ambling over to see what the fuss was about, he saw a man with video camera, a woman with a microphone, plus another man with a couple of cameras dangling from his neck. The cause of the interest was a man sat on the pavement, his back resting on the wall adjacent to the Beggars Way street sign. Sitting next to the man was a black Labrador, its paws resting either side of a bowl.

Graham recognised the dog. Through the dog he recognised the scruffy man. Graham had seen him in recent weeks selling copies of The Big Issue in the High Street. Today he wasn't selling anything. In front of him was a cardboard sign marked in broad felt-tip marker ink "HOMELESS, HUNGRY AND BROKE. PLEASE HELP". The beggar had constructed a makeshift tent, weighing down a dirty tarpaulin with bricks, stretched between the pavement and the top of the wall on the corner of Dave Grant's front wall.

Beggars Way had acquired its first beggar – or at least the first for centuries.

The cameraman was doing some setup shots. Graham walked over to the TV journalist and didn't hide his feelings.

'This is an outrage,' he blustered. 'Beggars on the streets.'

'I'm sorry,' the reporter said, interrupting, 'who are you?'

'I live here and we have a right to keep begging off our streets.'

The woman raised her hand to stop Graham. 'Perhaps we can do a short interview with you after we've finished with the, er, man on the pavement and the gentleman over there,' she said. For the first time Graham realised Dave Grant was standing waiting by his front gate and watching. Graham couldn't make out his expression exactly, he guessed a smug sneer.

The cameraman finished the setup and moved in with the reporter to film the beggar, donning headphones and plugging in the interviewer's mike. Graham poked his head over the cameraman's shoulder and listened to the interview. The reporter's immaculate shoulder-length red hair, clipped accent and expensive clothes, contrasted strongly with the beggar's unkempt spiky hair, rough speech, and holed jacket and trousers.

'Mr Benson, my name's Angela. I'll just ask a couple of questions before we start so we get the setup right, then I'll start the interview proper by asking why you're here.'

'OK', Mr Benson growled gruffly.

'Mr Benson, could I ask you your dog's name?'

'He 'asn't got a name. He 'asn't got nuffin', like me.'

An expression of frustration passed quickly over Angela's face, but she pressed on.

'Mr Benson, can you tell us what you had for breakfast?'

'I ain't 'ad no breakfast – I'm broke – see 'ere?' Benson said, stabbing his finger at the cardboard sign. 'And 'ungry.'

'Yes, quite,' Angela said, disapproving but not nonplussed.

'Is that OK for you Tom?' she asked the cameraman, who had his camera trained on Benson.

'No, I can't go out of the house without having something in the morning,' Tom said drily. 'But the sound and light's fine.'

Graham wondered if Angela's barely perceptible flush betrayed an amorous link with Tom.

'Let's get on with it then,' she said. She turned to Benson, 'Can you please explain to us why you have set up camp here this morning?' and pushed the microphone towards him.

'Well it's Beggars Way, innit?' Benson said.

'Can you tell us a bit more?'

'Like it says on this sign 'ere. I'm 'omeless and broke. This is Beggars Way. So this is where I'm stayin' from now on. It'll be 'ome like.'

'Isn't it illegal to solicit money on the streets? Aren't you afraid the police will come and move you on?'

'It's Beggars Way, see, historic rights, like. They can't turf me off.'

'But surely you'd be better off beg... er... soliciting help somewhere with more footfall?'

'I reckon regulars will get to know where me and Charlie live,' Benson said, apparently putting the lie to his earlier claim that his importuning assistant had no name. 'I've got nothing, so it can't get any worse, can it?'

Angela had enough for her needs. She switched the mike off and signalled Tom to stop the camera.

'Thank you Mr Benson,' she said without much enthusiasm.

Graham watched as Angela interviewed Dave. Dave put on a show of irate householder disgusted that the name of his street had attracted such attention. He was going to do something about it and get the name changed, or sue the Council for devaluing his property.

It was becoming clearer now. When Graham had met Benson on a previous occasion in the High Street and bought a Big Issue from him, Benson had been politely- if not particularly well-spoken, and was not clothed in the scruffy, stained and smelly-looking outfit he was wearing today. And Dave had shown mild satisfaction rather than purple anger before his turn to appear on-camera. But what to do? What to say when Graham's turn came?

CHAPTER 8

'Mr Ferguson, you live just over the road from here, can you tell us what your reaction is this morning?'

'It's an outrage. This is a decent neighbourhood and we're not going to stand by and let it be taken over by riffraff.'

'So you agree with your neighbour Mr Grant, the best way to deal with this is solve the problem by changing your avenue's name?'

Graham had been on a short fuse. He had planned what to say but had said something different, and now this question took him by surprise.

'No I bloody well don't. That man is a bloody troublemaker, only moved in a while back and now wants to overturn our bloody lives.' Graham's face reddened as he saw irritation flash over Angela's face. 'Oops sorry'.

Angela's voice changed from interview mode to conversational. 'I have no problem with you swearing, Mr Ferguson. I can tell you are probably an old hand at interviews, and know that any swearing is a ploy, the cue for us to drop that reply and edit it out. Merely a small inconvenience for us. OK I'll ask you the same question again.'

Her tone resumed interviewer's. 'Do you agree with your neighbours that the name should be changed from Beggars Way?'

Angela's introduction of the plural threw Graham. He wanted to say that Grant was only one person, and most of the residents had been happy until now. He didn't find the words.

'No I don't. I, that is we, all of us, er, oh bloody hell.'

'Don't worry, Mr Ferguson,' Angela said sweetly. I have all I need.'

'Oh bugger, can't I have another try?' Graham pleaded.

'No need thanks. Look out for us on Points West tonight. Bye.'

Graham swore at nobody in particular, raised his hands in frustration and stormed off towards his house. Grant watched him, a broad smile on his face.

Angela turned to Tom. 'Did you get the shot of him storming off like that?'

'Of course,' Tom said.

'Good, maybe we can use that, let's do me asking the questions.'

They selected their spot and Tom filmed Angela as she recorded new versions of the interview questions. They recorded a few more shots of Angela nodding in response to the now non-existent responses, then packed their bags and left. Dave went off to work.

'I made a right prat of myself,' Graham confessed to Lawrence, having calmed down enough to knock on Lawrence's door for a chat and some comfort.

Lawrence thought it not appropriate to rub salt into the wound by saying something like 'No change there then,' and surprised himself by saying something reassuring.

'I'm sure you did no such thing,' Lawrence said.

'Oh but I did, I swore and went off in a huff and didn't say anything I wanted to.'

'I'm sure it will be all right. Maybe when you saw what was going on you should have come and fetched me.'

'I didn't think.'

'Well like I say, I'm sure they won't put out anything awful.'

'It's going to be on Points West tonight. I can't bear to watch. I'll be a laughing stock.'

'I tell you what. I'll record it on the video. If it's not as bad as you think it is, you can watch it later on playback.'

'And if it is?'

'We'll get rat-arsed down the motel.'

'I can't go out if everybody's seen me mess up.'

Lawrence's tolerance of self-pity had been exceeded. 'Never stopped you before.'

'Like when?'

'Like when you fell over at the Round Table Christmas do and pulled the Chairman's wife's dress off.'

'That was different. Everybody knew that was an accident.'

'Caused by excess alcohol.'

'Fine friend you are, reminding me of that. It was years ago.'

'OK, OK, if you've messed up that interview we'll just stay home and get pissed. Happy? Shall we go down the off-licence and lay in stocks now?' Lawrence laughed and gave Graham a dig in the ribs.

'But this could be serious if I messed up and Grant wins.'

'So tell me more about how you think he wangled this. Or maybe better, if you think it's all a bit fishy why don't we go over and talk to this beggar guy and see what's going on.'

'Maybe he's gone.'

'All the better if he is. That proves it was a stunt.'

Jake Benson was not looking forward to carrying out his contract. Although Dave Grant had paid him well enough to sit here for a day, or long enough to make sure they had the right media coverage, Jake didn't want to catch piles from a cold pavement, and Charlie would miss his regular walk, although Jake supposed if he left the tent and sign in place, a temporary absence for walkies and Jake's own personal needs might be OK. The tent contained enough dog food and human food for two days, plus assorted drinks. The begging bowl contained a couple of pounds, but Jake had put most of that in himself.

Jake hadn't been given any specific instructions about how to tackle passers-by or neighbours, Dave had just said play the begging role. After the TV crew and newspaper snapper had left Jake was bored. He took a call on his mobile and failed to notice the approach and arrival within hearing distance of Graham and Lawrence.

'Sell Tesco, buy Morrisons,' they heard him say. 'Surplus to the bank.'

Jake suddenly became aware of a presence and snapped his mobile shut.

'Fell off the back of a lorry,' Lawrence suggested, pointing to Jake's mobile, 'since you're broke?'

Jake eyed the intruders and said nothing.

'And what's that about buying and selling?'

Jake felt obliged to parry. 'Plastic bags.'

'Plastic bags?' Lawrence's eyebrows raised in surprise.

'This new law about charging for plastic bags means there's a bit to be made.'

'And putting the profit in the bank?'

'I didn't say profit, did I, I meant the recycling bank.'

Lawrence laughed. 'Bollocks. You've been sussed, you're no more penniless than I am. We've seen you on the High Street. This whole act's a con. And we know who put you up to it. I think the best thing is for you to pack up and clear off, don't you?'

'Or what?'

'Either police or a watery experience. That's my house over there, second down. And I've got a long hose. It'll reach here from the front garden tap.'

Jake thought the threats were a little feeble, but he was bored and ready to compromise.

'Look, suppose you let me stay until teatime, that's when the evening TV local news programme's coming out, right? I'll make it worth your while.' Jake took his wallet out of his jacket and peeled off a fifty. 'Would this cover it?'

Lawrence looked at Graham. 'That'd well cover that trip to the off-licence tonight,' he whispered in Graham's ear, digging Graham in the ribs.

'It's not right,' Graham replied.

'The damage, if there will be any, is already done, and think how Dave Grant would feel if he knew we've got fifty of his cash in our pockets.'

Graham pondered the ethics. 'It would certainly defray some of our expenses.'

'Right then,' Lawrence said, turning back to Jake. 'You're on. Fifty it is and you can stay until teatime.'

Jake handed the notes over. Easy come, easy go. He had good earnings from his High Street operation and didn't want that scuppered. And Dave Grant had given him a couple of hundred.

'Anything you need, something to eat or drink?' Graham offered, kindly.

'No thanks mate, I'm OK, I've got provisions in there,' Jake said waving at the tent.

'Something for the dog?'

'No, Charlie's fine, he's got water and a tin or two of Chunky Chunks, his favourite.'

Graham's charity did not extend to offering bathroom facilities. And he could imagine what Laura's reaction would be.

'OK, we'll leave you to it,' Lawrence said, touching Graham's shoulder to signal it was time to go.

'Fancy a beer?' Lawrence asked Graham, as they walked off.

'I don't mind if I do,' Graham replied, his mind eased considerably, apart from the nagging worry of how he would appear on television.

Jake watched them walk down the road and when they were out of sight he packed his gear and rang for a taxi. Dave had had his money'sworth, in Jake's opinion.

As it happened Graham need not have fretted. Points West showed part of the Jake Benson interview, a sentence or two from Dave Grant, but nothing about Graham. Graham did not know whether to be relieved or cross that he had ended up on the cutting room floor, or the modern equivalent, a deleted file in the BBC computer screen trash bin.

Laura had coped with Graham's telling and retelling of his experience and concern for half the afternoon. Although she was beginning to wonder if Graham's swearing was getting out of hand, at least he had admitted today's misdemeanours, which, like a heavy drinker admitting the scale of the problem, was probably a hopeful sign.

'Maybe you just weren't made to be a TV personality,' she said with an affectionate smile.

When he returned from his office that evening, Dave was not best pleased to find Jake Benson had already decamped. But he was happy with the TV coverage, and was confident that tomorrow's regional and local dailies the Reporter and Gazette would cover the story, with pictures. In any event Connie had almost gone berserk when his glee in revealing his plot had led him inadvertently to tell her how much hiring Jake had cost him. Paying for Jake to stay longer was a definite no-no. Connie had asked him why he felt the need to shell out money at all. Dave couldn't answer. It had become a matter of pride for him. He didn't want that woman Hilary and that fatuous bore Ferguson to get the better of him.

Dave had already conveyed to Hilary the fact that his residents group were happy to accept any new name of the Council's choice. The only fly in the ointment was that letter from Fairbrace. He had to figure out a way to handle that one. Maybe his contacts knew something about Fairbrace that he could use, if fair tactics came to nought. But he remained confident of winning at the end of the day.

Dave's confidence in the Western Daily Reporter printing the story turned out to be justified. What he hadn't foreseen, though, was a trio of genuine beggars, two men and a woman (probably, it was difficult to be sure under the grime and shapeless coat) who, as Dave found when he left for the office, had occupied Jake's deserted pitch. They only had one dog between them, a lop-eared mongrel whose tousled hair looked decidedly less strokeable than Charlie's sleek coat. This was all highly disagreeable to Dave. A beggar for a day who was under your control was all very well, but he didn't want the genuine articles polluting the neighbourhood. On being accosted for money Dave told them in no uncertain terms they should leave immediately. He did not mince words. The reply was to tell him to do exactly the same as he'd told them to do.

Dave promised them he would call the police and get them removed. He was told to do his worst. The word had passed round last night – it had been on the telly. They had the right to stay. Historic rights.

Dave found himself in a dilemma. Getting the press to cover the new invasion would add to the media coverage and profile of the case. For free this time. But Dave imagined what Connie would say when she found out. He predicted the argument that would develop if he told her he was encouraging them to stay a while for his own purposes. And then there was the risk that the rash would spread. Against that, of course, was the fact that unless Beggars Way became a local tourist attraction, the beggars would have no income from passers by. But then again gypsies might move in. They would turn the grassy patch at the end of Beggars Way into a dump and pitch rubbish there. The local pets would all be garrotted and cooked.

No. Dave decided it was more prudent to use his contacts in the Force to have the police deal with this as soon as possible. Nip it in the bud.

Graham could not believe his eyes when he ventured out of the house an hour later and spotted the new arrivals. He scooted off immediately to Lawrence's, and the two of them crossed the road to tell the beggars, in more polite terms than Dave Grant had, that they should depart forthwith.

'How much is it worth?' the female said, displaying gaps amid blackened teeth.

'Not a penny,' Graham declared. 'Just clear off before I call the police.'

'No need, some other bloke said he was going to call 'em,' the woman giggled.

'Good,' Lawrence said. 'More complaints the merrier. They'll have you lot shifted in no time.'

'Maybe we should have offered them fifty,' Lawrence suggested with a grin, as he and Graham went back to Lawrence's house to make a call.

The police arrived a short time later and dealt with the situation, as Dave's masonic contact on the Force (or one of them) had promised. The condition was that Dave didn't organise press coverage. The use of truncheons isn't very photogenic and the police like to preserve their fair and upright public-friendly image.

In the event use of truncheons was not necessary. The trio of beggars valued what teeth they had left and gratefully accepted a couple of pounds each from the police community fund to move on without trouble.

Over the next three days the Beggars Way affair subsided into stalemate. The numbers of residents for and against name change settled down with a small majority in favour. The Devon Evening Gazette had indeed repeated the Jake Benson story on Thursday evening, with a picture of him sat alongside the street sign. Dave congratulated himself on a victory, but it was doubtful what effect his campaign spending had, since most Roselake town residents did not stay glued to their televisions in the early evenings and did not buy Devon and Exeter papers.

On Friday morning Graham received a letter from Hilary informing him that the person who had requested the name change to Cypress Avenue had now confirmed that any suitable name which the Town Council chose would be acceptable. Graham felt the need to visit the council offices and tell her that Grant did not speak for all the residents, as she well knew, and the new Residents Association would wish to be consulted. Hilary gauged from the answer to her question as to the status and membership of the new association that this was not yet a force to be reckoned with. Graham was also forced to admit that some of the signatories on the letter he had provided earlier against name change might now be having second thoughts. Hilary said not to worry, the dropping of Cypress Avenue as a possibility in her view rendered the earlier request null and void. She would continue to tell the council members that the residents were still divided on the issue. Graham came away somewhat encouraged. Hilary had not imparted the same information to Dave Grant, since she felt the less he knew the less energy he would expend in mobilising his troops. She saw Dave's hand behind the recent house price and beggar press splashes, and thought that feeding him information would only spur and rechannel his efforts. In particular she did not encourage him to put a new request in writing.

Graham and Lawrence could do nothing to counter the media coverage Dave had already achieved. It was pointless issuing a new press release as the one with the Quentin letter and the rebuttal of the price drop argument was still outstanding. Instead they set to work trying to rally their supporters and reverse the downward trend in votes against change, and were partly successful in that. Dave had similarly spent part of his weekend chasing support for his side, but had little success in swaying the opinion of the folk on the north side of Beggars Way, thanks to Lawrence's hint to them that Dave had used underhand tactics in setting up the beggar stunt. Whilst the residents were not committed in their stance against name change, the thought of dirty tricks being employed raised their hackles.

Where Graham and Lawrence were singularly unsuccessful was in stimulating enthusiasm for the formation of a residents' association. Graham had proposed an inaugural meeting for ten o'clock on Sunday morning at his house, and had received encouraging replies from the people he found at home on Friday and Saturday. He had dropped notes through letterboxes of people he had not found at home. But on Sunday morning he sat at home disconsolate. Not a soul turned up, not even Lawrence.

'Never mind dear, I expect they'll all rally round when the time comes,' was Laura's reaction to Graham's disappointment.

Graham was not sure what Laura was expecting. Some moment of crisis, when he would have to go round issuing pitchforks and clubs, and assemble materials for a barricade to prevent the powers-that-be from replacing the Beggars Way sign?

If action in the street itself slowed down over the weekend, elsewhere things were astir which would have significant impact on the Beggars Way affair. The publishing of the article in Wednesday's Midweek Gazette on house prices caused ripples that spread far from Beggars Way, and indeed the town.

The article caused rumbles in Butts Close, part of the Broadwood estate on the outer fringes of Roselake. On Thursday morning Celia Pascoe at number fifteen took a copy of the paper round to her neighbour Gwen Thorgood at number twelve. Over a cup of Twinings best morning tea they discussed the prospects of their cul-de-sac houses losing their value. The potentially unfortunate connotations of the street's name had of course been noted before by everybody living there, but it was not something you cared to discuss outside the privacy of your own home. But the Gazette was now forcing the issue into the open.

'I spoke to Hugh about this last night,' Celia told Gwen, after Gwen had read the article. She had not read it previously, her own copy having as usual gone straight into the recycling bin.

'We are rather concerned that this could apply to us, for reasons of which I am sure you are aware but don't need discussing.'

'Agreed,' said Gwen.

Celia wasn't quite sure as to whether Gwen was agreeing that she, too, was concerned, or that the obvious required no explanation.

'So what are we going to do about it?' Celia continued, assuming the former. 'Those people at Beggars Way asked for a name change, do you think we should do the same?'

'Change to what?

'I don't know my dear, anything that isn't associated with, er, shall we say, nether regions.'

'But they haven't even agreed to change Beggars Way yet. And that name is ancient. Our estate is new, so's the name. It's not like it was named back in the days of archers training for Agincourt or anything like that.'

The name Butts Close was indeed hardly ancient, although it did recall a time past, the use of the land in the middle of the twentieth century as an army test firing ground for small arms and modest artillery. A historical legacy remained, not only in the name Butts Close, but in archaeological artefacts. During excavations for the new housing a couple of large live rounds had been found. After these had been safely detonated the area had been thoroughly screened and pronounced safe. However the finding of the shells had been brought to prominent public attention, and still many local gardeners remained cautious of deep digging. The allotments created on part of the old range were only half used. Allotment seekers applied instead for plots on Roselake's more central site, where they were more likely to turn up a Roman coin than strike their spade into a bullet.

'The fact that the Council made a poor choice twenty-five years ago is no excuse for them not to make the right decision now,' Celia stated firmly. 'If the name is now costing us thousands of pounds each they must sort it out.'

'I suppose so, yes,' Gwen replied. Gwen, if truth be told, was not convinced. But she was willing to play along with Celia's concern because of their friendship. Celia and Gwen had made friends the day Gwen and her husband Lars moved in to the Close. Celia had come over to offer them hospitality immediately the removal van had departed. And when Lars passed away soon afterwards, Celia was the first to offer Gwen support and more than a little Twinings and sympathy.

'So what do we do? Write to the council?'

'Wouldn't it be a good idea to speak to the neighbours first? Get some agreement?'

Celia was an organiser. 'Excellent plan. I shall get cracking straight away. We could have a meeting tomorrow morning maybe, at my house. Ten o'clock OK for you?'

'I suppose so,' Gwen agreed.

Whilst one might argue that the residents of Beggars Way and Butts Close purchased their houses in the full knowledge of the name of the road they would be living in, one could also see that the residents of Isis Close had no idea at the time that their residence would be linked to Islamic fundamentalism.

At the same time as Celia and Gwen were sowing the seeds of change on the Broadwood Estate, so too was Ted Slater. Ted had harboured a bee in his bonnet about the potential linking of his address with terrorists for some months. Being himself of a bigoted right-wing persuasion, it might come as a surprise to find Ted's ally to be his near neighbour Sami Hasan, the Bangladeshi owner of the "Indian" restaurant on the High Street. Ted's views on many subjects were well-known to his neighbours, which was why he could not count on any of them as his friends. Ted had had no interaction with Sami since he moved into the cul-de-sac, so Sami remained unacquainted with Ted's bigotry, and would still greet him with a cheery smile when they passed each other on the street. Ted's wife gave him the inspiration to approach Sami for support, and Ted reluctantly set his prejudices aside, temporarily at least.

Sami had a more personal reason for wishing to publicly disassociate himself from extremism, and he leapt at the chance of running his moderate colours up the mast, in order to gain kudos as a good neighbour in the Close, as well as hopefully drum up more business for the restaurant. In his innocence Sami assumed that his neighbours knew he was a Moslem, whereas in fact, since Sami's family female members showed no sign of Islamic dress, most of his neighbours would probably have thought him Indian and a Hindu.

Unlike Gwen and Celia, and because of Ted's uncertain confidence in his neighbours' support, Ted and Sami had no truck with seeking consensus, and decided immediately to lobby the council and establish democratic rationale later.

Over on the west side of the town lies the Beaver Estate. The estate comprises blocks of council flats and a few streets of council or ex-council houses. It had enjoyed for many years a reputation for accommodating most of Roselake's undesirable families, not to mention the town's most notorious brothel. The latter fact drew some wry comments that the estate's name was entirely appropriate. The fact is, the estate was named after a Lieutenant Colonel Lionel Beaver, who moved to the area when Roselake accommodated an army training camp, and on retirement and disbanding of the camp Lionel demobilised, retaining his domicile and his military title. He became a notable town worthy, carrying out many good works, including, ironically, the attempt to expunge the town's prostitution trade, which had thrived under army patronage.

Although the Gazette article provoked much discussion in the streets and in pubs that weekend about the Beaver name, the cause célèbre generated more mirth than concern or call for action, especially as the only organisational skills many residents of the estate had acquired were already fully utilised in the fields of drugs and other minor crime. But a few of the estate's youth started to foment ideas for a bit of recreational fun.

The Midweek Gazette's coverage was not confined to Roselake, of course. It was distributed districtwide, and since Edward Cowley's warning on house prices was a general one, it struck fear in the hearts, or rather the pockets, of quite a few residents of Exebury, Rosemouth and Bradmouth, who realised, if they had not done so before, that their addresses, many of which were old and venerable such as Argus Back Passage, Spitup Lane, Old Camp Road, Dogger Lane, Hooker Court and Peaswell Street, could be wide open to ribald comment. A storm was brewing. Already by Friday the town council offices of Exebridge and Rosemouth had received enquiries as to the procedure for applying for name changes. The crest of the wave would break on Monday.

Monday morning in Roselake passed quietly on the streets. In days gone by the High Street and South Street would have been thronged with women shopping after the weekend for fresh produce at the many butchers, bakers and greengrocers. No longer. Although some old Roselakeians who lived within a couple of minutes walk of the shops still shopped locally in the one butchers, one bakers and one greengrocers that remained, the incomers drove to the edge-of-town supermarkets, and if they ventured into town at all it was to take a tea or coffee at one of the many tearooms and coffee shops.

Hilary, however, had a busy morning in the town council offices, trying to remain patient as she explained responsibilities, procedures, technicalities and facts to Celia, Gwen and another Butts Close resident, Janice Watkins, who had come to enquire, to lodge petition, and to lobby. Hilary had to go through the same procedure a short while later with Sami and Ted. She didn't mind that so much, as Sami was not only good looking but extremely affable, nodding or wagging his head with a smile on his face at Hilary's every utterance. Hilary took an instant dislike to Ted, however, as his opening words were on the lines of 'You've got to do something about this', and although Ted had never been in the army nor been in any service other than working in a hotel, he had that condescending air of those used to being obeyed.

At five minutes to twelve the arrival of another pair delivering a letter from the residents of Hanged Man Lane was more than Hilary could stand. She informed the couple that the office was closing, and when the couple remonstrated, pointing out that the official hours were until one thirty, Hilary hissed between her teeth that not today they weren't.

Hilary locked the door and retired to her office. She picked up the phone, rang the District Council and asked to be put through to Sue Eastwood. Her call was answered by a different voice she recognised as belonging to Eve Coombes. This was unexpected, but almost immediately confirmed.

'Planning department, how can I help? You're speaking to Eve Coombes,' Eve said.

'This is Hilary Jessop of Roselake Town Council here,' Hilary said. 'I was hoping to speak to Sue Eastwood, on a matter I was discussing with her last week.'

'Well you'll have to speak to me now. She's not here. In fact Sue may not be working in my department any more.'

'I thought you were on maternity leave,' Hilary queried.

'I was. I'm back,' Eve said, the tone of her voice indicating that she was not delighted by the fact of her return.

'I hope you had a good break, and that all's well with the family,' said Hilary, putting on a voice meant to charm.

'The family's fine, thank you very much for asking,' Eve said roughly, with no note of gratitude, 'but if you think it was a holiday you're mistaken.'

Hilary was a little miffed to find herself on the wrong end of a slightly difficult conversation. She decided to move on.

'Actually I was wanting to let Sue know we are facing more enquiries about changing street names.'

'You needn't tell me, I've had people walking in the door from Rosemouth and I've had to ship them off to the Rosemouth Town Council. I've had the Rosemouth Town Clerk on the telephone seven times this morning – seven – not to mention the clerks from Exebury and Bradmouth plus a couple of the villages. And it's all this name changing business you and your council sparked off. I was expecting a peaceful first day back at work, settling back gently into the old routine, and what do I get? Chaos!'

Hilary's back was up. She hardly felt it was her fault, nor her council's, if she had had to deal with a legitimate public concern, and told Eve precisely that.

'Deal with it? I wish. How did you deal with it? You cajoled poor Sue into falsifying the account of our dealings with Cosgrove Estates, who are respected developers here and provide a lot of local employment. I had to wheedle the full details out of her. She has gone home in tears, and may face disciplinary action, and it's all down to you.'

At least Hilary now understood Eve's attitude, although she thought Eve was being exceedingly unfair.

Hilary decided best not to argue.

'So what's the way forward?'

'You do nothing, you've done quite enough already. I will sort this my way.'

Eve put the phone down and congratulated herself on her performance.

Sue walked into Eve's office, bringing sandwiches. Two tuna sandwiches for Eve (she had developed a longing for tuna during her pregnancy and had not yet lost it) and an egg salad for Sue.

'That was a call for you from Hilary Jessop of Roselake,' Eve remarked, as Sue handed her her lunch. 'I dealt with it. I've had enough of these town clerks buzzing around today. Time they were put in their place. I ticked her off about persuading you to bend the record a little about the Cypress Way. I told her she had caused you to face the threat of disciplinary action, so act upset and reserved next time you speak to her.'

'Will do, Eve.' They smiled at each other. Sue had learned from Eve all she knew about how to blag lunches and proseccos. And how to fib once in a while.

After lunch Eve got to work. She met her chief planning officer, the treasurer and the chief executive, and when they arrived at the council offices after an obviously vinous lunch she spoke to Donald Cresswell, the planning committee chairman, or cabinet member for development control in modern parlance, and the leader of the council Stuart Parkinson.

CHAPTER 9

Dave and Josh were late arriving at that evening's Roselake Town Council meeting, and couldn't find a seat. Dave had dragged Josh along with a promise of a beer afterwards. Josh had survived a tiff with his wife – just - and with no darts match tonight was at a loose end. They had checked the agenda, and the possible renaming of Beggars Way was the first item after agreeing the last council meeting minutes and receiving last Monday's planning committee report. Graham and Lawrence were again to be seen sitting in the public gallery. The main event of the evening, discussion of the plans for the community complex, had attracted a large audience, and even the extra rows of chairs put out didn't provide adequate accommodation. The issue was a hot potato, and supporters of both sides of the argument wanted to demonstrate that they didn't lack numbers. After nearly twenty years one might describe the heat as from smouldering embers rather than blazing firebrands, but there was a sense that matters were at last coming to a head under Brian's control of the reins.

The meeting began as usual with prayers. Gloria had recovered from her fall, and since her accident she had been careful to negotiate successfully Church Lane's detritus of beercans, used condoms and syringes. She also successfully negotiated arrangements with the police and the District Council to take action on cleaning up this alleyway of sin, and was promised either video cameras as a deterrent to inappropriate behaviour, night lighting or both in the near future.

As Gloria stood up to offer prayers, Graham and Lawrence couldn't help looking at each other and snickering like schoolboys. After Laura had forgiven his verbal lapse in front of the knitting circle, she had related to Graham the content of Katherine Leach's gossip. 'Just between us, mind, I don't approve of scandal mongering,' Laura had said, but Graham couldn't help pass what he'd heard on to Lawrence, with similar proviso, to be similarly broken, of course. Graham and Lawrence knew exactly what the question was in the other's mind. 'What colour are they tonight?'

Dave saw Graham and Lawrence's suppressed giggles, and wondered what that was about.

Gloria finished her prayer for God's guidance to descend tonight and illuminate the Council's deliberations ('That would be a first,' she thought to herself cynically, and the observant listener might have noted that she addressed her prayer to the Dear Lord, rather than Almighty God, and that this correctly interpreted her opinion that He had an occasional lapse in authority when it came to imposing reason on Roselake Town Council debate). Gloria departed to enjoy a glass of Chardonnay, which her friend, that rather nice Mr Cole had brought round to share with her. Martin Cole had a mysterious acquaintance who occasionally generously gave him a case of wine in token of friendship, and Martin occasionally offered Gloria a bottle in recognition of one of the supposed laws of Moses. A twelfth is not ten percent, thought Gloria, but God isn't too fussy about a percentage point or two, and she accepted Martin's offers and company with enthusiasm. The wines were always soooo much nicer than the plonk she bought in for the church, although of course it became something of an entirely different quality when consecrated. Gloria didn't offer, and Martin didn't expect, the same gratitude in kind that Hilary gave Oscar of Roselake Bin Ends. Gloria had felt a slight twinge of disappointment when Martin showed no amorous intent, and had given up any hope she might have had, too, about welcoming Martin into her flock. But they became friends. It was Martin whose underwear colour she had inadvertently let slip at the Parish Women's Group. She had only discovered it on her first meeting with Martin, when he had climbed a ladder to paint her ceiling, forgetting that he had just been involved in an escapade which left a large tear in his jeans, revealing his underpants, but fortunately nothing else, to Gloria's gaze.

With Gloria gone the council meeting commenced in earnest. The minutes of the last meeting were agreed without comment, and discussion of the planning committee's report on the result of the Beggars Way inspection was merged with the main agenda item which, as we said, was coming next.

'To summarise, Mr Mayor, councillors,' Hilary began, but Mr Mayor interrupted her.

'Excuse me Ms Jessop, but I have some new information for the council on this next item, which I think I should relay before we start any discussion.'

'Excuse me, Mr Mayor, if you have new information why wasn't I informed?' Hilary was still smarting from the rebuff she had received from Eve Coombes, and was feeling raw.

'I'm sorry, I only learned about it this evening, on my way to the meeting.'

Although this slight fib would appease the councillors, Hilary was not impressed. On arrival Brian had found enough time to have a pre-meeting fondle and grope in the mayoral office. Hilary would have preferred to be properly briefed. And she had a sneaking suspicion that Brian was making a mocking reference to the similar way Hilary had introduced news from the District Council at the planning meeting.

'Anyway, the situation is this,' Brian continued. 'The District Council has decided to alter the procedure for street name changes.'

'So they're cutting us out as usual, I expect,' Donald Ridgeway grumbled to his neighbour. 'At least we can move on quick to the next item.'

'Councillor Ridgeway, if I could continue without interruption. It's the opposite to what you imagine, actually. They have decided to leave the question of street name changes entirely in the hands of the town and parish councils. I'm sure that will please you, Councillor.'

Donald flapped his hand and the mayor invited him to stand and speak.

'No it doesn't please me, Mr Mayor. Not if it means we've got to waste more time on this Beggars Way business. If it's up to us I move we leave the name as it is and get on with something useful.'

Donald sat down and nudged Ken Baker. 'Seconded,' he said, and closed his eyes again.

'Let's put it to the vote,' Don Ridgeway suggested.

Hilary was inclined to bide her time. If this motion were carried it would ease matters with Eve Coombes, and she would be pleased for Mr Ferguson.

Frank Parton rose to speak.

'Mr Mayor, I really don't think it's good enough to just vote on this issue without debate, when we have spent quite a lot of time and effort on this, and some of us have devoted considerable endeavour in researching the history of the name Beggars Way. You may or may not recall my previous comments on this matter, the fact that from the sixteenth century…'

'Yes, have the courtesy please to credit us with good memories, Councillor Parton,' Brian said wearily. 'Let's move on.'

'Very well. There is another factor to be taken into consideration. The democratic rights of the residents who wanted a name change. We should respect that and go through due process. We have done that so far, and should continue in that direction, rather than undermine our dedication and commitment to the people we serve, our electorate.'

'Bollocks,' Don Ridgeway was heard to say.

'Did you wish to come back, Councillor Ridgeway?' Brian asked with heavy irony, but fearing the reply would be yes.

Don rose again. 'With respect, Councillor Parton doesn't know one bit of his anatomy from the other. Last time he was arguing for the name to stay Beggars Way, now that's exactly what I'm suggesting and he's arguing the opposite. What sort of a nonsense carrying on is that. He's like a push me pull you. Either he wants the name to stay or he doesn't. Let him make his mind up and have done with it.' Don sat down again.

Frank's colour rose and he raised his hand to speak again but Brian waved him down.

'I'm not going to have the level of discussion descend to personal abuse. As I said, let's move on. Yes Councillor Harker, you want to say something.'

Judy's ears had pricked up at the word democracy. Democracy being towards the pinnacle of her Green ideals pyramid, she couldn't let the word be mentioned without speaking up.

'I agree on this occasion with Councillor Parton. This is a matter of public accountability. Democracy and the rights of the residents are of paramour importance.'

Hilary's eyes rolled at the malapropism but Judy continued with uninterrupted flow.

'If the District Council would have put the issue to a formal poll of residents then so should we. Otherwise we are denying local input, subverting democratic emancipation and steamrollering over communal suffrage.' Judy sat down. Which was a relief to more than one of her fellow councillors, whose foreheads had started wrinkling in fear of Judy's speech becoming an unintelligible rant, which wouldn't have been the first occasion. For one or two of the listeners it had already gone through the orange light.

'At this point I think our clerk wishes to say something,' Brian said. This was not an act of clairvoyance, as Hilary had given him two hefty kicks under the table. Stronger and more painful than necessary, Brian thought.

'Thank you Mr Mayor,' Hilary said, smiling sugar-sweetly, but hoping she had indeed inflicted some pain. 'I have further information to share which might be particularly relevant if what you say about the District Council's intention is true.'

Brian felt the need to interject. 'Ms Jessop, if you are questioning my accuracy, you will find out soon enough when this is official.'

'And when will that be?' Hilary asked.

'The new policy will be in force by Wednesday after the next District Council cabinet meeting.'

'So it is not yet in force. I am not sure this council can decide matters on what may or may not turn out to be the case, whether that would be right and proper.'

'Ms Jessop, I am informing you that the official policy will be in force on Wednesday. But with immediate effect there is a moratorium on the District Council agreeing or denying any requests for street name changes. That's an end of that doubt, I hope. We can make whatever recommendations we want to the

District Council today, but they will throw it back at us on Wednesday.'

Hilary tried hard to conceal her irritation.

'If you had not interrupted me Mr Mayor…' Hilary began.

'I only interrupted to advise you of new information which could have affected what you were going to tell us.'

'If you had informed me before the meeting or given a full explanation at the start of this agenda item we might have got to the point a bit quicker.'

'Hear, hear,' came from Peter Galway's direction.

A few of the councillors looked round at each other. A public spat between the mayor and the clerk was a novelty.

'Please continue, Ms Jessop,' Brian said. 'In your own time.'

'I have to advise the council that there have been two new firm requests to change street names in Roselake. Plus one or two further enquiries. This was sparked by a rather unfortunate article which appeared in the Midweek Gazette last Wednesday. The point is, we are facing perhaps not just one request for a change but several. In view of what the Mayor has kindly shared with us this evening I suggest this means the Council might consider instituting a policy on the matter, rather than deciding one-by-one piecemeal.'

Peter Galway asked to speak and rose.

'I think we are a responsible council, and are capable of judging each application on its merits. That isn't so much piecemeal as recognising that all rules may have exceptions.'

Hilary kicked the mayor once again. Brian was inwardly fuming but smiled pleasantly. He ignored the kick, but Hilary interrupted proceedings anyway.

'With all due respect to Councillor Galway, I think if he understood the true scale of the furore that the article regarding street names has caused, he might realise that the best and in my opinion only way to deal with this is to make a clear statement on the issue. And that is best achieved by implementing an agreed policy.'

'With all due respect to our clerk, Mr Mayor, I suggest that if we do not understand the full extent of public concern, this is because it was not presented to us in the agenda papers nor by the clerk's introduction.'

Hilary was fuming and made to speak. Brian took the unprecedented step of kicking Hilary's leg under the table.

'I tend to agree with you, Councillor Galway,' Brian said, rubbing salt into Hilary's wound. 'But I have explained the situation from my viewpoint. I was only informed today of the impending District Council decision.'

Peter Galway scowled and sat down.

Derek Hunt rose. 'This is all very well, Mr Mayor, arguing the toss about whether we should have a policy, but we just don't have the information before us. This has been sprung on us just five minutes ago. And what about the cost to the Council if we are to start administering a new scheme? You've said not a word about that Mr Mayor. And if I know the District Council they will shove not just the responsibility but the cost onto us, you mark my words. Stands to reason. Tory council. Tory policy. Our budget will not stretch any further this year. We're fully committed.'

Brian groaned inwardly. Hunt was right, the dig at the Conservatives apart. When Donald Cresswell had tipped him the wink about the imminent policy change, Brian hadn't thought to check out the details. He (and Cresswell, who also had his finger in the community complex pie) were anxious to get a motion approving the complex through the Town Council this evening, and Brian had hoped to skate over the Beggars Way issue as quickly as possible without dissent.

'I propose from the chair,' Brian said, 'that we postpone further discussion of any street name changes until our next meeting, when Ms Jessop will no doubt be able to brief us properly on the details and implications of the new District Council policy as by then implemented. She will also be able to apprise us of the full public interest in the matter, and it will give time for her to liaise with Councillor Hunt over any potential cost implications.'

'Just one moment,' Judy Harker rose. 'Could we please, for the record, have Ms Jessop confirm the status of the Beggars Way application. Councillor Parton was right, we have had site inspection and two debates on this issue and we need to know how things stand. I still feel we owe it to the residents to give a clear indication of our stance on this particular issue.'

'The situation is as was reported to last week's Planning Committee, Councillor Harker,' Hilary answered. 'The name Cypress Avenue, Way, Lane or Cypress anything is not possible because that is already reserved for a new road on the Badger estate. I have received no alternative suggestion, although one resident of Beggars Way has told me informally since that he would be happy with any new name the Council proposed. Of course it would be open to the Council to discuss alternative name suggestions this evening.'

This met with groans.

'However, I would just remind councillors that we have a heavy agenda tonight,' Hilary concluded. What she meant was, of course, that if the Council found it hard to answer yes or no to a straightforward question they were hardly likely to get anywhere with making a list of alternatives and coming to a decision in one meeting.

'In which case it seems to me,' Brian said, hoping to cut debate, 'the original application has lapsed, and we should advise the residents who sent us the original letter that they should submit a new suggestion to be determined under the Council's new policy. As and when we have one.'

'But Mr Mayor,' Don Ridgeway said, after asking to speak and being allowed to do so despite a groan all round. 'The Council has an opportunity here. We can honour one of our recently deceased aldermen, and worthy citizen of Roselake, former ex-councillor Baker. I move we suggest the name should be Baker, er...'

'Baker Way?' Frank Parton suggested, with a sneer. 'Sounds like a TV cookery programme.'

'Lane. Baker Lane. That's it,' Don declared. I so move. He nudged his neighbour.

'Seconded,' Ken Baker chirped, exhibiting appropriately on this occasion his Pavlovian dog reflex.

'Mr Mayor,' Frank Parton leapt to his feet. 'This is outrageous. With all due respect to the late councillor Baker, and his brother who sits with us this evening, I think we need Ms Jessop's advice.

Should not Councillor Baker declare an interest in this and take no part in the debate?'

'Since he's asleep most of the time, chance of him taking part in debate at all would be a fine thing ,' Councillor Owen whispered to her neighbour, Peter Galway.

Hilary signalled to the mayor to speak. Brian winced, in expectation of minor assault, which didn't come, but refused her, raising his hand to signal he was losing patience.

'I repeat, we are in no position to decide on this matter tonight, and Councillor Parton is correct. The motion is not validly seconded, Councillor Ridgeway,' Brian ruled. 'I move we defer for a full report at the next meeting. Have I a seconder?'

'Seconded,' deputy mayor Paul Hart chirped up, his own conditioned responses springing into action.

'Agreed?' Brian said hopefully.

'Agreed,' came a chorus of bored voices.

'Anybody against?'

No-one said yes, but Don Ridgeway was heard muttering something about another effing total waste of time and more to come.

Dave Grant was furious. Hilary had put him down, making it seem that he was only one individual, not the representative of everyone who had signed the original letter. Now he was back at square one.

'Bastards,' he said to Josh. 'Let's go get a beer or two down us.,'

Graham and Lawrence also stood up to leave. Two people behind leapt in to claim their now-vacant seats.

'Does that mean we've won?' Lawrence asked, as they made their way out of the senior citizen centre door.

'We've seen them off for now it seems,' Graham said with a smile on his face. 'Let's go over the road for a pint.'

Unfortunately, both pairs chose to visit the Lamb and Flag, since it was immediately over the road from the Senior Citizens' Centre. Dave and Josh, who arrived first, were carrying their pints over to a table when Graham and Lawrence entered and made their way to the bar. Dave was seething and lost more than a mouthful on the floor when his hand trembled with anger. He plonked his beer down on the Montague table and strode over to the two Capulets.

Graham turned at Dave's approach, and had his chest stabbed by Dave's finger.

'If you think this is over you have another think coming,' Dave stuttered, his face flushed.

Following the incident with the youth in Budgens, and being embarrassed by his reaction, not to mention his faux pas when he arrived home, Graham had searched the internet and found an article on anger control – Ten Top Tips To Tame That Temper – and had found it useful.

He now followed tip number one, to calm himself, and after a moment or two attempted tip two, to express his discontent in an inoffensive manner designed not to escalate the situation.

'I am really not happy with your finger stuck in my chest, and I would be grateful if you would be so kind as to remove it.'

Graham had no time to progress to tip three, to start an approach towards conflict resolution.

Dave hadn't read the same web page. 'You pompous little ass,' he snorted. 'And you, you're as bad,' turning his gaze to Lawrence. 'Both a pair of useless tossers. I'm going to sort you two out. In fact I'm in a mood to do it right now.'

Alex, the barman, judged from Dave's body language and Lawrence's response, that it was appropriate to intervene.

'Come on now guys, let's not create a stir.'

'Guys?' Lawrence blurted. 'What sort of language is that? Where did you get your training in customer relations? Costalot Coffee?'

Alex raised his hands in mock surrender. 'Don't turn on me. It's not my argument. Whatever your problem is, sort it out friendly fashion. Have a nice day,' he said, 'guys,' with emphasis. Alex turned and walked down behind the bar to serve a young tattooed girl who looked disappointed not to see fisticuffs.

Lawrence turned to Graham. 'Let's go and find a pub with some staff with manners. Beer's pisswater here anyway.'

Dave was still spoiling for a fight, whether verbal or physical, but Josh was tugging at his sleeve, so he let Graham and Lawrence go with just 'Screw you two!' addressed to their departing backs. Plus a finger gesture.

Back in the council chamber, debate had moved on to the community complex issue. Brian asked Paul Hart to present an update on the situation. Paul did as rehearsed by Brian.

'Councillors, we now have an updated report which I am sure you have all read.' Paul was not at all sure the councillors would have waded through a report extending to three hundred and twenty three pages, but in council-speak this meant he hoped they had read the executive summary. If they hadn't read the detail, and questioned the validity of the summary, they could be easily squashed by the equivalent of an 'As you will know well, having read section 3.2.3, your question was fully answered there'. Except this would require Brian's intervention, he being the only one with the necessary grasp.

'The report demonstrates,' Paul continued, 'that all the issues raised on planning grounds have been met by the revised plans which now have the full agreement of the District Council, and the County is happy on highways grounds. The loans and funding partners for the venture are confirmed, and the ongoing viability issues have been addressed.'

'Bollocks,' came a comment from the public seats.

Brian felt obliged to pound his gavel. 'I will tolerate no interruption from the public gallery.'

This drew some ragged applause from the supporters of the project.

'Just trying to wake some of you buggers up,' was the reply from the heckler.

It was a fair point, Brian had to admit, as he looked round the table. 'And may I remind the councillors here present,' he felt the need to say, 'that this being a vital issue for the town it is crucial that our fullest attention is given.'

Don Ridgeway nudged Ken Baker. 'Seconded,' Ken said. Don had a word in his ear.

On the other side of the room, where the councillors representing St Mark's parish were seated, Councillor Owen gave her neighbour

Councillor Wilson a similar nudge. Godfrey Wilson reacted not by a snort and wake-up blink, but by falling face first onto the table in front of him. Jane Owen bent forward and shook Godfrey. He made no movement in response. She tried again, but he remained motionless.

'I think we may have a medical problem here,' she said, looking in Brian's direction.

Peter Galway leapt up and with 'Make way, I'm a trained paramedic', which rather overstated his first aid qualifications, rushed round and started prodding Godfrey in the neck. He pulled him upright and pulled down an eyelid.

'I think we have a problem,' was his verdict.

'I just bloody said that,' Jane thought.

Hilary dialled 999 and Brian announced a recess.

Peter got Godfrey laid out on the floor with the help of a couple of members of the public. He debated whether to give Godfrey the kiss of life. Unfortunately scout leader training hadn't brought him to face the reality of mouth-to-mouth resuscitation with a real person rather than a plastic dummy. And evening post-course practice with a willing Girl Scout leader had been hardly the same as engaging orally with an old decrepit well known for his halitosis.

Peter decided to fall back on the training he himself had received years ago as a cub scout and started manipulating Godfrey's arms and pounding them deep into his chest.

Truth to tell, there was little Peter could have done. Godfrey was stone-dead before his head hit the table, in fact he had been out of this world for some five minutes or more while his body had stubbornly remained seated upright.

In the public gallery, Doctor Ramsay, having been nudged and successfully woken from light slumber by his neighbour, made his way through the public seating to take charge. Harvey Ramsay was a senior doctor at the Roselake medical practice, respected for his age rather than his medical judgement. He waved Peter aside and performed a quick examination. He stood up. Peter asked if he should continue his resuscitation attempts. 'Nothing to lose,' Dr Ramsay said. What he meant was it would be better for the public gallery to remain hopeful. He didn't want the further chore of attending to women swooning at the realisation they had just witnessed a death. Men neither, come to that. Although many of the elderly audience were widows, to whom death's appearance was not that of a stranger, better safe than sorry. He approached the mayor and had a word in his ear. 'Dead as a doorpost. Heart.'

'So why is Peter Galway still thrashing away?' Brian asked.

'Good for the troops, if you understand me. Don't worry, I'll explain the post mortem damage to the pathologist if needs be.'

Brian declared the meeting closed but asked the public to remain seated to keep the way clear for the paramedics. The ambulance team duly arrived, had a quick look at the corpse and a quick word with the doctor, placed an oxygen mask over Godfrey's face and trolleyed him away.

'Well, what a performance,' Hilary said to Brian in the confines of the mayoral office after the council room had cleared.

'Indeed,' said Brian. 'Peter Galway was giving it some welly with that artificial respiration. I distinctly heard a bone crack.'

'I didn't mean that,' Hilary said crossly. 'I meant you not briefing me about the District Council policy change and then having the nerve to chide me in public.'

'Oh,' said Brian.

'Is that all you can say, "Oh"?'

'Like I said, it all happened a bit late.'

'I see. Obviously it's expecting too much for me to receive an apology. Which I also deserve because of your abominable manners to me during the meeting. So I'll say goodnight and consider my position.'

'As clerk? You can't leave, you're too valuable.'

'No, not as clerk, I need the money. As your bit on the side.'

'Oh.'

'All you can say yet again is "Oh"? Obviously my sexual services are not too "valuable" to lose. So be it.'

Hilary grabbed her coat from the stand in the clerk's room and left without another word. Brian glanced wistfully at the Jesus plastic statuette. There would be no flashing tonight.

143

Meanwhile, Arnie and Jessica, having no wish to let their parents catch on to the fact of their liaison, had made their ways separately to the London Inn, where they had arranged to meet at eight. They'd had no weekend assignation. Arnie had declared Saturday nights were reserved for him to get together with his mates, in other words drink themselves senseless down the Volunteer, and Jessica was happy to similarly meet her girlfriends on Sunday evenings at the wine bar to discuss the details of their week's romantic adventures.

When they were settled at a table with a drink in front of them, Arnie plucked a Tesco plastic bag out of his backpack.

'I got something for you,' he said with a grin.

'What?'

Arnie passed the bag over. 'What you wanted.'

Jessica looked in the bag and found a squeeze pack of Tesco honey.

'Oh.'

'Is that it? Oh?'

'What do you want me to do with this?'

'Well, you know, what you said the other night.'

'I meant what do you expect me to do with it now?'

'Take it home for, er, next time.'

'After what happened on Thursday I'm surprised you think there'll be a next time.'

'It wasn't that bad.'

'Let's forget it,' Jessica said. Arnie's sexual performance that evening had been decidedly unimpressive, but she was prepared to forgive him once, at least. 'Anyway, what I meant is, you think I'm going out and I say to my mum "Oops, nearly forgot my honey", and pull it out of the fridge?'

'Keep it in your bedroom then.'

'Why don't you keep it in your bedroom?'

'My mum might find it and start asking questions.'

'Well so might mine. Anyway best keep it where it'll be used.'

Jessica scrutinised the label.

'Organic eh,' she said.

'Cost me an extra quid for organic. Worth it to save the world, my mum says.'

'Every time she drives down to Tesco, and fills the boot with loads of organic stuff she doesn't need, she saves the world I suppose,' Jessica remarked.

Arnie shrugged. He and Jessica had argued about green issues before. He knew nothing and cared less, she knew a little and sort of cared, mainly because some of her friends did, or pretended to. Amongst them only her friend Katy was a zealot, but the girls put up with Katy's proselytising because she was very attractive and drew boys to the group when they were out together.

Jessica passed the squeezy bottle of honey back to Arnie. Arnie returned it to the shopping bag and stuck it in his backpack. He'd figure out where to hide it later.

'I still don't get why you were asking about where my mum and dad get their wine delivered from,' Arnie said, changing the subject a little.

'Oh that,' Jessica remembered. 'And?'

'And what?'

'And did you find out?'

'I did actually. I think.'

'You only think?'

'Well I looked in what mum calls her cellar – it's only a cupboard in the utility room really – and found some bottles of Sainsbury's Pro… Prosomething, whatever, the fizzy stuff she drinks when she's cooking. So she must get her wine from Sainsbury's, right?'

Jessica giggled. 'That's a relief.'

'What is?'

Jessica told all she knew about the tale her mum had been told, every time the man from the wine shop made a delivery to this woman she gave him more than the price of the wine.

Arnie twigged. 'And you thought my mum might be…' Arnie blushed.

Jessica shrugged. 'Funnier things have happened. This woman the wine man bonks is supposed to be all butter wouldn't melt, but she's at it.'

Jessica didn't see Arnie's mum as the butter wouldn't melt type, more the come-and-get-me type, judging from the revealing clothes she wore, but she didn't share that with Arnie.

'Your dad might be interested in this woman,' Jessica continued.

'What you mean, you think my dad's up for it with her?' Arnie blustered, blushing again.

'No I didn't mean that, silly. I meant he knows her. My mum and dad have been talking a lot about this changing the street name business, and my dad says yours is not best friends with this woman. She works at the town council offices.'

Arnie was well aware his dad was in the middle of a crusade, his mum was complaining about it every day. 'What's her name?'

'I forgot. I just know your dad has had a row with her.'

'Oh. Do your mum and dad want the name changed?'

'No. My dad wanted to get it changed when there was that news that the price of our house would fall, but my mum went ballistic and told him that was crap. He gave in when that other letter came round from that estate agent, and yesterday that bald man with the moustache came and dad promised to support him, help keep the name.'

'My dad's gone potty over this. Can't see why. He was dancing a jig in front of the telly on Thursday when they had a minute of him on the news prog.'

'He was on the TV?'

'Yes.'

'Wow.' Jessica's eyes widened. Anybody who had appeared on TV went up in her estimation.

'No big deal,' said Arnie, a note of jealousy in his voice. 'That beggar didn't stay long did he?'

'Dunno.'

Jessica's forehead creased for a moment.

'I think it's romantic,' she said.

'What is?' Arnie was puzzled, unsurprisingly.

'Me and you,' Jessica replied.

It was Arnie's turn to frown. No way was he prepared to return a declaration of undying love and devotion. Nor offer a ring.

'Like how?'

'Like Romeo and Juliet. Star spangled lovers. Like in the film. Her parents are on one side and his on the other, and they shouldn't be seeing each other but they do and they love each other and someone finds out and he kills someone and… I forget what happens next exactly but they both die in each others arms.'

'Doesn't sound romantic to me. Dying and stuff.'

CHAPTER 10

Not surprisingly, events at Roselake Town Council dominated the week's issue of the Gazette. The Echo, out on Tuesday, had to content itself with printing a photo of a hand (Dave Grant's) offering alms to Jake Benson, and a short account which stated simply that Beggars Way had been invaded by beggars. Tom Woodacre, general do-everything except make the tea, which was down to his secretary and advertising assistant Brittany, gnashed his teeth as he read the Gazette and realised again by going to press a day earlier than the Gazette he had missed another good story or two.

The paper's front page carried a portrait of Godfrey Wilson. And very handsome he looked. The more unkind of the Gazette's readers commented that it must have been taken a very long time ago, which it was.

The headline was "Councillor Collapses at Council Meeting". The details of exactly when Godfrey passed away were glossed over and reduced to the comment that he was found dead on arrival at hospital. There followed some biog, and tributes from three fellow councillors, chief of whom was Brian.

Brian had found it rather difficult to eulogise. He stressed the length of Godfrey's service on the Council (twenty nine years) and declared he had made an enormous contribution to the Town's public life. When pressed by Anna Shale to give some detail of this achievement Brian's brow furrowed. He had to content himself and Anna by saying Godfrey Wilson was a long-standing respected member of the Council when Brian first joined it, and he would be much missed. In truth Godfrey had never been a mover and shaker. He joined the Council because his friend Leonard Fairchild invited him to stand, so that they would have an excuse for getting away from their wives for another evening, in addition to their get-togethers at Rotary and British Legion meetings. By the time

Leonard passed on, being a councillor had become a habit for Godfrey. Godfrey occasionally spoke his mind on issues close to his heart or his neighbours', but it was too early to pass judgement on whether he would be a loss to the Council, which would depend on the aptitude of his replacement.

"Natural causes" was quoted as cause of death. It had been decided by Godfrey's doctor that in view of Godfrey's medical history he would sign the death certificate without need for autopsy. His opinion was that Godfrey had died of a massive stroke. You may think that this doesn't actually accord with Harvey Ramsay's assessment, but what the heck. If you're gone, and go at the age of eighty-two, no-one is going to get too upset about the exact cause unless they have spotted a dagger sticking out of the deceased's back.

An inside article covered the street name affair in depth, extending to a full two pages (give or take a small advertisement or two – actually eleven, par for the course on the news pages). Illustrated by another picture of Jake Benson, the first part of the article concentrated on the rumblings at Roselake Council. This was followed by confirmation that the District Council was handing over responsibility for street naming to the town councils "in the interests of democracy and the principles of localism". What did not come from the promotion department of the Council was a large box on the opposite page listing the names which residents in towns across the District wanted changing. Anna Shales had been busy on Tuesday morning, but her boss Carla had thought it worthwhile employing another junior reporter on the job, Jackie Smith, and had also pitched in herself to get quotes from the District Council at senior level, in order to meet the paper's deadline.

Carla also decided the issue was now escalating to serious reader interest level. Part of the double spread was devoted to announcement of a reader poll. After a few lines sketching the conflicting advice estate agents were giving on the likelihood of a scandalous name dipping house values – not enough to satisfy Graham, who had been hoping that Quentin's letter would merit more than a sentence and a half – a panel read *'Tell us what you think. Should historical names be preserved or should our towns move with the times, respecting residents' wishes and supporting their concerns about property values?'* the poll was, of course to be conducted primarily online. Or votes could be cast by SMS (charge per text £1.80 in addition to your provider's normal charges etc etc).

After the Gazette dropped through the letterbox at number fourteen, Graham's first move was to grab, read and digest it. Laura commented that he would do better to eat his dinner and digest that, but she knew it was a lost cause. Graham went off to the spare room, his study as he called it, fired up his computer and looked at the Gazette's website. He duly cast his vote, then after a brief kiss on Laura's cheek thanking her for dinner equally briefly pecked at, he scurried round to Lawrence's house. Lawrence was still eating, and Pat, after a scowl at the interruption, offered Graham a coffee, or a glass of wine from the box they had just opened. This came as a surprise to Graham. He knew Lawrence as a beer-drinking man. The wine-drinking was down to Pat. She had looked in the mirror one morning, decided she wasn't getting any younger, and thought she might as well enjoy life a little more. Anyway her sister Grace, with whom she spoke infrequently as she lived in New Zealand, as even Skype can't change the time difference between NZ and UK, had recently asked her if she preferred Chardonnay or Pinot Gris with her meals, and Pat had been hard pressed to answer, which she found uncomfortable and a little embarrassing.

Graham opted for a coffee. A glass of wine would have pleased Pat better as all she had to do was hold a glass and push a button.

After Lawrence declared his dinner delicious, he and Graham retired to the lounge. Lawrence read the Gazette and asked Graham what was important enough to make him come rushing round disturbing his dinner.

'But there's this poll.'

'So?'

'We need to do something.'

'Like what? We can't travel all over the area telling people to vote. Anyway it's a load of nonsense. Nobody will take any notice of that.'

'The Council might.'

'Or might not.'

'So we sit and do nothing?'

'No, I'll humour you. I'll go upstairs and do a bit of voting.'

'What do you mean a bit?'

'All right a lot.'

'I don't get it. You can only vote once.'

Lawrence tapped his nose. 'Watch me.'

He led Graham upstairs to the spare bedroom where he kept his computer. He powered it up and navigated to the Gazette's page. He clicked on the "save our heritage" button.

'That's brilliant,' Graham said, 'the result is 100% in our favour.'

'That's probably because only you and me've voted so far,' Lawrence said. 'But we can help ourselves a bit more than that.'

He did a bit of fiddling Graham which didn't understand, and went back to the voting page. He voted again.

'I couldn't do that, it said I'd already voted.'

'These newspaper polls are all a lot of cobblers,' Lawrence said. 'My nephew showed me how to do it. All you do is this," Lawrence performed a few clicks of his mouse, which left Graham bemused, "and lo and behold you can keep voting again and again.'

'Isn't that a bit, er, unethical?'

'Yes. A tad. But Roselake was a famous rotten borough historically. Precedent set, eh? Following tradition?'

Graham scratched his head.

'OK. Good point. Could you show me how you do that?'

'Sure.'

Graham spent that night into the early hours voting repeatedly on the Gazette's poll webpage. Lawrence had not the same stamina and gave up after about twenty votes.

Next morning Arnie Grant was surprised to see his father appear in the kitchen for breakfast. Dave rarely showed before Arnie had left for his early shift at the Co-op supermarket where he stacked shelves with overnight goods deliveries. In theory Arnie was on a government apprenticeship scheme, but after a year he hadn't progressed to a higher level than stacking the top shelves. Dave had hoped for greater things for his son, but recently he had revised his expectations, and was content that Arnie appeared happy enough, earned enough to get by, and, best of all, didn't seem to have a drug habit.

'What you up so early for?' Arnie asked as he chewed his bacon sandwich.

'Thought we might have a little chat,' Dave said.

Arnie looked at his watch. 'Best be a short one.'

Dave brought a chair alongside Arnie and sat down. 'See this?' he asked, showing Arnie a web page on his smartphone.

'Yeah? What's that?'

'The Midweek Gazette web poll about name changes. Right now it's showing 78% to keep old names and 22% for changing and modernising.'

'What happens if you don't give a toss?'

'There's no box to click for don't give a toss. But we do give a toss, don't we.'

'Speak for yourself, Dad,' Arnie said, 'Me, I've had it up to the eyeballs with all this talk about it lately. Can't see why you're so fussed.'

'It's a matter of principle,' Dave said. Quite what principle he had in mind he would be hard put to say. 'Anyway I want that vote changed. There must be some way we can rig that poll. I don't know about these things but I thought you might…'

Dave assumed all young people were experts in information technology, seeing how they spent so much time playing with their toys. In this case he was wrong, Arnie hadn't a clue how to fix web polls. But he knew someone who had.

'Sure. It'll cost you.'

'I figured that.'

'You said you'd help me buy a motor. I could use a motor. Like now.'

Arnie particularly had in mind back-seat adventures with Jess, as his parents didn't go out often enough for his liking.

'I said I'd maybe help, not buy you one. How much you got saved?'

'Not a lot.' Arnie couldn't be criticised over his honesty.

'You do this for me, we'll see what we can do.'

'It'll have to be tonight.'

'No problem. And there's another little job I have in mind for you.'

'You'd better go to the cashpoint today then,' Arnie said with a grin. 'No, wrong, there's a daily limit. Cash a big cheque.'

'Don't get your hopes up.'

'Actually, I've a bit of info that may be of use to you. Worth a bit, know what I mean?' Arnie said, grinning still. 'Added value. About that woman at the Council you've got it in for.'

'What sort of info?'

'Damaging,' Arnie said with a pantomime wink. 'Got to shoot. Later.'

'Brush your teeth, you've got some bacon stuck there,' Dave said - a rare bulletin of paternal advice.

If Graham and Lawrence had been disappointed by the failure of Quentin Fairbrace's letter on house prices to gain prominence in the press, they would have been pleased it did have one effect. This was to have some minor influence on the outcome they wanted. It prompted Lisa Thornton, who had finally tracked her father down, to get her parents to put their house Glendale Cottage on the market. Now that she was in contact with both her parents, Lisa hoped that the divorce and separation of property could be achieved as soon as possible. Lisa was not prompted by family concerns. She had recently met a young man. A whirlwind romance led to his begging her to marry him. He was a little naïf but comfortably off with his own home in the country. Lisa saw which way her toast was buttered. If she could get her parents to cash in on the house value she might expect a generous wedding settlement from both her parents, who would no doubt vie to outdo each other in their generosity.

Lisa had always had the ability to get what she wanted from her father, and her mother had proved amenable to selling Glendale Cottage on the understanding that Jack Thornton would cease legal action against her on the matter of her emptying the NatWest account.

Within a couple of days Quentin Fairbrace had a board up advertising the house for sale. This provoked the expected response from the neighbours, those on the south side swearing it would never sell, those on the north wondering and gossiping about the whereabouts of the Thorntons. The most malicious rumour was that Lisa had murdered her parents, and buried them in the garden. This was scotched by local handyman Jeff Barker, who did gardening for Lisa, and her parents before her arrival, and swore he would have noticed any untoward ground disturbance. Or if he didn't, his dog Harry would have for sure. Harry was a great one for digging up bones.

Celia Pascoe, having enjoyed success in rallying the troops of Butts Close behind her, and finding it was now the Town Council who were to decide the name change issue rather than the more remote and less approachable District Council, was in campaigning mood. She contacted Dave Grant, Ted Slater and Sami Hasan with the view to forming a group to lobby the Council on formulating a policy which would accord with residents' wishes. She suggested the name Roselake Residents for Progress to represent the ambition of the proposed new group. Sami expressed the view that this didn't exactly roll off the tongue easily. Celia kept her thoughts on that choice of phrase to herself, having visited the Indian subcontinent on one and the last occasion as far as she was concerned, and replied that Sami was welcome to make alternative suggestions. She was organising a meeting in the Methodist Hall on Monday evening, having had the good fortune of a cancellation by the Roselake Reptile Enthusiasts Society. Their chairperson had been arrested by the police on suspicion of illegal imports of endangered species (rare locusts for his epicurean snake), and other members of the group naturally wished to adopt a low profile for the time being.

Celia had received Dave, Ted and Sami's contact details from Hilary, who had at first been reluctant to divulge their identities, but found her match in Celia, who said it would save a lot of time and trouble if Hilary acquiesced. She was sure Hilary did not want a formal Freedom of Information request to tease the information out. Hilary was unaware that she might have been protected by the Freedom of Information legislation from being obliged to divulge personal data, as any such request would have been a first as far as she was concerned.

Her reluctance was formed due to her fears that it would damage her position on the Beggars Way issue if she encouraged other name change applicants. But then she considered that if she could repeat her suggestion to the Council that the floodgates were about to open, they might throw their hands up, veto the whole proposal, and impose a restrictive policy which would incidentally favour the retention of Beggars Way.

Meanwhile, an opposition camp was being set up. Frank Parton had been lobbied by several members of the Roselake History Society, including its chairman Bob Peters, and cajoled into addressing a special meeting of the Society on Monday evening, at the Roselake Baptist Church. Being a long-standing member of the Society, Frank found it hard to refuse. He protested that it would be wrong for him to be seen to have a view on an issue before it came up for debate in Council. Bob Peters said nonsense. Having a view on things was what you got elected for in the first place.

Over the next couple of days posters were displayed around the town advertising the two meetings. Celia Pascoe stole a march on her opponents by organising a petition on Saturday, which, being market day, was the busiest day in the High Street. Celia found that busy shoppers were willing to sign anything if a smile and ten second explanation were given them. She and her team, numbering one and named Gwen, ended the afternoon with two hundred and thirty two signatures, which Celia considered an excellent haul.

Despite the efforts of Graham and Lawrence, and the parallel efforts of Dave and Arnie, the Gazette poll remained a frustration to both parties. By the weekend the public seemed fairly evenly divided on the issue, and the fact that casting a few more votes failed to upset the stubborn percentage figures suggested that across the Gazette's distribution area a large number of people had voted. The alternative theory was that a few people on both sides knew how to perform the multiple voting trick.

Arnie had earned his money by getting his geeky friend Zing to tell Arnie how to fix the poll, which wasn't actually much of an insider's secret. Fortunately for the security services and banking establishment, Zing was no hacker. He just had a bit more IT nous than most of his friends. Enough to earn him a reputation.

On Thursday night, had Graham looked over the road to Dave Grant's house, he would have seen the light on in Arnie's bedroom. Arnie was up until the small hours and was pleased with his result, having not only restored parity but established a small percentage lead in the survey.

On Friday the tide turned again, and Dave found to his displeasure that his side was losing, but Arnie was happy to work late hours again to earn more cash.

It was Saturday evening before Dave shared with him his next assignment. Dave had earlier travelled to an Exeter retail park to make a couple of purchases.

Arnie, being aware of his ASBO record on file still, was a little reluctant, but some extra cash persuaded him.

'And while we're at it, settling accounts, what's that tale you were going to tell me about the Council woman? What's her name?'

'I forgot. But she's the clerk. The one you were in a rage about Monday night. When I went to bed you were half way through the second playing of Zulu and half way through the whisky.'

'OK. So spill the beans.'

'She's only having it off with the wine shop delivery man. Regular. Once a week he brings a case of wine and gives her one.'

'What wine shop?'

'The one in the High Street.'

'Who told you that then?'

'Can't reveal my sources. Confidential,' Arnie replied.

'You're not a bloody journalist with a Hippocratic oath or something, come on, who told you?'

Arnie was not willing to reveal Jess as his source of information and stubbornly shook his head.

'Come on,' Dave spluttered, 'you can't just give me a story like that without backing it up. No confirmation, no cash.'

'Aw Dad, you promised. This is gospel. Anyway if you want to prove it why don't you go round to her place on Thursday night and check it out for yourself?'

'Thursday?'

'That's when the van comes. I think. Or was it Wednesday?'

Dave handed Arnie his mobile. 'Call your source and find out which.'

'As if. You don't catch me that easy,' Arnie said. 'It's Thursday. I think.'

'If this is good info it may be worth a bit.'

'How much?'

'I don't know. I'll have to think about how I can use it.' It was interesting news, but at the moment Dave really couldn't think how he could take advantage. Could it help him find a way to swing the name decision? Provide a blackmail opportunity? Or maybe he could just embarrass his enemy big style.

'Perhaps we should go down to the car lot tomorrow. I'm getting fed up with ferrying you around all the time.'

Arnie grinned. A result.

'Only if you get that little job done tonight, mind,' his dad said.

It was Graham's turn to have his breakfast interrupted. Lawrence appeared at the door of number fourteen in a slightly dishevelled state.

'Have you seen what someone's done to the sign?' he asked.

'What sign?' Graham asked, puzzled.

'The Beggars Way sign.'

'No, what's happened?'

'Come and see.'

'Lawrence, I'm in the middle of breakfast.'

'Invite him in for a coffee,' Laura called from the kitchen. 'There's a full pot.'

'So what's up?' Graham asked as he mopped up his egg yolk with half a slice of toast.

'They've only gone and defaced the sign, haven't they?'

'I don't know. Have they? Who? How?'

'Let's put it this way. If you changed the first vowel in Beggars Way what would you get?

Graham thought for a minute. It dawned.

'No!' he said incredulously.

'Yes,' said Lawrence. 'And they changed the second vowel in order to be spelling perfect.'

'But who would want to do that?'

Lawrence sipped his coffee. 'Must be them across the road, who else?'

'But why?'

'Warped minds? Beats me. Maybe they just want another picture in the paper, keep the issue live, so to speak.'

'Maybe it was just a lad out on the town last night, fancied a laugh.'

'So according to you, lads go out for a bevvy with a can of paint and a paintbrush do they?'

Graham finished wiping his plate and hmphed. 'I suppose not. It could be a decorator with a bit spare in the boot.'

Lawrence guffawed.

'What'd I say?' Graham asked.

'More likely a bit of spare in the back seat on a Saturday night.'

'Oh ho ho. Lawrence this isn't funny. What are we going to do?'

'We can try wiping it off but it looks well dry to me. Have you got any white spirit?'

Graham's nostrils flared. The imagined odour of white spirit and the real odour of cooked bacon was not a good mix.

'I have some in the shed but you'll have to do it. The idea makes me queasy just after my breakfast.'

'I've just finished mine too, you know,' Lawrence informed Graham.

'What did you have then?'

'Porridge and egg on toast.'

'Ah, well it's the bacon that's the big turnoff. You'll be OK after just egg.'

Initial attempts by Lawrence to remove the blue paint had little success.

'This'll never come off,' was Lawrence's opinion, after carefully brushing then energetically rubbing the affected area. 'All we'll do is make a smudged mess, or damage the sign.'

'Paint stripper?' Graham suggested.

'Even more likely to mess up the sign. I don't want to get lumbered with a fine for damaging Council property. A sign like this must cost two or three hundred at least. I paid best part of a hundred just for a metal house number sign for number fourteen.'

'Good job you don't have a number in the hundreds and a house name, then.'

'The house did have a name when we bought it,' Lawrence said. 'Mon Repos.'

'Sounds like a funeral parlour.'

'Right. I ditched that straight away when we moved in. Pat found me shedloads of renovation work to do – not much repose there then. And the owners weren't even French. An ex-bricklayer from Clapham. His wife looked as though she'd worked the streets.'

They fell silent for a moment. Graham was wondering what a street worker looked like these days. Hard to tell, he supposed, since all the girls wore skirts with hems up to their bottoms, and plunging necklines almost meeting bare midriff.

'Maybe the Council get a discount for quantity,' Graham suggested, moving the conversation back. 'On the signs I mean.'

'Like how many Beggars Ways are there?' asked Lawrence.

'Just one, I guess.'

'Well then.'

'So what do we do if we can't fix it? We can't leave it like this.'

'Your suggestion being?'

'Inform the Council?'

'It's Sunday.'

'Report it to the police? It must be criminal, vandalism like that.'

'And do we tell them who we suspect?' Lawrence asked, cocking his head in the direction of Dave Grant's house.'

Graham frowned. 'I'm not sure about that.'

'Me neither. Talk of the devil.'

Striding over towards the pair came Dave.

'Oh dear oh dear, who could have done that?' he asked with a look of mock concern on his face. 'You two. Caught red-handed, it seems, with brush still in hand.'

'As you'll see, if you care to use your eyes,' Graham said, 'We are trying to remove the offending letters.'

'Felt guilty then after doing it, did you?' Dave smirked.

'Don't be stupid. I'd have you know we are considering reporting this to the police. And we have ideas of our own who's responsible.'

'I hope you don't mean me,' said Dave. 'And I warn you that if you go casting... whatstheirnames... slandering me I'll have your balls for breakfast. I am telling you flat. It wasn't me.'

'Then who? One of your lot?' Lawrence said.

Dave raised his hands in a not-knowing gesture. 'Beats me. Mind you, if the police come noseying around and bothering me I might ask them who nicked those two cypress trees from the bank last week.' Finding the trees gone had been an annoyance to Dave, who had no doubt about whom to blame, but realised there was little he could do.

'Maybe we could ask who planted them to hoodwink the Council,' Graham said, inadvisedly.

'Only because some buggers chopped down what was there before. If you want dirty linen washed in public it won't be mine hung out to dry.' Dave wondered for a second whether he had used the right phrase or metaphor, but felt he had made his point when he saw Graham and Lawrence look at each other guiltily.

'I suppose you've called the press,' Graham said.

'Nope, how could I? I only just found this like you, didn't I?'

Dave's wife Connie approached the trio. 'Dave there's a call on the BT for you. Wesley somebody.'

'Tell him I'll call back,' Dave said.

Connie saw what the fuss was about. 'Oh Dave, for heavens sake!' she said in irate tone, turned and returned to the house.

'Looks like your missus points the finger in a certain direction,' Lawrence offered with a grin.

'Like your missus, too, is always right, hundred per cent of the time?' Dave replied.

'Fair point,' Lawrence conceded.

'It wasn't me, got it?' was Dave's last word on the subject. He took a picture of the sign using his mobile and went home.

Graham and Lawrence returned to Graham's to put the white spirit, brush and rag away, wash hands and think over what to do. Laura made another pot of coffee.

After two cups each they still could not decide whether to call the police, leave it until tomorrow to inform the council, or take the initiative and contact the press.

The decision was taken out of their hands. There was a firm rap of the knocker, and Graham was surprised to find PC Middleton at the door.

'Mr Ferguson, I'm calling about a bit of vandalism to your street sign, and I understand you might be able to help with my enquiries.'

Graham's heart dropped. 'It wasn't us, officer.'

'Your partner in non-crime being Mr Stone, I suppose.'

'And I suppose that troublemaker from over the road has been telling stories.'

'If it's my turn to suppose, then I suppose you mean Mr Grant. Actually, I haven't had the chance to speak to him yet.'

Laura came to the door and chided Graham. 'Fancy leaving PC Middleton standing outside. Come on in, would you like a cup of coffee?'

'Wouldn't say no,' PC Middleton said.

The interview continued around the kitchen table. PC Middleton explained the situation. 'Mrs Jackson at number two saw you with Mr Grant, and when you left she saw the sign had been defaced. She was angry and called us.'

'That was blooming quick, you coming round,' Lawrence said. 'I reported a break-in once and it took three days for someone to turn up.'

'PC Middleton lives just round the corner, don't you Bob,' Laura smiled. 'How's Sheila and the baby? Not a baby any more, I'm sure.'

'You can say that again, right little tearaway. I'll be having to arrest him and lock him up soon,' Bob smiled at his own joke, obviously well rehearsed, but not a strong chuckle-inducer. 'Sheila's fine. Number two on the way.'

'That's good, I always say two's better than one,' Laura said, with a slight re-awakening of her wish that one would have been better than none. The pang went away almost as soon as it came.

Graham and Lawrence explained that they had been disturbed to find the vandalism this morning and had made a brief and unsuccessful attempt to clean off the new paint.

'Would you be willing to speak to the press?' Bob asked.

'Who's brought them in?' Graham demanded, his voice rising.

'Well my boss, actually,' Bob said. 'He saw the opportunity for a bit of promotion, rapid response to a community call, that sort of thing. He was wondering if someone would tell the paper how quickly we responded and had a bobby on the scene. Mrs Jackson wouldn't do it. Shy of having her name in the paper.'

'And if we're too shy?'

'No problem, I'm sure Mr Grant will oblige. I saw him on the telly the other night.'

Graham and Lawrence looked at each other. If the option was them speaking to the papers or Grant doing it there was no argument. They had to do it.

'I'm sure we'd be happy to oblige.'

'Excellent. And Mrs Ferguson, you make a good cup of coffee.'

'Call me Laura,' Laura said with a smile.

CHAPTER 11

On Monday evening Anna Shales, having been alerted to the two rival pressure group meetings, had to opt to cover one or the other, or try to catch the flavour of the two. She intuited that if Frank Parton were to address the Roselake History society meeting, as billed on the poster, there would be ample time to visit the meeting at the Methodist Hall first and still be able to catch any debate and get some quotes at the Baptist.

She arrived early at the pro-change meeting to get a statement from the organisers, and found Celia only too willing to talk.

'We want the name Butts Close changed, and we support everybody else in the same situation as ourselves - residents whose lives will be ruined if their house price values collapse.'

'Just what objection do you have to the name?' Anna asked, playing the innocent.

'What's wrong with it? I'd have thought it was obvious to anyone of your generation who watches a lot of American television.'

Anna had to hide her dislike of being patronised.

'I thought it was just a sort of firing range thing, actually.'

'It has other connotations I'd rather not mention.'

'OK I'll google it,' said Anna innocently. 'That's what people of my generation do.'

Celia looked at Anna sideways, wondering if Anna were being facetious. 'You do just that,' she said.

'What do you say to those who have the opposite view?' Anna continued. 'Can you appreciate their point about preserving the town's history?'

'The town's history my... Er.. What I mean is, the Council destroyed the Town's history when it gave planning permission. Our Close is only a fragment of the old army training ground. Why should we have to suffer, when others have nice leafy names like

163

Primrose Walk, and Foxhill Chase? We have the backing of many of Roselake's residents. In only a few hours on Saturday we collected over two hundred signatures in our support. Now if you'll excuse me, Miss er… it's time we got started.'

Anna sought a chair near the exit. Seven thirty arrived, and Celia, although casting an anxious look towards the door for latecomers, decided to commence proceedings. She had cajoled Ted and Sami into joining her behind the table on the dais at the front of the hall. Dave had needed no cajoling. Celia, naturally, chaired the meeting, although this rubbed Dave up a bit.

Anna made notes. "Good turnout" was the first. (The hall was small so that even a modest attendance merited that comment, without need to count or divulge the figure).

'Good evening, everybody,' Celia announced in a stage orator manner, 'and welcome to what I hope will be the inaugural meeting of a new Roselake organisation, which will lobby for the rights of residents, for local democracy, and in particular for preserving the value of our property. As you are aware, we are facing a crisis. The Town Council is to be given the right to overrule residents' wishes and retain old street names which are a blot on Roselake's townscape. Fashions change. Times move on. We can not allow history to interfere with fairness and progress.'

'Hear, hear,' came from her right. From the mouth of Dave Grant to be precise.

There was a movement in the body of the hall. Two people made their way to the exit. Celia stared at them sternly. Another couple followed. Anna crossed out "good turnout" in her notepad and substituted "hall half full". Five minutes later the entry of another three people to boost the attendance caused her a moment's thought as to whether to amend her note yet again, but she was more interested in making a record of the debate regarding the name of the birthling organisation and its tactics.

On the first point, Celia's suggestion of 'Roselakes Residents for Progress' was not over-well received. Dave, in particular, was vocal in condemning the proposal.

'Doesn't do it for me. We need something with a bit more oomph.'

Sami wagged his head. If Celia hadn't had a minimal experience of the orient, and if she hadn't already heard Sami's opinion she might have thought he was disagreeing.

'How about Roselake Forward?' spoke up a voice from the hall.

'Sounds like a fascist political party,' Dave said.

'Punchy though,' Ted said. 'Sounds pretty good to me.'

Sami sat expressionless wondering about the rights and wrongs of getting into bed with people like Ted.

'Any more suggestions?' Celia asked.

Seconds passed by without any new contribution.

'In which case,' Celia continued, 'I suggest we move on. It's perhaps more important right now to agree to form a committee and delegate a few matters to them. So much easier to decide in a small group. Agreed?'

There was a murmur of what Celia took as assent, although it concealed a mix of views.

'In which case let's focus on what action we propose to take. We can come back to the committee question later.'

'How about Roselake Action Group?' the man who had made the earlier name suggestion said.

'Excuse me?' Celia was thrown.

'For the name,' Garry Packer said. 'That's what it's about you say, action.'

'I thought we'd moved on,' Celia said, exasperation showing on her face. 'And I'm not sure an acronym of RAG is very flattering. But we can go back to considering that suggestion later if the committee here agree.' Ted, Sami and Dave nodded in agreement. Gwen was rightly querying whether it was right for Celia to already have determined the committee's composition.

So was Garry Packer. 'Hang on a minute, I didn't know of any committee being agreed yet. You talk about democracy but democracy starts here, right? On the floor of the hall.'

Another murmur came from the assembly. Its intent could be interpreted either way.

Celia realised her faux pas. 'Of course, you're absolutely right. We'll come back to the name and committee issue later, with everybody's consent.'

'Seems all we do is move on without deciding anything,' Garry Packer said.

Anna sighed and decided to move on herself.

Anna arrived at the Baptist Church hall to find Frank Parton still in speech mode. Anna looked around the audience and spotted the quartet who had left the Methodist Hall earlier. She twigged what had happened. They had got their churches mixed up. As had, no doubt, the three late arrivals at Celia's meeting.

'Ah welcome,' Frank broke off his speech to say. 'It's a positive sign that our esteemed local media is taking an interest in the proceedings.'

Whatever she thought of Frank's remark, Anna smiled gently, bowed her head briefly in acknowledgement and sank her bottom into the nearest available chair. Frank shuffled his notes, prepared to resume his lecture.

In fact, Anna was wondering why Frank had, for the first time to her knowledge, attempted a pleasantry.

The truth was, Frank had taken rather a fancy to Anna. His state as a confirmed bachelor, which had led some to wonder about his sexuality, was brought about by an early life indifference to the opposite, or indeed any, sex. His life had been filled with the desire only for knowledge and learning. As he was now in advancing years, or at least beyond his best, perhaps the tide was turning, but although he was not conscious of any desire to make up for lost time he had suddenly found himself viewing Anna, on her appearances at Roselake Town Council, with interest. He thought of her in architectural terms, not for nothing had he spent time in his youth, during the university summer long vacation, in Italy studying its historical remnants from Classical to Renaissance. He thought therefore of Anna's rounded cupolas, her curved Corinthian columns, her....

He did not, of course, ever imagine - in his waking hours at least - that his appreciation could ever be reciprocated. Only occasionally at night did his fancy take flight. For her part, of course, he remained an old bore. More emphasis on the noun than the adjective, as Frank was no older than Brian. Brian was masterful in Anna's eyes, Frank was dry and, well, just sad really.

The pause allowed an interruption from one of Frank's audience. He signalled the chair, Bob Peters.

'Yes what is it, Mr er...' Bob asked.

'Len Savage is the name. Excuse me, but from those posters pasted up over town I thought we were coming to formulate some sort of action plan to press the Town Council to see our point of view, not for a history lesson.'

Bob groaned. Len's name had appeared several times as signatory to some strong letters in the local press. Bob objected not so much to what was said as to the way the strong views were expressed.

'We *are* the Roselake History Society, Mr Savage, and Mr Parton *is* amongst our most knowledgeable members.'

'That's as may be, but I came here expecting some positive strategy. And I'm blowed if I know what relevance the story of digging up a rhinoceros fossil has to do with pressing our views on the Town Council.'

'Hear, hear,' was repeated several times. One could only imagine this was from non-members of the Society, as members would surely not have wished to offend Bob Peters, not so much because he was well-respected as because although on the face of it mild-mannered he was known to have a temper on a short fuse and a wicked tongue when roused.

'We will have ample time for discussion after Mr Parton has finished his overview of the situation. In the meantime I hope you will give him the courtesy of an uninterrupted hearing.'

Frank, who was distracted by Anna's removal of her coat, and the words flying buttresses which had entered his mind unwillingly and architecturally irrelevantly, had lost his thread. 'Thank you Mr Chairman, I think I have made my point. Roselake has a rich and varied history which should be, nay demands to be, recognised and remembered.'

Frank's sitting down was met with mild applause.

'Thank you so much for that, Mr Parton, most illuminating and instructive,' Bob felt obliged to say.

'Now we come to the main part of the evening, deciding on a course of *action*, in view of the Town Council proposing a new policy on renaming of some of our historic road names, and what form of words the Society should use in its letter to the Council.' Len stood up again and was waving his hand. Bob expected trouble and groaned. 'Yes, Mr Savage?'

'Excuse me, but sending a letter is hardly a course of action, and frankly I was expecting a bit more than that. And if it's only to come from your History Society, plus you don't want our suggestions for some real action, you seem to have decided already, and if so I don't know why the rest of us have bothered coming here.'

'I should have thought that was fairly obvious, Mr Savage. We want to gauge public opinion, and incorporate constructive comments in our response.'

'Well your Society hasn't exactly got a good track record of writing letters. Your submission didn't stop the planning permission going through for the town centre supermarket. You didn't stop the old mill being knocked down, and you didn't stop the water channels down the High Street being closed down. It ...'

Frank Parton winced. The stopping of the historic water flow down the channels either side of the High Street was for him a running sore, an issue he had battled on over a considerable period and on numerous occasions. He had lost the vote at the Council every time. The water flowed no more, and never would again.

'May I stop you there, Mr Savage,' Bob said, his hackles rising. 'I said a moment ago that I was seeking positive comments. If you can't do that, and insist on continuing to vilify the Society I shall have to ask you to leave. And, frankly, I'm not sure why you came in the first place, if what we've heard so far is the level of your contribution.'

'I came to do something. I care about our town's past as much as the next man. It's going down the pan because of inadequates like you lot. Too right I'm going, it's clear there's bugger-all point in wasting my time here. Anybody who wants to discuss some practical ways of achieving something positive can join me down the London.'

Len made a show of storming out. Bob's relief at his departure turned to annoyance as half the room emptied.

'Maybe we should have served some free beer,' the Society secretary whispered in the treasurer's ear.

'Maybe we need a new chair,' the treasurer replied.

Anna was in two minds for about ten seconds, then left to join the deserters in the London. That promised to be a lot more lively than staying on here. She could ring Bob Peters for a quote in the morning.

The London had a room available and offered its use free to Len, naturally expecting the group would be consuming. Which was a good guess. Graham and Lawrence were first at the bar.

'I like his style,' Lawrence said, as they waited for their pints.

'Who?' Graham asked.

'Len Savage. Got his head screwed on. Not like those history society people.'

'Well I'm not sure,' Graham said. 'I mean that Frank Parton's a councillor, and maybe on our side. We don't want to put his back up.'

'You worry too much, mate. If his natural inclination is to do the decent thing, what's the harm in giving him a little push?'

When they had all convened in an upstairs room, Len opened the proceedings.

'If we're all sorted out for refreshment let's get on. I'm assuming we're all here because we want a Town Council policy of no changes to historical names, am I right?'

This met with a chorus of assent.

'So I may have my own ideas, but this is a democratic meeting, not like the one we've just left, so let's hear from round the table first.'

A serious-looking lady with an orange juice on the table in front of her offered the suggestion that they should form a new organisation, called something like Preserve Roselake's Heritage.

Len was encouraging and said great idea for the future, but maybe they needed to get things moving right now so they could get some influence on next week's Town Council debate.

Lawrence felt the need to butt in.

'Why delay? We need to put something to the Council, official, like, a proper formal democratic representation.' Lawrence carefully avoided the word "letter" which had put Len's back up at the RHS meeting. 'So let's go with this lady's suggestion. Straight away. Call ourselves the Roselake Heritage Preservation Society or whatever it was, agree what we want to say and bang it in.'

The serious-looking lady, Ellen Parfitt, was not very happy at the idea of anything being banged in, not her style, but was grateful for support and said so.

'How about,' a young man, which in this company meant he was probably mid-forties or so, said, 'us all going to the meeting next week and displaying placards, make a real physical presence.'

'I'm not sure we want to give the impression of intimidating the councillors,' Ellen Parfitt opined.

'Good idea. All for it. Democratic process, visibility, show the public mood,' Lawrence observed in shorthand before he rushed off to use other pub facilities.

'And did you hear those people from Butts Close got a petition signing going last Saturday?' the young man continued. 'We could do that. Get some people out on the streets collecting signatures. Saturday's best, but we could do it any or every day.'

'That's more like it, a lot of positive thinking there,' said Len with a grin.

Anna scribbled away at her notes, smiling. This was much more productive for her purposes too, garnering her plenty of material for an article in the Gazette's next edition.

When it appeared, Dave was disappointed at the content. The front page headline story, which continued to occupy most of pages two and three, was an attack on a chihuahua by a seagull. The main article on the name change affair appeared on pages four and five, but Dave scanned it for mention of the sign vandalism without success. He was further discomfited to find the story devoted far more space to the Len Savage meeting than the Celia Pascoe event, partly due to the fact that Len had plied Anna with gin and tonic after the close of the meeting. The headline "A Town Divided" set the tone of the Gazette article, but the strong suggestion was that battle honours were not equally divided.

The paper relegated the vandalism of the Beggars Way sign to a couple of column inches on page eight, with no picture. The headline was "Police hunt sign vandals", which of course was pure media-speak as the police had, naturally, no intention whatsoever of devoting resources to the job. The article stated that the Beggars Way street sign had been defaced (in an unspecified manner) by graffiti. Local houseowner Graham Ferguson commended the police wholeheartedly for their speedy response to a resident's complaint.

The sign vandalism article had suffered its cut at the hands of Carla Davis. She was obligated to print something, as the tip-off and information had come from the police, and previous experience told Carla if nothing were printed her boss, the owner, would soon be breathing down her neck asking why. But she reined in on the idea of giving the full detail, and printing a picture of the offending defacement. She pondered printing a picture blurring out the offending vowels, but under time pressure decided against using a picture at all. Her snapper was anyway far too busy taking pictures of swarming seagulls, plus mini-pooches and cuddly babies, suitable prey at risk from seagull terrorism, and people holding placards reading "CULL THE GULL".

The weekend's events provided more sustenance for the Gazette's future news columns. The two rival groups RAG and PRH had both decided to augment the number of signatures on their petitions by fielding teams of signature collectors on market day. This led to confusion on the High Street, with shoppers and visitors being asked more than once to sign petitions, leading them to make the natural assumption they were being accosted twice to sign the same one. It also led to anger and frustration, in particular in RAG member John Johnstone. He became so incensed at being repeatedly told that the people he approached had already had their signature collected by the man along the street, PRH's Garth Symes, that he took it on himself to remonstrate with Garth. The discussion turned to argument, and the argument turned to an exchange of blows before they were parted by an elderly lady wielding a walking stick. Witnesses reported blood streaming from Garth's nose, which was a bit of an exaggeration, although it did leak a little.

Later, down the pub, Garth blamed the walking stick rather than a punch for his injury. This did not stop Len Savage suggesting he should call the Gazette and report that one of his group members, innocently collecting signatures to preserve the Town's heritage, had been the subject of a vicious and bloody physical attack, without warning, by a member of a cabal who wished to destroy the Town's past and turn it into a ghetto for refugees from the South-East. Garth was persuaded after a drink or two to go along with Len's version of the story and was later snapped by the Gazette's staff photographer holding up a blood-stained petition page. Actually a splash of tomato ketchup from the London's counter, but it made a good picture and story.

Dave had still not decided what to do about the information Arnie had supplied regarding Hilary's amorous trysts. A man should perhaps trust his son, but Arnie's tale was second if not third hand, and Arnie was steadfast in refusing to reveal his source. A little detective work to see if Dave could prove for himself the truth of the delivery man tale would have been good, but this week it hadn't been possible. Dave had been obliged to go to Leicester for an insurance product release meeting and training session which kept him away from Roselake overnight on Thursday.

During the return journey on Friday afternoon, though, he had an idea on how to ramp up the profile of the defaced sign, which still remained in its damaged state, the District Council not having taken action. He needed Arnie's help again. The first visit to the local car lot had not resulted in a purchase, and although this was not good for Arnie it suited Dave in that it kept Arnie on the hook. By Sunday night the picture Dave had clicked of the Beggars Way sign had gone viral on social media. Something the Echo and the Gazette could not now ignore, Dave reasoned.

Relations between Hilary and Brian remained extremely strained. Brian had not apologised for his perceived slight, not to mention his admittedly retaliatory kick, and Hilary was not prepared to forgive and forget. The input from the District Council on the new street sign policy had kept Hilary's mind occupied, and her meetings with Brian on the matter were not private, as Paul Hart and Derek Hunt were sitting in to draft an appropriate town council policy.

Hilary also faced representations, which she regarded as unnecessary interruptions to her normal work, from Celia Pascoe and Len Savage. Why can't they be polite and just put their views in writing in two or three sentences like the Roselake History Society, was Hilary's thought.

Both Celia and Len handed over a sheaf of paperwork – their petitions – to Hilary, with the proviso that they would add to the numbers on Monday morning. Being of an orderly mind, Hilary would have loved to submit the petitions to computer analysis, but she did not have the time. It seemed from even a cursory glance that the petitions contained signatories declaring out-of-Roselake addresses, and she detected more than one signature common to both petitions. She would have been surprised, too, if Arnold Schwarzanegger had been in town to sign either.

As the issue had now escalated far beyond Beggars Way, Hilary no longer saw it as a personal conflict between Graham Ferguson and David Grant, and she felt obliged to assume a more neutral stance. Which, interpreted differently, meant she was considering it more important to judge how much extra work would be imposed on her, and how (without extra pay) to minimise this by encouraging the appropriate council policy, or in any event to stake a claim for overtime.

Monday evening's council meeting promised to be a protracted affair. Which explained the unusually high number of apologies Hilary received from councillors. And this, since the agenda contained at least one item of vital importance to the town, might be perceived by the cynically minded as dereliction of elected duty by the jobsworthies.

The first item was long-scheduled, and could not be skipped. The congratulations due to the election of the year's Carnival Royalty. Pomp and ceremony, with the Roselake Town Crier in attendance in full regalia. This year the carnival committee had responded to accusations of sex discrimination by adding a Carnival Prince to the titles awarded. A carnival king would have aroused speculation as to whether he was having it off with the carnival queen, but the committee decided, in private, that the public should and would assume that at their age the prince and princess were not incestually tied. The committee was not, of course, politically correct enough to realise that the carnival queen title should be available to a male. Roselake was not ready for this, the committee might have thought, if they had thought about that at all, which they didn't. But they would have been a hundred per cent correct.

Gloria Paynton was in two minds as to whether to include in her opening prayers reference to the Lord's intervention in the last council meeting by calling to his side one of the members. This was a tricky one. Gloria sought advice from on high but was disappointed when she had no response. She called her friend Martin Cole, and asked his secular advice. Martin said his cat Tyger had just brought a dead mouse home. He hadn't felt able to tell Tyger how to change his approach to the inevitable nature of cat and mouse relations, so had let it be, and given Tyger an affectionate pat whilst binning the unfortunate mouse's entrails. Gloria asked why Martin hadn't answered her question. Martin said he thought he had. In a way. Gloria said she was in no mood for enigma. Martin said surely the Lord always answered through enigma. Gloria told Martin mere mortals should speak plainly when their friends asked for advice and put the phone down on him in a huff.

Gloria in private duly and dutifully commended the Lord for exercising His wisdom, and in public, at the commencement of the council meeting, delivered a prayer omitting reference to the last one's unfortunate outcome.

The celebration of the award of carnival titles also passed without incident. Town crier Barry Sutcliffe was a handsome figure, with white mutton-chop whiskers and dressed in full gaudy uniform, red jacket with gold-braided edges and emerald green pants cut off at the calf, his legs white stockinged below, blue shirt overlain by Roselake lace, and with a tricorn hat on his head. He drummed the floor with a long mace with ornate head, performed his 'Oyez Oyez pray silence for the Mayor' speech, and stood twirling his moustaches, leaving it to Brian to present the certificates and gift of the freedom of the town for one year to the carnival royalty trio.

Sharon Bailey smiled sweetly as she received her queen's crown and certificate. Jan French smiled, not quite as sweetly, as she was still nursing a wound. Last week Sharon had attempted to steal Jan's boyfriend.

Carnival Prince Hal Ashley sashayed onto the stage and gave a little bow before receiving his certificate. Hal needed no introduction to one or two of his male admirers in the audience, or probably more, judging by the applause he received. He was a good-looking lad. And willing.

After the presentations and congratulations a few members of the public gallery departed, namely the parents of the carnival royals.

A substantial number of people remained. Indeed the vacated seats were fought over, enabling the unsuccessful people at the back of the hall to at least enjoy a little more standing room.

Hilary opened the first of the two main agenda items by giving an account of the effect of the District Council's new street naming policy, and the thrust of the proposals that were now before the Council. She also outlined representations that had been received from the public, not concealing her broad-brush criticism of the worth of the petitions.

This was the prompt for the unfurling of a large banner "PRESERVE ROSELAKE'S HERITAGE" at the back of the hall. A number of members of the public, some of whom stood, revealed smaller signs they had carried in, variously worded, but summarised as originating from two camps with key phrases "Keep our Heritage" and "Roselake Progress".

Brian hammered his gavel to enforce attention and said whilst the Council appreciated that this agenda item had obviously aroused strong views, debate should be carried out in a calm manner, and the public should respect that. He called on Paul Hart to open the debate.

Paul obeyed Brian's order to keep it short and sweet. To excess. He moved the policy recommendations detailed in the agenda be agreed. He sat, and Edward Harding seconded the proposal.

It was expecting too much to think this would be passed without discussion, and indeed Frank Parton signalled his wish to speak. But he was prevented from doing so by a vociferous interruption from a member of the public, who asked 'What recommendations? This is a travesty. We came here tonight to hear a proper public debate. And have our views taken into account, I'd add.'

Brian banged his gavel and stated that the agenda and its included reports had been posted on the town noticeboard, and had been available as required by law, including at the Council offices and in the library.

Celia Pascoe stood up. 'That's as maybe, Mr Mayor.'

Brian pounded his gavel again/even harder. 'This is not the time for interruptions from members of the public. If you wished to speak you should have notified the clerk in advance in accordance with standard procedure. Please sit down.'

Celia was in no mood to be hushed. 'I will not be silenced. That agenda report does not take into account the representations made to the Council. It does not state that over five hundred signatures have been collected in support of changing inappropriate street names and protecting decency, and the town's reputation. And property values. If you think you can just pass the recommendations, which give overwhelming priority to preserving the status quo, you are mistaken.'

Celia sat to some applause.

Brian had further recourse to the gavel. 'As I said earlier, I appreciate that this issue seems to have aroused strong feelings, but I will not tolerate any unruly behaviour. If there are any more interruptions I will ask the town crier to clear the members of the public from the room.'

Hilary kicked Brian's shin to indicate her wish to intervene. Having no wish to have his leg suffer the same bruising that had lasted days after the last meeting, and not being quite sure how to handle an unruly public, nor an unruly Hilary, Brian asked Hilary to speak, but she was prevented from doing so by Len Savage rising to his feet.

'Mr Mayor,' he began.

The gavel was used again. 'I have warned you, I will tolerate no further interruptions.'

'But that woman had her chance to speak and I want mine,' Len continued, to a chorus of 'hear, hear's and 'right' and 'well said, Len'.

'We have a majority of residents on our side. We will not be ignored. We had more signatures on our petition than the priggish money-grabbing self-opinionated and selfish newcomers. We are not willing to lose...'

'Sit down and shut up, you rude sod,' came from an unknown source.

'I will not sit down. I will say my piece,' Len insisted, to a chorus of boos and 'sit down'.

'That's it,' Brian said, nodding to Barry Sutcliffe. 'Please clear the room.'

Barry was nonplussed. This was the first time he had been called upon to do anything other than make an announcement. In theory Brian was within his rights. If Barry had read the small print of his job description, he would have realised that hidden in the responsibilities paragraph was mention of his duty to "uphold the peace" at ceremonies and town meetings. However the last time the crier had been called on to perform a peacekeeping role was back in the 1900s when two Roselake suffragettes attempted to chain themselves to the mayor's table. In fact they had succeeded, but hadn't taken account of the fact that if the table were lifted the chains could easily be slipped down and off the legs. Miss Thresher refused to reveal where she had concealed the key to the padlock, and the then crier Alfred Brock, although he could guess, was quite properly not willing to perform a physical search in that region of the girl's anatomy. The two young ladies were escorted out of the building still chained together.

Town history records that Miss Thresher made several more rather unsuccessful attempts to draw attention to women's rights. She enjoyed her moment of triumph later, however, when, having achieved suffrage, Emily Thresher was elected to the town council and indeed became the first lady mayor of the town.

Tonight's disruption was a little less principled and a lot more aggressive. Barry tried an 'Oyez Oyez' to draw attention, but Len was in full flow, and was being cheered on by his supporters on one side and heckled and booed by Celia's supporters on the other. In particular John Johnstone made his way over to Len and started shouting at him and jabbing his finger in Len's chest. Len did not take kindly to this and after a strongly worded request to desist proved ineffectual, he swung a punch, catching John full on the chin. John staggered, but a moment later came back at Len with a haymaker, missing wildly. Pete Symes, who had been standing next to Len, saw the opportunity to gain revenge for John's assault on him in the High Street, and leapt into the fray.

Barry oyezed in vain, and flagged by Brian to 'Do something' made his way over to the fracas waving his mace high in the air and calling for order. He tapped Garth Symes on the shoulder and Garth turned round lashing out with a punch. This caught Barry only on the shoulder, but he was not standing for that. He whacked the mace over Garth's head and there was a resounding crack which caused general dismay. Fortunately it was the staff, weakened by decades of being used to stamp the floor, which had cracked, not Garth's head, but Garth let out a few choice swear words and a groan. Barry continued to wave the broken stick threateningly. Len referred to Barry's uncertain parentage and morals of his mother, and, picking up from the floor the remainder of the mace pole, thrust its bent head into Barry's chest. Barry fell backwards and sat down on the floor with a loud thud.

Hilary raced over and tried to pull Barry away from what had become a general brawl. The meeker of the public were scurrying out of the door, while a few of the non-partisan remained to enjoy the show. One or two were tapping away taking pictures with their mobiles.

The fracas seemed to end as suddenly as it had begun. Len had gazed in horror at the sight of his action having torn a priceless and historic piece of Roselake lace. He pulled Garth Symes away and the pair ran for the door. John Johnstone and two of his friends waved fingers at their departing backs. Barry regained his wind and stood up, shaking his head at the ripped lace.

'Meeting closed,' Brian announced wan-facedly to those councillors who had remained seated.

'That town crier gear will cost a packet to repair,' Derek Hunt remarked, shaking his head.

Graham and Lawrence were among those who left immediately the violence broke out. Fortuitously, the high public attendance this evening had relegated them to a back row pair of seats. As the first punch was swung, Graham went pale. He and Lawrence looked at each other. Graham tipped his head towards the door. 'Time we went.' Lawrence removed the smile from his face, he would have looked forward to a bit of fun, but in deference to Graham's timidity nodded approval. They made their way over the road to their usual refuge, where they enjoyed a pint to the background of Arctic Monkeys and police and ambulance sirens.

CHAPTER 12

Hilary was in no doubt who was to blame for the evening's events. 'We shall speak about this in the morning. I will leave you to lock up,' she told the mayor, took her paperwork back to her office, collected her coat and left.

Anna Shales waited until everyone but Brian had gone, and told him she thought he might like to give her one or two quotes for the paper. Brian nodded, closed the door to the street and suggested they sit down in the mayor's office. Anna followed Brian in. He flopped down in his chair and motioned to Anna to take a seat.

'Fancy a drink?' he asked.

'What have you got?' Anna asked.

Brian reached down in a desk drawer and pulled out a bottle.

'Marc,' he said. 'Our French twinning friends always bring over a couple of cases on their annual visit. Good stuff.'

'I'm not sure I've ever had it,' Anna said.

Brian got a couple of glasses from the mayor's window-fronted cabinet, which contained apart from glassware various gifts to the town. He poured a good amount from the bottle into each tumbler.

'Try it,' he said. 'If it's not to your taste I've got this.' Brian pulled another bottle out of the drawer and showed Anna the label.

'Don't tell me,' Anna said, 'Your German twinning friends bring over a couple of cases each year.'

'Spot on,' Brian smiled. 'Of course we always respond in kind with some top quality Scotch.'

'Actually,' Anna said after a sip of the marc, 'this is rather good.'

'Yes it is isn't it? Now who is that?'

The last remark was due to a ringing of the bell. Brian asked to be excused for a moment. A couple of minutes later he returned and resumed his chair.

'Police. Somebody called 999.'

'That must have been over half an hour ago,' Anna remarked.

'Yes,' Brian agreed. 'Pretty speedy response tonight, eh? Anyway I'll call the powers that be and smooth things over tomorrow morning.'

'No investigation, no charges?'

'I don't think we want to get involved in that sort of thing.'

'But I saw the town crier's mace was damaged, and his lace. Are they insured?'

'I will have to check.'

'But presumably the insurers will want to see a police report?'

'I'm hoping that won't be necessary. I am hoping, too, I can persuade you to write something rather, er…'

'Fictitious?'

'No, just rather mild. Oil on troubled waters. "Roselake council meeting curtailed due to an accident", something like that. Short and sweet. Or maybe nothing at all.'

'I can't do that. My editor will be breathing down my neck tomorrow morning for a good piece. This name business and the community complex are big stories for us. Of course we'll have to cover the awards to the carnival queen anyway. I took pictures.'

'Did you take pictures of the disturbance?'

'Of course,' Anna smiled. 'But I doubt we'd print them. My boss Carla might print a pic of the broken mace.'

'I think I need to make a call tomorrow morning to Carla's boss. Straighten things out.'

'I'm not sure I know what you mean.'

'Good. Would you like a refill?'

Anna's glass was empty. 'Unless you want me to try the schnapps.'

'Of course, I'll get clean glasses.' Brian got up and turned to the cabinet again.

For the first time Anna noticed the Jesus statuette .

'What's that on top of the display cabinet?' she asked.

'Ah that,' Brian smiled, 'was a gift from the Church. It lights up and flashes.' He returned to the desk and filled Anna's new glass with the German offering

Anna took a sip, nodded, and took another longer. She gazed at the statuette.

'Could I see it working?' she asked.

'Of course,' Brian replied. He switched on the wall socket. The lights started their travels. 'It is more impressive with the room light off,' he added.

Anna didn't reply but smiled and nodded. Brian crossed over behind Anna and switched the main light off.

'Wow,' said Anna, after a minute, 'that is really quite er.. unusual.' What she meant was, the flickering pulsating lights were having a similar effect on her as they had on Hilary and Brian.

Anna stood up and walked round the desk to take a closer look at the flashing Jesus. Brian followed her. His left hand strayed to her right buttock.

'You're a very attractive young woman, Anna,' was all he found to say.

'May I call you Brian?'

'Of course.'

Anna turned. Brian put his arm round her.

'Brian, I'm not sure we should do this.'

To be fair to Brian, he would have respected a refusal of his advances. But Anna's response was hardly a "no", was it?

Brian did not get much sleep that night. It was not the length of his encounter with Anna, nor that with his wife when he finally arrived home, that minimised his rest time. At two a.m. he received a telephone call. After a few moments of confusion, and what are you thinking of ringing me at home at this time of night response and equally indignant counter-response, he realised Hilary was not calling on a whim. She was passing on the news that the Senior Citizens' Centre was on fire. Hilary had been called by the duty fire chief immediately after he had assembled his volunteer troops and sent them in response to a 999 call.

'I'll be there in fifteen minutes,' Brian said.

Hilary was half minded to tell him he would not see her there, her job description didn't involve attending fires. After all, she had no personal belongings left in her office to speak of, and all her computer data was carefully backed up on removable memory cards and safe at home. However, her curiosity was aroused.

Moreover, if the fire were serious this could have a significant effect on her work.

'I'll see you when I see you,' Hilary said, non-committally, to preserve her options in case she decided to go back to sleep. In any event she was not racing out without a cup of coffee.

The Centre was well ablaze when Brian arrived at the scene. Firemen were getting to work connecting hoses and one hose was already playing through a broken window.

From what Brian could see, the main area affected was to the left, namely the public reception area, Hilary's office and his own, as he had come to regard the Mayor's quarters, away from the main hall and the kitchen.

'How's it looking?' Brian asked the chief officer, Carl Parkin, who introduced himself, shook Brian's hand, and then shook his head.

'Not good, to be honest. It's well alight. We may be able to save some of the main hall. Roadrunner's got the breathing apparatus sorted and he should be going in to take a look any second now. Jerry will have to axe the main door down.'

'Roadrunner?' Brian asked, baffled.

'My best man, Gary Crowcher.'

'But Roadrunner?' Brian asked again.

'Sorry. Yes. We've all got nicknames. Cartoon characters, like. Gary's Roadrunner.'

'But Jerry's the other chap's real name?'

'I just told you, it's all cartoon characters. Jerry as in Tom and Jerry, get it?'

'Who's Tom?'

'Tom's not on call-out tonight.'

Carl suddenly bawled, 'Play that hose a bit higher And get that frigging kink out of that second hose PDQ Donald.'

'And who are you?' Brian felt the need to ask, when Carl came back from giving Donald a hand.

Carl frowned. 'Carl Parkin. You've a short memory.'

'I mean your nickname,' Brian replied.

Carl squinted and winked. 'Popeye.'

Brian thought for a second. 'I've got the keys to the door, maybe there's no need to break the door down.' There was a crash as Jerry broke the door open.

'Too late,' said Popeye. 'Anyway the lock would be hot. Don't want the Mayor burning his hands, do we?'

'Might have saved the door.'

'I'm guessing the door is well charred and smoked up already,' Popeye said. 'Just best leave it to us. Ah, here's the police. That's good. It'll keep the Munchkins out of our hair.'

'Munchkins?'

'Civilians. Public.'

Brian puzzled a moment. 'Hang on, the Munchkins aren't cartoon characters.'

'Funny that,' Popeye said. 'Walt Disney never did an animated version of Wizard of Oz, did he? Should have. Someone cornered the rights I heard. Sold out to the Japs. Typical. Not that I've seen their version. Anyway, public is Munchkins to us.'

Roadrunner reappeared after less than a minute inside the building. Popeye left Brian to get a report and signalled two firemen to run a third hose inside the main door. Jerry broke down the door to the public entrance lobby, releasing a sheet of fire. A fourth hose crew played a stream through the opening.

Popeye rejoined Brian. 'You want to get a window made facing the street when the place is rebuilt,' he opined. 'Makes it so much easier to get a hose playing inside straight away.'

'When it's rebuilt?' Brian's heart sagged. This was worse than he had thought.

'Might not need total demolition first,' Popeye said, winking in what he hoped was a friendly and reassuring manner. 'These old buildings can withstand quite a lot. Unless the roof beams collapse. Then the walls might throw a wobbly.'

Brian preferred not to think of the walls falling down. 'Any idea how this could have started?' he asked.

'Anybody's guess until we've got it under control and Jessica Rabbit has been down to take a look.'

'Jessica Rabbit?'

'Head of the county fire investigation team.'

Brian felt like tearing his hair out but regained his composure as he spotted Hilary's arrival.

'The summary is, the place is doomed,' Brian told her. 'Your office and mine will be ashes. I guess we've lost all our files. This is a disaster.'

Hilary was still in the mood to score points. 'The loss of your records may be a disaster. Mine are not lost. Everything we need that could be computerised is safely stored. Everything since I assumed office, that is. What happened before I can't answer for. It is possible some historical records could be recovered from the library's files, I know Barbara Middleton keeps archives. Of course the recovery is subject to negotiation and changes regarding my contract, hours of work, rates, that sort of thing. I assume that despite the penny-pinching when it was purchased, the fireproof safe with the legal documents will be proved to have been just that.'

'Of course,' Brian replied, his attention distracted by a plume of black smoke now rising from the building.

The following morning Brian was not allowed a late sleep-in. His phone rang at eight.

'Hello it's Popeye here.'

'Who?' Brian's brain was not yet in gear.

'Popeye, you know. Carl.'

'Ah Popeye .'

'Right. I wanted to tell you Jessica's been over the scene and wants a word.'

'Jessica? Oh Jessica yes. When?'

'Well I wouldn't be ringing you now if it could wait until next week, would I?'

'OK, so when?'

'This morning. Like straight away. At your office?'

'I haven't got an office any more, remember?'

'Oh. Right. Down the fire station, then?'

'OK.'

'I'll tell Bart to put the kettle on.'

Brian had never visited the fire station. He looked in vain for a greased pole. A fresh-faced young man asked his business, and punched a single digit into his desk phone.

'Diamond Joe's here to see you,' he said into the handset. He turned to the wall, pushed a button, and a door swung open.

'First on the left,' he said to Brian, who was still puzzling over the introduction.

Brian had imagined Jessica to be voluptuous and curvy as befitting her soubriquet. He was disappointed. Olive Oyl came to mind. Becky Grayson introduced herself, by real name, peered over her glasses and said she felt obliged to ask Brian some questions about last night.

'Why exactly?' Brian asked, his suspicions roused. He kicked himself for not calling Anna and warning her to keep stumm about their after-meeting tryst last night.

'The fire, as you might have seen, mainly affected the offices side of the building, and probably originated there. I just wondered if you had any idea how a fire could have started in that area.'

'I see. No. No idea at all.'

'Who would have been the last to leave the building?'

'That was me.'

'And you turned lights and all electrical equipment off, locked up as normal?'

'Yes. Definitely.'

'You see the problem is I have reason to believe the fire was assisted in gaining control by the presence of some accelerant.'

Brian knew in fireman parlance what this meant. The suspicion was that someone had doused the place with petrol. Arson.

'Accelerant?' Brian played dumb.

'Yes. Inflammable liquid.'

'What sort?'

'I don't know yet. Unfortunately our C.A.D. is off sick so we will have to wait for an analysis.'

'C.A.D.?'

'Canine Accelerator Detector.'

'A dog?'

'That's what canine implies, Mr Quimby, er.. I mean.. Mr Mayor.'

Brian's forehead creased again.

'Hasn't he got a nickname, like Pluto, say?'

'Actually it's a she called Perdita, but since this is a serious matter I suggest we avoid frivolity.'

'Suits me. Just how serious?'

'Crime, naturally.'

'You're thinking arson?'

'I see you have a sharp mind,' Becky said, with a trace of condescension creasing her lips. 'Yes, I can't rule it out at this point of time.'

'But who on earth would want to torch the building?'

'You tell me. I hear there was a rather unpleasant incident last night causing the meeting to be abandoned. But I am not the police. That's an issue for them. I can only provide them with my report and my forensic evidence.'

Brian groaned as his brain sprang into action. Incident equals violent affray. Tempers roused. But enough passion to set light to the centre? Surely not. Police involvement certain. He needed to hush up Anna's presence. He needed to speak to his lodge colleague, local Geographical Area commander Superintendent Broughty, fast.

Brian sat back in his seat and feigned relaxation.

'I am sure all that had nothing to do with the fire. And it's also not for me to speculate. I've told you all I can. But when I got there the centre doors were locked, as they were when I closed up. I can't see how someone could have broken in.'

'Good point. But I have to consider everything. When was the last time the Centre was rewired?'

'You'll have to ask the Town Clerk that question.'

'I already have. She can't remember. She says the records went up in flames. She says it was before her time.'

Leaving the fire station, Brian lost no time in calling Anna's mobile. They agreed a story to tell Becky or the police. An interview yes, but no drinks and two-person sex party. Anna could genuinely back up Brian's claim to have locked up and left. Of course the police might say he could have gone back into the offices on his own. But only if they had him in the frame as a serious suspect. And had he turned off everything? Lights yes, for sure. He relaxed.

Anna protested he had given no quotes for an interview. Her story for the paper was incomplete. Brian suggested they meet to remedy that, soon. In fact at the Rosebridge Motel in an hour. Anna said no, just a couple of sentences would do, over the phone, now. She was, in truth, a bit put out that Brian had not called her in the night so she could get a scoop, a pic of the blaze, and this made itself felt in her tone. Brian asked Anna to tone down her reporting of the council meeting events, Anna said no, it was a good story, although she expected her editor would do the toning down. Brian figured his relationship with Anna would prove to have been a fleeting one, and gave Anna the desired couple of quotes.

Brian's call to George Broughty was equally unsatisfactory. George's mind was occupied by what he enjoyed least, poring over spreadsheets figuring out how he could comply with the Chief Superintendent's request, read demand, to make financial savings. George assured Brian with a note of humour in his voice that if he were charged, he would supply a character reference. Brian protested the whole point was to prevent any suspicion, never mind any charges, regarding Brian's involvement in the fire. And to play down any suggestion that there was any case to be made for arson.

George finally got the message as to the seriousness of Brian's concern and said he'd see what he could do. Which was not a lot, at least not before the Fire Service's FIT report came in, or if anybody raised complaints about assault and criminal damage on Monday night. Brian heard a question mark in George's voice and assured him that no complaints would originate from him. Brian was also privately pretty confident that no complaint would come from the council's insurance company, regarding claims for damage to the town crier's mace and lace. The broker was local to Roselake and knew how to handle that, if he were to keep in Brian's good books.

Over the next couple of days speculation was rife amongst the Roselake public as to the cause of the Senior Citizens' Centre fire.

Gossip spread about the events which took place at Monday night's meeting and it was inevitable that conclusions were drawn about the fire being linked to those events.

On Wednesday, despite Anna Shale's prediction, the Gazette hyped the story and fuelled the arson theories by publishing a no-holds-barred account of the Monday night altercation, and the indiscreetly shared opinion of Becky Grayson that it was possible an accelerant had contributed to the blaze.

Both RAG and PRH spokespersons were adamant that none of their membership had sparked off the violent events during the council meeting, and absolutely denied that any of their members had returned to the Centre later that night.

A newcomer to the public debate, Stan Grierson, had sent an email to the Gazette letters desk suggesting that the torching of the Senior Citizens' Centre could be down to the proposers of the community complex, who were no doubt substantially discomfited by the fact that the last two council meetings had resulted in failure or postponement in advancement of their cause, and who might believe the loss of the town council premises would add pressure for a new building to be erected with all haste. Carla Davis took the letter away from the letters editor, but built a less scandalous and less libellous article around the theme, complete with outraged denials from the chair of the Roselake Community Complex Association of any suggestion that a member of his group could possibly have descended to the level of torching the council's building to advance their cause.

Unfortunately the article gave some authority to an already-planted seed of doubt, and fuelled speculation from some of those who suspected that the mayor's pursuit of the community complex plan was based less on altruism than personal gain. They did not keep their thoughts to themselves, and the rumour of the mayor's involvement in the fire spread.

It was perhaps fortunate for Brian that since the events of Monday night he had no time to respond to or worry about the hints that his acquaintances shared with him about the rumour-mongering. He had been propelled into action to help rescue the situation for the Town Council. To give Brian his due, he was not a person to shirk a crisis. And his contacts stood him in good stead. By Thursday he had secured a lease on new Town Council office premises and negotiated a deal for hiring a replacement for the Senior Citizens' Centre as a meeting venue for the Council. Truth to tell, there had been casualties, the Roselake Photographic Society and the Roselake Crochet Club were severely put out by having their regular meeting venue, the Scouts Hall, snatched from them until further notice, but every crisis has its collateral damage. Brian assured the societies he would push them up the priority list for the Council's next round of community support grants. The Scouts had suggested, with an eye on income, that they could also provide accommodation for the senior citizens, but Brian told them he had already made arrangements with the Red Cross. Brian had thought it a good idea to separate at last the link and resulting public association between the wrinklies and his dynamically-led council. Anyway, the Red Cross Hall was an ideal place to station the seniors. At least they were likely to get some immediate emergency treatment if they fell asleep and took a bloody tumble whilst munching their dunked ginger nuts.

Hilary had been willing to agree a truce with Brian, given the circumstances of the week's events, and given that she believed Brian's cross-my-heart assertion that he had not participated in the burning down of the Senior Citizens' Centre. There came a sticky moment when Hilary realised that Brian had secured as temporary offices the premises which until very recently had been those occupied by Roselake's sex shop. She saw Brian's point in that it was very convenient, being only two doors down from the still-smouldering Centre, and she saw his point that a replacement telephone landline renumbered as the old Council number could be installed in a jiffy (Hilary hardly wanted to use the existing sex shop number with the likelihood of people ringing and asking for items outside the Town Council's remit). She also saw his point that the discreetly blacked-out shop windows suited Hilary's need for some privacy when receiving visitors.

Hilary was, however, not sure she wanted to occupy premises with "His 'n' Hers" in bold letters and "Your Every Need Supplied

Within" in smaller letters below on the shop front. In the past, argument over the naming of the shop had caused some delay in Alan Perkin's plan to occupy it. His original suggestions were considered too cheeky for Roselake to countenance, and His 'n' Hers was a compromise on all sides. The subtext was not subject to agreement, but complainants were forced to admit that it could have been worse.

Hilary insisted on an immediate sign change. Brian assured Hilary he would get someone to adjust the frontage in due course. Hilary told him to give her a ladder, a can of paint and a brush and she would deal with it herself. Brian said no panic, he'd get it done.

Paint and paintbrushes were also on Dave and Arnie's mind. A new phase of action kicked off with a successful attempt by Dave, by again dangling the prospect of a new car for his son, to get him to perform another little duty. Arnie had a short evening out employing his signwriting skills. Dave promised him without fail the keys to a motor in his hand by the weekend if Arnie did him one last little favour. Actually on this occasion Arnie used a spray can.

Arnie and Dave were sat enjoying a drink late that evening, a can of Stella for Arnie, a glass of Jack Daniels for Dave. Dave was not totally content, as his own evening out had not been an unqualified success, but at least he wasn't in the Zulu zone. He and Arnie sat back to do men stuff. Texas Chainsaw massacre.

There was a doorbell chime. Connie being out on another hen party or widow's wake equivalent, Dave didn't remember which, he had to answer the door himself.

He faced Detective Constable Pratt on the doorstep.

'Can I come in?' Pratt asked, sticking a foot through the door and attempting to wave Dave aside.

'Excuse me, no you frigging can't, who the hell are you?' was Dave's response.

'Ah,' Pratt replied. He had neither social graces nor an extensive vocabulary, and his removal from the force was high up on the list of cost-saving measures his colleagues would like to implement.

'DC Pratt,' he said, showing Dave his credentials. Dave wanted a closer look. Pratt would not release the document and Dave was not wearing his reading glasses. Pratt looked a mean man and wore large steel-capped boots, so Dave assumed he was indeed a member of the Force and let Pratt in. He led him through to the lounge.

'Police,' Dave told Arnie.

'Shit,' was the mild reply. Arnie turned back to the film.

Dave turned back to Pratt and shrugged, in a gesture he hoped evoked a common spirit, two people of the same generation having similar views about the attitudes of the younger.

'I can assure you my son and I have been in all night,' Dave told Pratt. 'Watching television, as you can see. My son hasn't left the house.'

Dave had leapt to a wrong conclusion, and a moment later wished he had buttoned his lip. He blamed Jack D.

'It's not your son's whereabouts I'm interested in, Mr Grant,' Pratt told him. 'It's yours.'

'Ah,' Dave said, light dawning.

'Where've I been, Arnie?' he asked, turning back to his son.

'Here,' Arnie said, munching a couple of crisps noisily.

'What've we been watching?' Dave asked.

'You can see, Chainsaw Massacre.'

'And before that?' Pratt asked, not at all impressed by this charade.

'Zulu, wasn't it,' Arnie suggested. Arnie reached for the remote and put Chainsaw on pause.

'Right, Zulu,' Dave confirmed with a smile. Arnie knew that if asked, Dave could rehearse every scene and recite almost every line of dialogue, if required under interrogation.

Pratt reached in his jacket pocket for his notebook. He read out a car licence number.

'That your car's reg number, sir?' he asked.

Dave nodded. A little difficult for him to do otherwise since the licence plate was personalised. The "DG" rather gave the game away.

'Can you tell me who was driving it tonight, between, say, about seven and nine o'clock? .....while you were watching Zulu?' Pratt added with a smirk.

'Ah well,' Dave blustered. 'I might have popped out for a bit of fresh air.'

'Funny your son didn't notice you popping out,' Pratt commented.

'Zulu sucks,' Arnie said in his father's defence. 'Boring. Not enough action. I might have dropped off for a minute or two.'

Pratt said nothing for a while.

'Suppose I told you that your car was reported parked in Brandon Gardens for the best part of two hours tonight? The driver's description…' Pratt tapped his notebook, 'tallies with yours. Average build, middle age, average features, mousy hair.'

Pratt was exaggerating a little. Rose Newby had described the car's occupant as youngish, quite attractive looking, brown-haired. And of course since Dave had been sat in the driver's seat all the time, Rose had formed little impression of his height or build. Of course if Pratt were reciting his own impression, now meeting Dave for the first time, he was sticking to the letter of the truth.

Although stung by Pratt's words Dave was not fool enough to let it show.

'Brandon Gardens, you say? Yes, that's possible, now I come to think of it. It couldn't have been that long though.'

'Near as dammit,' Pratt said. 'Are you denying you were there?'

'Er, no,' Dave said, after a moment's thought. He couldn't see any way to wriggle out of it. His mind was already fast-forwarding to his asking his police contacts of higher rank than this DC to help him out of a hole. If he were indeed in one. 'I am not sure why this concerns you, though, constable. Parking up for a while isn't an offence as far as I know, it's not like it was on any yellow lines or anything. I fail to see why a detective constable should be involved.'

'I'm involved because I happened to be in Roselake, investigating another incident this evening. An act of criminal vandalism. Defacing public street furniture. Namely a road sign.'

Arnie shuffled in his seat.

'But that needn't bother you.' DC Pratt was not a community officer. He knew little about social or community activity on his patch. He did not therefore link the vandalism of the sign to that earlier of Beggars Way. 'I was called in to investigate a complaint not of parking, but what the driver was doing in the car. Can you explain to me why you used a pair of binoculars on several occasions to spy on the occupant of number nine?'

Dave thought of an inspired answer. 'I bought a new pair of binoculars this week from Amazon. Good for night vision, the webpage said. I was testing them out. I can show you the receipt if you like.'

Not that inspired though. 'And can you tell me why you need a pair of night vision binoculars? For what purpose exactly?'

'Well for, general purposes, like. I might fancy some birdwatching. Every man needs a hobby.'

'Like playing Peeping Tom and looking in ladies' bedroom windows? Seeing what frilly items are left out on washing lines at night?'

'No, of course not.'

'For what then do you need night binoculars? Let's get it straight. You were caught spying on a house at night. Now either you're a Peeping Tom or you are a stalker, Mr Grant. Stalking that young woman at number nine. Either way we could be looking at a serious offence, you see my point now? Six months in prison maybe for a summary conviction. Maybe more if you argue the toss in court.'

Dave was not prepared for this, not least by Hilary being described as a "young" woman. He gulped. Of course Pratt was exaggerating again, but Dave had not been prepared to have his hour or two of what he thought of as amateur sleuthing defined as a criminal act.

'Of course if you've been harassing and stalking this woman continually that's another situation again. We'll have to see what she says when she gives a full statement to us in the morning. But come on Mr Grant, have you got a thing about this woman, Ms Jessop? You're obsessed with her, right? She well built?'

Arnie, who had been listening to this conversation with some confusion, now twigged. He couldn't stifle a guffaw. The idea of his dad having an obsessive crush on the woman he had been verbally chastising for the last couple of weeks was just too funny.

'You got something to laugh at, son?' Pratt asked coldly.

'Think I've a cold coming on,' Arnie improvised.

'Cold my arse,' Pratt muttered.

'Hold your arse?' Arnie replied. 'You should be so lucky. You hear that, Dad? Bit of a perve this one.'

Pratt scowled. He was good at scowling. He had had a lot of practice.

The distraction had given Dave an instant to recover his wits. He realised Pratt had nothing on him beyond a neighbour's say-so.

'DC Pratt, I am stopping this conversation now, and asking you to leave my house. You are going a step too far, making unjustified and frankly laughable allegations. You are harassing my son. I've admitted I was in Brandon Gardens and stated that was for entirely innocent reasons. So your little bit of detective work is complete, and I hope we hear no more of this trivial matter.'

'You think staring through windows with binoculars at women naked and in their underwear is a trivial matter?' Pratt asked. Although the remark was not addressed to him, Arnie shrank into his chair. He had done a bit of that in the past, as we know. Arnie was a little puzzled as to how women could be naked and in their underwear at the same time, and let his imagination dwell on this problem for a moment or two.

It was news to Dave that Hilary had been dressed scantily inside her house. 'It seems, Detective Constable Pratt, that your informant knows more about the inside of number nine than I do. Perhaps you had better ask Ms Jessop's opinion on how her neighbour watches her movements and monitors her being in the noddy. I think you've been looking in the wrong place for the Peeping Tom. Goodnight.' Dave ushered Pratt to the door.

Pratt could have bitten his tongue at letting out the information he had found, that Rose Newby had an interest in watching through lace windows that extended rather beyond neighbourly protection. He had no answer to Dave's chide.

Dave slammed the door behind Pratt and returned to the lounge, with a detour to the kitchen to revisit his Jack Daniels bottle.

Arnie gave him a broad smile as he parked his bottom on the sofa.

'What you smirking at?' Dave asked. 'This is all your fault. If you'd told me where you got the info from I wouldn't have got into this shite.'

'Oh so it's all my fault is it, you go spying on women with binoculars when they're undressed at night?'

'She wasn't undressed. That's bollocks.'

'But you were spying on her, eh? I thought all you needed to do was see if she had a visit from the van man.'

'He hadn't turned up. You never told me what time he usually came.'

Arnie sniggered.

'Less of the smut,' Dave continued. 'I had to do something while I was waiting. Make sure she was still in the house and hadn't snuck out round the back.'

'Yeah, yeah. Sure.'

Dave had in fact taken not a little pleasure in spying on Hilary. Even though she had remained fully clad, watching her had drawn Dave into an inexplicable regard for his nemesis. With distance and double glazing separating him from conflict and angry words, Dave felt a stirring of interest, in Hilary's physical form at least.

'Watch it lad. If you'd told me the full monty I wouldn't be in this mess.'

'It's no mess. The cops can't pin anything on you with that neighbour's evidence. I bet it's the same one who shopped the Jessop woman for having it off with the wine shop delivery man.'

Dave thought. 'Good point. That might have legs, if it comes down to it. But I'm still in the slimy if Jessop tells the police she wants to press charges.'

'Nah, it'll never happen. Anyway if it did, you'd likely only get an ASBO. I'd put in a good word for you with my mates in the Masons.' Arnie chortled.

'You want that motor, yes or no?'

'Yes. A definite yes.'

'So watch the lip.'

'But I did the business at Fore Street, remember? Good one, that.'

'You posted the pic yet?'

'No but I will when I go to bed. None of my mates do social media before midnight. Don't worry, I got it covered. I wouldn't mind another beer from the fridge, since you're asking.'

'Just why would I get you another beer?'

'Cos I'm worth it? Your glass is empty again anyway. Figured you're heading that way.'

CHAPTER 13

Brian had had so much weighing on his mind that it wasn't until that night it clicked that however the fire might have started, he might have made a significant contribution to its getting a hold in the Town Council offices. Finally he linked accelerant with alcohol, and remembered that his torrid fling with Anna had involved the accidental emptying of the contents of two bottles of high quality and decidedly high ABV content marc and schnapps onto the mayoral carpet. Brian spent much of the night worrying, or dreaming of cartoon characters occupying the witness stand in court.

Fortunately for Brian, he received a phone call early the next morning which put an end to agonising internal debate as to whether he should share his revelation with the fire brigade or police, and if so, how. His police link George Broughty had news for him. The conversation started off awkwardly for Brian, with his anxiety in recognising that the call might be an invitation to a formal interview showing in his voice. George took advantage of the situation and, rather unkindly, led very slowly to the point.

'Brian, I'm calling because I have some news on the fire situation. Not all good, I'm afraid.'

Brian's heart sank. 'Best get on and tell me then, George.'

'I now have Becky Grayson's report on the likely cause of the fire, and the chief officer's assessment of the damage.' George paused.

'And?'

'And the damage is assessed as severe, with some major rebuilding required. No surprises there, the insurance assessor came to the same conclusion, I gather. The full fire team report will be with the District Council this morning. As the owners, of course, they should have the detail first, but I made sure you'll get a copy this morning.'

'Delivered to your sex shop,' George added with a half snigger half snort. 'Anyway I thought I'd better just call to let you know that the centre isn't going to be in use again as a meeting room or tea, biscuit and chinwag centre any day soon. But of course you've already made temporary arrangements. So that's it, really.'

'But the cause of the fire?'

'Oh, nearly forgot,' George lied. 'Becky Grayson has written off the fire as probably caused by a wiring fault. Some equipment left on in the kitchen, she wouldn't wonder. Blew a fuse in the office part and a fire started there.'

'Is that it?'

'What else were you expecting?'

'Er, nothing,' Brian fibbed.

'Oh, if you mean about the booze, Ms Grayson says that for sure helped the fire along. Says it wasn't a bright idea to have that much inflammable liquid lying around. I agree with her. You should have shared it out with your friends. Maybe next time you will, if you get my drift.'

'She never asked me about booze.'

'Didn't need to, your clerk told her you had a stash hidden away in the mayor's office.'

'Disloyal bitch,' was Brian's thought which remained unsaid. He thanked George for the update and was about to put the phone down when George stopped him.

'By the way, I hear you've got another Roselake street sign defaced.'

'Oh? News to me,' Brian said.

'Last night someone changed the name of Fore Street,' George told him.

'To what?' Brian asked innocently.

'Something vulgar. Best go see yourself. If it's linked to that Beggars Way business it's time you put the lid on that.'

Brian didn't take kindly to having his management of the Town Council come under fire. 'I'll bear that in mind, George. But you'll be aware that's exactly what I tried to do at the last couple of Town Council meetings. First time a councillor kicked the bucket, second time there was a public disturbance. That's something I hope you can put the lid on yourself, by the way George. Let me know if I have to put in a formal request for police office presence at future meetings. And I hope you'll crack down on this vandalism. Maybe you should up the numbers of boots on pavements.'

'I take it that was a feeble joke, Brian. You know as well as I do how overstretched we are already.'

'But I think we know the boundaries of our responsibilities, that's all I'm saying George.'

Brian put his mobile down. A moment later its ringtone warbled again. It was Donald Cresswell informing him that his leader Stuart Parkinson wanted an urgent meeting. Brian agreed to be at the District Council offices in Rosemouth in an hour's time.

Brian's absence from Roselake this morning was welcome for Hilary. She had what seemed hundreds of tasks to do before her office formally opened to the public next Monday morning. She had already organised the basics, installation of chairs, table, wooden cabinets, filing cabinets and new computer equipment. It had been fun, almost like furnishing a new home. Muscular removal men had delivered the furniture, and a very pleasant, intelligent and helpful young man called Adam attended to her computer's installation. Very attractive to Hilary's eye, too, especially when he removed his glasses.

There was a mountain of paperwork to do, itemising the Council's losses under two headings – immediate need for replacement and insurance contents claim – and putting together an agenda for the Council's Emergency Committee meeting which had been called for the beginning of next week. Hilary would have had no time to paint out the worrisome shop name on the shop fascia and, truth to tell, she was wobbly and practically swooned if she went above three ladder rungs. Her boast to Brian about wanting to rejig the shopfront herself had only been a ruse to get him to speed up the required sign changes.

Now she needed time, too, to make herself familiar with the new computer Windows version and new hardware, for example to find out how to use a network printer. And to check out fully the compatibility of software that Adam had loaded with her files, and organise a transfer of some information on paper files from the library up the road.

This police business last night was a nuisance. The whole affair sounded like another one-man-band, or one-woman-band, neighbourhood watch scheme gone wrong. Hilary was used to seeing Rose Newby's curtains twitch, and when that odious detective constable Pratt mentioned her name Hilary was at first inclined to write off the incident as insignificant. But when Pratt asked her if she knew a man called David Grant she was thrown. Why would Grant be watching her, if indeed Rose's report to Pratt was accurate? It occurred to Hilary that it was fortunate that Oscar from Bin Ends had not been able to carry out his normal weekly delivery last night. That would have been embarrassing. Luckily for Hilary, Oscar had been detained. Literally, by police in Northamptonshire investigating his possible involvement with a suspected stolen consignment of wine which had disappeared somewhere between Newport Pagnell and the M6 junction with the M1.

After Brian had called in to collect the copy of the fire report, Hilary received another visit at His 'n' Hers (as we shall continue to call it, despite Hilary's attempt to stamp the Town Council's interest in the premises by printing an A4 poster and fixing it to the door glass). It was from a young female community support officer. Hilary surmised, rightly, that this implied the peeper affair had been scaled back in its importance, and was now regarded as a matter for filing in a folder and forgetting.

However, Julie Woodman wanted to do more than write a note or two, close her notebook and wave goodbye. She had recently received training in "women's issues" and thoroughly enjoyed the three day course at the police training centre, especially as she was also able to involve herself in men issues after class. This morning Julie demonstrated to Hilary her feminine sympathy at being harassed. Her instructor would have been proud, this came straight out of the course material word-perfect. Julie's mistake was that immediately following the stock paragraph she made it clear that she didn't believe a woman of Hilary's age could possibly have attracted a heavy-breathing stalker. Hilary gauged her response to

Julie accordingly, and expressed her thanks for the police interest. She had not been threatened, or under surveillance as far as she knew. She had not at any time last night bared herself to public view, she did not believe for a moment that David Grant, whoever he was, had any interest in her, and Julie should perhaps contact social services to investigate Rose Newby's mental health.

'Ungrateful bitch,' was Julie's reaction as she slammed the door on leaving Hilary's office.

Hilary lost no time in calling Dave. 'We need to talk,' she told him in an I-shall-not-be-denied voice.

Dave was not expecting a call from her. From the police maybe, regarding last night's escapade, but not from Hilary. 'What about?' was his unrehearsed reaction.

'You know very well what about, Mr Grant. You will meet me at the Lamb and Flag at eleven o'clock. I shall not take no for an answer, and you had better be on time. You had also, more importantly, better have a good story to tell me about why you were sitting in your car watching me at my home at night, and moreover give me a good reason why I shouldn't ask the police to lay charges against you.'

Hilary did not wait for a reply and terminated the call.

Dave had a little time to think things out before his appointment at the Lamb and Flag. Surely Hilary wouldn't want the whole story about her liaison with the wine man to come out in public? So why was she in a strop, threatening charges? Only one reason occurred to him. She wanted to meet him because she hadn't a clue what it was all about.

Hilary made a point of arriving at the Lamb and Flag after Dave. In fact she had been waiting for his arrival. The sex shop was almost opposite the pub, and with a little judicious scraping of the dark wrapping film which obscured the plate glass window, Hilary was able to squint through the gap and watch the L&F's entrance.

She met Dave at the bar, as he was waiting to buy himself a drink.

'While you're at it, mine's a glass of white wine. Sauvignon for preference,' she added for the benefit of the bartender, a pigtailed girl called Lucy, 'provided it's freshly opened. Otherwise red will be acceptable.'

'It's all freshly opened today,' Lucy said with a smile. Dave would have been charmed by Lucy's smile if he hadn't had an aversion to tattoos, prompted by an adverse physical reaction after his own first expedition into body art, involving painful skin graft and, even worse, a course of powerful antibiotics which required abstinence from alcohol.

'I'd prefer it if the bottle wasn't opened at all before my glass came out of it,' Hilary said, knowing full well that freshly opened in pub terms meant sometime in the last week. 'You can bring it to the table,' she added for Dave's benefit. Or Lucy's, she didn't mind which. Hilary turned and went over to a table in the bay window.

Lucy's "get her" conspiratorial look designed for Dave's benefit missed the mark. Dave was watching Hilary's rear as she sashayed across the room.

'Just open a new bottle of Sauvignon Blanc,' Dave told Lucy.

'Large or small glass?' Lucy asked, feeling snubbed.

'Large,' Dave replied, absentmindedly. 'And a large scotch for me.'

'Any preference for brand?' Lucy asked.

Dave scanned the row of optics. He had experience working as a barman. 'Forget it, I'll take a pint of Sheep Dip.'

Dave sat at Hilary's table and she offered a curt 'Thank you' in return for the drink. Not quite sure as to how to open the conversation, Dave took a draw of his pint and let Hilary do the job.

'So let's get down to it. Why you were playing the Peeping Tom last night? If you were disappointed not to find me frolicking around naked I can't say I'm sorry.'

'You mean you have no idea why I was there? On a Thursday night?' Dave added pointedly.

'Of course not,' Hilary replied. 'I wouldn't even be spending my valuable time with you if I knew why you were stalking me. And unless you get on with it and tell me, I shall be perfectly happy to let the police take over. I shall of course tell them that we had some very unpleasant exchanges in my office, you were abusive towards me and I had to ask you to leave.'

'And I shall tell them exactly why I was there last night, that day of the week particularly,' Dave said, with what he hoped appeared as a smirk. 'And maybe the press, if the police want to charge or caution me and I choose to make an issue out of it.'

Hilary twigged. Thursday night was the night she expected her wine delivery. But how had Dave got to hear about that?

'I have no idea what you are talking about,' Hilary said to draw Dave out.

'I think you have. A little bird tells me you normally have a certain visitor on Thursday evenings. A married man. Who stays rather longer than necessary to make a goods delivery.'

Hilary sucked her cheeks. 'That's true. Oscar is a good friend of mine. He always stays for a cup of tea. Or an occasional glass of wine.'

'Where does he take his tea?'

'Excuse me?'

'What I hear is that when he arrives an upstairs light comes on and curtains are closed.'

Hilary by now had beamed in accurately on her neighbour Rose as being the source of Dave's information.

'Ah I see what you're getting at. Wrong, of course. Where do you keep your spare cash, Mr Grant?'

'What do you mean? I don't have spare cash. I use plastic.'

'Well call me old-fashioned, but I prefer bank notes. I keep my spare cash in my bedside drawer. That's how I pay for my purchases.'

'You expect me to believe that?' Dave grinned.

'Frankly I don't give a monkey's, as you might say, whether you believe me or not. But I can assure you that the only person you would be damaging by any groundless allegations such as you're hinting at would be Mrs Parsons, Oscar's wife. The poor woman has enough to put up with without hearing spurious slanderous allegations about her husband's infidelity.'

Dave had only guessed that Hilary's putative lover was married. He had no ammunition to counter Hilary's assertion that Mrs Parsons was a "poor" distressed woman.

'Sure. I wouldn't want to hurt anybody.'

'Except me?'

Dave ignored the remark. 'Why don't we both just forget the whole thing?'

'How can I? You haven't explained yourself. Were you intending to blackmail me?'

Dave didn't like that word. 'No, of course not. It's just that I was told a tale and I wanted to see for myself whether it was true.'

'Who told you this tale?'

'I can't say. It came third-hand at least anyway.'

'You mean there's a rumour about me going round?'

'Seems so.'

'And you wanted to take advantage of it for your own purposes. But what you're refusing to tell me is what your purposes are. If not blackmail, then what?'

'Straight up, Ms Jessop, I didn't know. I just thought I'd better find out my facts first. I didn't think beyond that. If the story was nonsense I'd have said so and that's good for you, no?'

'I don't believe that was what you were thinking at all.'

'But will you let the matter drop? My wife doesn't want problems because of unfounded allegations about her husband being a pervert, does she?'

Dave was not bad-looking when he smiled. Hilary suppressed a smile herself.

'On one condition.' Hilary fanned herself. 'It's hot in here, don't you think?' She unbuttoned her cardigan and exposed flesh below. Dave, as Hilary guessed, was a sucker for the sight of a bit of cleavage. And he was not careful to conceal it.

'Er, condition?' Dave asked, reaching for the tie he wasn't wearing.

'Yes. You just forget the whole business of getting Beggars Way's name changed.'

'Is that it? The only condition, I mean?' Dave asked.

Hilary nodded. 'I have far too much work to do now to waste any more time on this trivial matter.' Which better represented her reason now for opposing a change. Her memory of Graham Ferguson now, compared with Dave at least, was of a rather inconsequential fellow.

Dave thought for an instant. Not whether to agree, but how to put the response.

'I think, in the interest of eliminating the aggro between us...'

'You mean the petty antagonism?' Hilary suggested as an improvement, her expression changing.

'Yes, right. Maybe I should just ditch the whole idea. If it's better for you, I mean,' Dave continued, having half his mind on Hilary's cleavage and the other half on her lips, which up to now he had thought thin and intimidating. Now he had seen a smile on them he was reconsidering his view.

'I think, all things considered, that is the best way forward.' Hilary agreed.

Dave, essaying his best boyish grin, asked Hilary if she would like another glass of wine. Hilary thought that an excellent plan, so they could toast the elimination of their animosity.

'Friends then, you mean?' Dave asked.

Hilary nodded. 'Why not?'

Dave collected their empty glasses from the table and made his way over to the bar. Hilary watched him. She noted his broad shoulders and his firm rounded buttocks. She thought to herself she could do worse, now her relationship with Brian was looking doomed, and maybe her free wine too. She wondered if Dave had the money to go with his swagger, which might be the icing on the cake.

When Dave walked away from the Lamb and Flag he felt relieved that he had avoided any retribution from the last night's excursion. Indeed it had turned out rather well, and although Dave had not yet worked out the rights and wrongs of any dalliance with Hilary, never mind the technicalities of any liaison, he felt a few years younger seemingly having an offer on his plate.

He meant what he had promised Hilary. The decision to abandon his pursuit of Cypress Avenue or any other replacement name for Beggars Lane had not been an incredibly difficult one – on his way to work this morning, Dave had noticed that at Glendale Cottage the "For Sale" sign, now had "Sale Agreed" tacked across it.

At his office Dave had lost no time in calling Quentin Fairbrace. The two did not know each other, and Dave was able to introduce himself as a resident of Beggars Way wanting to put his house on the market. Quentin, scenting another easy sale, was not backwards in telling Dave how successful he had been only this week in selling a property in the road at only a fraction off the full asking price.

'And how much was that, if you don't mind me asking?' Dave asked.

'I don't mind you asking,' Quentin replied. 'But I am sure you appreciate there are issues of client confidentiality.'

'Except that a month or two from now the selling price will be all over Rightmove and the rest on the internet.'

'Well I suggest you wait for that to happen,' Quentin replied. 'Anyway, many a slip, as it were.'

'Of course,' Dave replied. He would have to be content with the information that the offer on the property was near the asking price. Which he didn't know. 'How much was the asking price then? That can't be a secret.'

'Three fifty.'

Dave made his excuses, said he'd be in touch about his own property, and ended the call. Quentin might not have been telling the truth, maybe gilding the lily a little. Dave toyed with the idea of calling Eddie Cowley to see if he knew more, but decided against it. Eddie might not want to discuss Quentin's success, especially after Eddie had tried to shoot down the prospect of selling a house in Beggars Way.

Dave imagined that the news of a house selling so quickly, and at a decent price, would be certain to decrease support for his crusade to get the name changed. So when Hilary offered a way out which meant he wouldn't have to lose face with Josh, Connie and Arnie, Dave was quite willing to let go. Dave knew it was doing him no good to work himself into a stew every day, and Zulu was beginning to pall.

After his meeting with Hilary, Dave figured that the Fore Street affair was now best kept under wraps. He called Arnie, in the hope that he would say he was too knackered last night to make a splash on social media. Arnie disappointed him.

'Nah, it's ace,' Arnie told his dad. 'Gone viral. Shouldn't be surprised if we see a bit more action from my mates over the weekend, know what I mean?'

Dave groaned. He wasn't very sure now why he had thought an attack on Roselake's street signs would help his cause, neither with his Beggars Way neighbours nor with Hilary. Hilary might not associate him with any escalation of the name issue, but then again she might, and after today he wanted to keep his social options open.

He could of course act now to make peace with Graham Ferguson. But that would be too humiliating. Dave decided to keep quiet and see what happened. See if the ripples settled. Maybe Arnie's mates would not cause a stink. Maybe Hilary would contact Graham to update him anyway. Do nothing, wait and see, best plan.

As it happened, Arnie was mistaken in overestimating the influence he had on his friends. Out with his mates the night after the visit from DC Pratt, he had crowed about the police visit and in bragging mood talked up himself as being the reason for the call. When he went to visit the pub facilities his mates had a quick discussion which resulted in unanimous agreement that risking police visits to their homes was not a good plan. Especially if the cops came with sniffer dogs. What Arnie's friends said later on social media wasn't matched with action. The outbreak of sign vandalism in Roselake was to prove short-lived, although it blossomed gloriously elsewhere in the district.

For Brian there were still choppy waters ahead. Although relieved that no formal blame had accrued to him because of any contribution to the Senior Citizens' Centre blaze, he was surprised to find on his arrival at the District Council offices that Stuart Parkinson was in aggressive mood. Stuart had played a role in Brian's exit from that Council, but they had not borne each other grudges. Fortunately for Brian, Donald Cresswell was also in attendance.

'Brian, we have a bit of a problem,' Stuart announced.

Brian kept his mouth shut. He knew well what was coming in general, if not in detail. Stuart meant Brian had a problem.

'We had hopes,' Stuart continued, 'that Roselake would be able to help us make a transition, progress towards a streamlined, more cost-effective council bringing benefits across the whole district.'

'Maybe you could be a bit clearer, give it him straight,' Donald offered.

'OK here it is. In our view the present District Council premises are no longer fit for purpose. The interests of the council taxpayers will be best served by relocating the offices to a new build complex, with major opportunities giving added value.'

The District Council offices were located in what was originally an old extensive manor house on the outskirts of Rosebridge. It had been acquired for a very modest sum for the establishment of the District Council on local government reorganisation in 1974 and was now a prime piece of real estate.

'You mean you want to flog off the majority of the existing site for housing development and redevelop the existing council offices as a leisure and hospitality complex,' Brian added helpfully, in further clarification.

'OK, so it's not a new idea,' Stuart agreed, grudgingly. 'But I am getting close to going to Council for agreement. And this includes a new build at Roselake, on our industrial estate land. Good for us, good for Roselake, right?'

'Right,' Brian agreed, although this planned removal to Roselake hadn't been flagged up before.

'Do our Roselake District Councillors know anything about this?' Brian asked. If the answer were yes he would not be happy that he had not been informed.

Stuart looked at Donald. Stuart shook his head. 'The time wasn't right to let them know, during sensitive discussions, if you know what I mean.'

Brian knew exactly.

'So when's it going public?'

'The agenda for next week's policy meeting will be mailed out this weekend.'

'Which is why you're telling me now. The time wasn't right to inform me either before. Betrays a certain lack of trust, Stuart.'

Donald looked at the ceiling. He had been hoping the note of discord would have been dropped.

'The problem is, Brian, recent events in Roselake, in particular the last week's, haven't helped my, I mean our, cause. Roselake has become something of a thorn in the Council's side. Trouble over street name changes which spread to other towns is one thing, but fisticuffs at council meetings and burning down of town council offices doesn't do much for your reputation, and hence for our plans to give Roselake the big prize.'

Brian pondered his response. 'But Roselake is the obvious choice for relocation. Central to the district, good communications, etc., etc.'

'This isn't a matter of logic, Brian. I have to get the plan past fifty or more councillors who don't represent Roselake, and who will fight their own corner.'

Brian wasn't sure about that point. The majority of the leader's party were, like Roselake's own current three district councillors, happy to get elected, sit on their hands, and do what they were told without doing a thing for their town or any other.

'So what's the reason for calling me in? What do you want me to do?'

'I received a précis of the fire officer's report this morning. It seems you were keeping booze on the premises and that contributed to the fire.'

Brian laughed. 'Are we talking pots and kettles here?' He pointed behind Stuart to the glass-doored cabinets hosting many bottles of no doubt high-alcohol drinks donated by overseas visitors. The bottles formed the centrepiece of a display which occupied the whole of one wall. Various trinkets and objets d'art, scrolls and photographs occupied the shelves either side of the colourfully labelled spirit bottles.

To the side of the main wall was another cabinet exhibiting larger offerings from foreign groups who had visited to perform at the annual music festival. Drawing most interest and comment was a single cabinet containing a Zulu assegai and shield. The contents had a certain notoriety. The assegai had put an end to the political life, or life of any description, of Harry Jeffreys, who for many years had ruled the roost at the District Council serving as leader and chairman. He was rumoured to be a descendant of Baron "Hanging Judge" Jeffreys, although no-one ever dared to ask. If he was a descendant the baronetcy had suffered a serious decline, as Harry was a hairdresser by trade and had maintained ownership of a barber's shop until his demise, leaving his staff to perform the cutting as he busied himself with District and County politics, where he became a sizeable fish, albeit in a small pond. He developed new lucrative business interests as a sideline to his political career. Unfortunately his rule of the District was brought to an end by a wronged councillor. Hell hath no fury like a woman scorned. Especially when she sees a newly-arrived assegai resting on the Leader's table whilst he is dismissing her from his team and casting aspersions on her sexual prowess.

'It's not alcohol,' Stuart said, bringing Brian out of his reverie.

'What?'

'The bottles on show. I'll let you into a secret. When the bottles are handed over they are emptied and refilled with an innocent water-based liquid of similar tint.'

'And the original hooch?'

Stuart shrugged. 'Use your imagination. This was, of course, on the advice of our own fire officer. Needless to say, he enjoyed and enjoys still some of the benefits resulting from his advice.'

'You're pulling my dong, Stuart,' Brian was prompted to say.

'Be that as it may, questions about the Roselake fire were raised by the press, and questions are being raised by councillors. In particular, whether it suited the mayor's purpose to have the place torched.'

'That is bollocks. The whole idea is ludicrous. That's what came out in the police and fire department's report, right? No. End of.'

'I have to say, as we are the landlords, the question remains about the state of the wiring in the building. Whether you acted with proper diligence.'

'And I have to say, Stuart, that due diligence was employed. Even though we were not officially responsible for the maintenance, we did have the wiring checked two years ago. It was declared fine, no problems, give or take a minor bit of rewiring.'

'You have evidence of that?'

'Indeed I have. My clerk gave me the full details, and a rather singed but still legible document rescued from the safe confirming the situation. It was a guarantee for work done offered by a company called Parkinson Electricals Limited. Ring any bells?'

'Ah,' Stuart replied, caught off-balance. 'Of course you realise I have little involvement in the day-to-day running of the company.'

Just took the backhanders, Brian thought. Nice one, Brian, thought Donald. We make a good team.

'But getting back to the issue at hand,' Stuart insisted. 'Just how are we to rebuild up from the ashes? It seems to me we have the option to scrap our involvement by flogging the site off for redevelopment, or rebuilding as it was. We'd want the Town Council to commit to continuing its use of the premises. But I guess you don't see that as an option?'

'No I don't. We're far too close to getting agreement to start work on the new complex.'

'Not near enough, some of my councillors are saying. It looks like the town is divided on the issue, so is the Town Council. You couldn't bring home the bacon in the last couple of meetings, what guarantee do I have you can do it next time?'

'If nobody dies at the Council table, and if the public don't start a riot, I've got a good chance. There's little I can do about the first risk, but I can ask for some police presence to reduce the chance of fights breaking out again.'

'But will you carry your councillors with you?'

'I'll try my damnedest. It's now or never. I'll find a way.'

'But back to the old premises. What about option one? Rebuild for a new purpose?'

'And the senior citizens?'

'Can't they move to the new complex with you?'

'For heavens sake, Stuart, you know damn well how many times we have rejigged the complex plans. This version is final. And it doesn't include space for senior citizens. They didn't want to move, when it was put to them years back, I'd remind you.'

'I still don't see why they can't use a room in the mornings.'

'When did you last look at the plans, Stuart? We don't have space. And if we did, by kicking the crèche out we'd be losing a significant income stream. Mothers pay well for the opportunity to leave their kids in safe hands while they are at work. And besides, the new site is uphill, well away from the High Street.'

'It's only a couple of hundred yards.'

'Or so. The "so" counts a heck of a lot when you're elderly and frail. Of course if you'd passed planning for the Town Green site we'd have had a more viable complex as well as an ideally located one.'

'You know that wasn't an option.'

'Only because the Rugby Club bent the ear of the planning chairman. Before your time, of course. No disrespect, Donald,' he added for Donald Cresswell's benefit.

'But,' Stuart persisted, 'it wasn't only the Rugby Club who objected to losing their pitch. We had a whole pile of letters from others bemoaning the potential loss of a historic public facility.'

'You know that was nonsense. It's only the Rugby Club and Hockey Club who use it. And dog walkers.'

'Maybe you shouldn't underestimate the attraction of poop scooping,' Stuart said with a grin, in a typically pathetic attempt at humour. In all the time Brian had known him the only occasion on which people had laughed at Stuart's jokes was when he positioned himself in a rather unfortunate manner in front of a sign advertising a circus visit, next to a revealing and provocative photo of a busty trapeze artist.

An idea surfaced in Brian's brain.

'You've got me thinking. What I need to do is get the town moving in one direction, together, right? Council in tune with public opinion?'

'Right,' Stuart replied. Donald nodded agreement.

'Well after twenty years of tussle over the complex, which would be the best thing ever for the town, I can't unite the public behind a positive and useful project. When does the public unite? When they are up against a big threat. So let's create one.'

'So where's this big threat coming from?' Stuart asked.

'From you. The District Council.'

'What?'

'Well not really. There doesn't have to be any substance to the threat. But I'll need your help.'

'You're not making sense, Brian,' Stuart worried.

'How about this. A rumour, a rumour only mind, spreads that now the town council building has burned down, the idea of building the new complex on the town's Green has resurfaced. The plan is to shift the Rugby Club out of town to the greenfield site beyond the industrial estate, and build a new bunch of houses on the Green to finance the new complex. Nearby residents, as always, will be inflamed, the Hockey Club will be stick-waving like blood-hungry St Trinians schoolgirls, and the Rugby Club will be livid. Everyone will agree the whole idea is a crock. I sneak past the existing complex plan and I guarantee I can get a majority, in the face of the alternative.'

Stuart looked at Donald. 'Might work,' Donald said. 'But no way am I sticking my neck out proposing a plan to build on the Green.'

'You don't have to,' Brian said. 'Nor do you, Stuart. I will find a way to leak a rumour around town, making sure it gets headlines in the press. When asked I will deny knowledge of any such plan. All you two have to do is suggest there is no current plan to build on the Green, without actually categorically denying that such an idea exists. You just reiterate that the Rugby Club operates under a lease which will remain in force. As always any plans involving Roselake would receive full consultation with local councillors and public.'

214

'OK, I'll go along with it. Let's see how it pans out,' Stuart agreed reluctantly. Donald nodded. 'But if there are repercussions they will be on your head.'

'I'll take the risk,' Brian said.

'Pity the Green idea doesn't have legs,' Donald mused. 'Would have been a good plan. Relocate the Rugby Club, generate the cash to build them a new clubhouse, which they've been moaning on about for years, raise the funds for the new complex, and put some life into the swimming pool, which we'll have to close down if it doesn't do more to pay its way. And maybe make a nice park for your seniors.'

Brian started. The news that the swimming pool was under threat came as a surprise to him. 'Excuse me, the swimming pool is due for the chop?' he asked.

'Hopefully not. Provided the money can be drummed up from somewhere.'

'Same question I asked you before. Do the Roselake district councillors know the pool is under threat?'

'They ought to,' Stuart said. 'If they read their agenda papers for the finance and leisure services.'

'Bloody hell. I'll take that as a no, then,' Brian said.

Stuart shrugged. 'Once in a while, just once mind you, I miss someone of your calibre on the Council, Brian,' he said wistfully.

'That's the nicest thing anybody's said to me all week,' Brian responded, with a smile.

CHAPTER 14

'This all still leaves the question of rebuilding the old council building,' Stuart moved on. 'Use for the Senior Citizens' Centre alone wouldn't justify it. We can use insurance money for the rebuild but we'll miss the income. Another loss leader.'

'I have a plan,' Brian told him, waving a forefinger in the air. 'Over the years the community complex organisation had discussions with the Roselake Surgery, based up South Hill, as you know. The doctors saw the advantage in keeping the main surgery near the hospital, but having an outstation, or should I say instation, in the centre. When the plans for the complex moved on, necessarily downsizing, any idea of building facilities for the medical practice fell through. But maybe if I resurrected the idea with the docs, an occasional surgery and a pharmacy built adjacent to the hall and kitchen for the senior citizens might be an idea to catch hold.'

'Surgery next to the senior citizens, nice one,' Donald approved. 'Convenient for the old, and a captive market for the quacks and chemists. Change of use no problem,' he added with a glance at Stuart who briefly nodded.

'Precisely,' Brian said.

'Would help us make a financial case for a rebuild,' Stuart agreed.

'If the doctors don't go for the plan maybe the funeral director will,' Donald said, which jocular remark ended the meeting.

Donald offered to buy Stuart and Brian a drink. As Donald had been anticipating, Stuart declined, claiming things to do. Donald did need to speak to Brian, and Stuart knew that. The prospect of the possible relocation of the District Council offices to Roselake had not been one to which Donald had been party. This rankled, as it had with Brian. But Donald was intelligent enough to realise that this meant that Stuart had previously had other irons in the fire, but now his Plan A had fallen through. Today Stuart was, correctly, assuming fallback Plan B, to involve Donald and Brian, would work. He knew Donald and Brian would be miffed not to have been involved at stage one, but that wouldn't let them stand in the way of opportunity. If Donald and Brian could get a consortium together quickly to get the design and building contract for the new centre, there was money to be made. A substantial amount. Donald and Brian drove over to the Fox and Hounds, on the Roselake road outside Rosebridge. After a couple of drinks a sketch plan was agreed.

Brian's problem now was how to plant an unfounded and unsubstantiable rumour which carried enough weight to get press coverage, without its origin being traced back to him. He sought for an answer to this conundrum without success. Then he fell back on an oft-used method. Deny the truth of a rumour and others will assume no smoke without fire.

He needed a dupe to help spring his trap. He chose Anna. Brian spent ten seconds wondering if this constituted journo-abuse or sexual abuse or both, but decided this was beyond his power of moral reasoning, and anyway the benefits outweighed the concerns. He rang her.

'Anna, I've got a bit of a problem,' was his opener.

'Like what, Brian?' Anna asked. 'Like it's not as if I'm not pleased to hear you but I am rather busy you know.'

'I know you were cross because you thought I didn't give you a scoop on the fire, but this is new. Might turn out to be a big issue.'

'Like the guy who pretended to be a beggar on Beggars Way sells on the High Street?'

'Ha ha. No this is big I mean B-I-G. Of course I could talk to your boss, Carla, if you prefer.'

'No, no,' Anna rushed to say. 'What's the story?'

'How about we meet?'

'Can't we do it over the phone?'

'Would you like to rephrase that?'

Anna giggled. 'OK, I'm passing through Roselake in an hour. I could drop in to your office for ten minutes or so, I guess.'

'I haven't got an office, remember? Not any more.'

'Where then? I'm not coming to a sleazy hotel room, if that's what you have in mind.'

'No this is above board. No shenanigans. Not today anyway. Which direction are you coming to Roselake by?'

'Blackleigh.'

'How about the Green Man in the village centre?'

'OK. I'll be there, say, four fifteen.'

Brian thought more about the challenge of making the rumour stick, and made another call, to Tony Goodman, one of the three councillors representing Roselake on the District Council. The three were Tory jobsworths, and frankly never lifted a finger after election except to pick up their council salary cheques, or more accurately to log in to their online bank accounts and check that the money had arrived electronically.

Whilst Brian might have preferred in an ideal world to have better direct representation for Roselake on the District Council, he was happy – as he was on the Town Council – not to have any serious rivals who might prevent him from imposing his will and getting his way on matters affecting the town.

Brian chose to share the rumour with Tony Goodman for the simple reason that Tony was known as an indiscreet old gossip. Les Ford was known as a Parkinson Puppet as he did everything he was told to by the council leader, but little else. Not much at all was known about the last of the trio, Keith Eastham, as he was new to the town, in the real sense and not in the decade-or-two minimum sense, and seemed to spend most of his time elsewhere.

Brian started his phone call to Tony with a question. 'Tony, is it true? What I'm hearing about the District Council wanting to build on Roselake Green?'

Tony hadn't a clue, of course, what Brian was talking about. But then he wouldn't have known either, if such a plot were indeed being hatched at District level.

'News to me. Just what are you hearing, Brian?'

'The whisper is the District wants to build a housing estate on the Green and dump the Rugby Club out of town. And I tell you now if it's more than a whisper I am outraged that I as Mayor have not been consulted, or even informed.'

'But Brian, I don't know what you're talking about.'

'Well frankly you bloody well ought to. You're the senior Roselake member on the Council and I'd have expected you at least to keep yourself informed.'

'Slow down, Brian. If all you've heard is a rumour then it's bloody unfair to start having a pop at me.'

'I suppose you know nothing about plans for Roselake Swimming Pool, or the Council offices, either?'

'What?'

'Just do the job you're paid for, if you want to keep your seat at the next election, is my advice,' Brian said huffily. 'I will expect you to chase this up right now.'

Brian clicked off the connection. He smiled to himself. By planting two genuine issues, the pool and the relocation, alongside the Green deception he had boosted the credibility of his false rumour.

The Green Man is a pleasant enough village pub, unremarkable perhaps in this area with its many delightful cosy hostelries, except for its pub sign graphically displaying a remarkably and self-evidently virile man with foliage sprouting out of his head. Less threatening than the Incredible Hulk, less young and effeminate than the Green Giant of the sweetcorn brand, and definitely less dressed than either. Inside the pub the beer was excellent. You could always rely on a good local brew such as a Thirsty Foxhound or a more recent arrival, the Beaver, named when a wild colony of the rodent was discovered in a local river.

Brian was left clicking his fingers on the tabletop for a full fifteen minutes as he waited impatiently for Anna to arrive. He tried not to show his irritation, and responded likewise to her smile of greeting. He bought her a spritzer.

'So, what's this problem of yours, Brian?' she asked after a sip of the drink.

'Apart from not being able to get you out of my mind since the other night, you mean?' Brian said with a voiced enthusiasm which wasn't matched by his real thoughts.

'Apart from that,' Anna said. 'Not that I believe that for a moment.'

'It's been a busy week,' Brian admitted.

'Normally it takes two weeks for a man to forget me,' Anna chided. 'But can we move on, please? I have a busy schedule.'

'OK, here is my problem. There is a rumour circulating.' Brian was sure he was technically correct, being right in thinking that Tony Goodman would have by now been active.

'The rumour is the District Council wants to build on Roselake Green,' Brian explained, and outlined the non-existent plan.

'So, just to be clear,' Anna asked, 'why is this such a problem for you?'

'I don't want the public, or the Rugby Club in particular, thinking I had a hand in this at all.'

'Why should they? You say it's a District Council thing.'

'I bet you, if you do one of your surveys, that you'd find the majority of the public hasn't a clue what the difference is between the Town and District Council,' Brian's opinion probably being spot on. 'I will get the blame. Just like the rumours about me and the fire on Monday.'

'What rumours?' Anna asked, flushing as she imagined any such rumours could also involve her.

'That I started it, to move the community complex project on.'

'But that's nonsense,' Anna said. 'I know that.'

'So that's another way you can help. Get it in the paper that the fire has been written off by the fire brigade investigators and the police as an accident, caused probably by an electrical wiring glitch.'

'That's no problem. But what's the first way? You've lost me.'

'Do a bit of investigation. Leave me out of it. Find out if this rumour is true or not. Come to me for a quote when you find out more. I know this town. The story will be big. Big news report with your byline. Could help you up the ladder.'

'How?'

'Your reputation as a reporter.'

Anna was not experienced enough to know that Brian knew less about her promotion prospects than she did, but was flattered. Her mind already leapt forward to bylines which no longer referred to her as a junior, but as "Anna Shales, Senior Staff Reporter", or even "Anna Shales, Deputy Editor". No, scrub that "deputy", Anna thought. Tanya Blackman had reached the top quickly from a standing start, why shouldn't she?

'OK, I'll do it.'

'But leave my name out of it until you've come back to me with some more info, for an interview. You don't want Carla Davis knowing you had the story on a plate from me, do you? She'd be pretty quick to strip your name off the article if she thought it was just a mayor's press release.'

'I can see the sense in that. OK. But,' she said, looking at her watch, 'I must go.'

'OK. The chairman of the Roselake Rugby Union Club is Jack Gray, by the way, I can give you his number should you need it.'

'That's all right, I'll find it.' Anna had not got where she was without standing freezing on Roselake Green watching the Rucks, aka the Mastiffs, playing their rivals, and waiting for a post-match quote or two, without having RRUC contacts in her files.

'And by the way, Brian,' she added, standing up from her seat. 'Great as it was, I think maybe it's best if we consider last Monday night as just a one-off, don't you?'

Brian tried to look severely disappointed. How good his acting was he didn't find out, as Anna had already twirled and was heading for the door.

The next days went rather nicely according to Brian's plan. Tony Goodman had lost no time in making a series of calls, including to Jack Gray, the chairman and effective boss of the Mastiffs. Jack Gray let him know with an injection of expletives into his response exactly what he thought about the plan, as Jack assumed it to be

221

rather more than a rumour. He told Tony to get his finger out and get something done. Jack himself lost no time in spreading the rumour amongst club members. By the weekend the "news" was all over town.

On market day once again shoppers found themselves approached, this time requested to sign a petition. "KEEP THE GREEN GREEN" was the heading of the appeal organised by the Rugby Club. The subtext was 'I the undersigned state my wish to have Roselake Green remain in its entirety as a recreational area for the Rugby Club, the Hockey Club and the town as a hole.' The misprint caused some amusement among the more astute member of the public and some embarrassment when this was pointed out to the signature-collectors.

Jack, his vice-chair and secretary had in fact argued long – maybe too long - over the text. Jack was for having the signatories demand that the Council (unspecified) keep the Green as it was. John Briers, the vice-chairman, suggested it would be more tactful to request rather than demand. The Hon Sec Pam Russell, had no opinion as to which he preferred. In desperation, and frustration at Pam's silence not giving Jack a majority, Jack told John let's not waste any more time on the wording, and leave it to Pam. Pam groaned, as he knew as soon as he walked away from the meeting he would receive a call from Jack telling him what to write. This didn't actually happen, but only because Jack's mobile battery had run out. Pam was forced to improvise, and she came up with the wording as it eventually appeared. Unfortunately, although she was no doubt skilled in writing as a secretary should be, honourable or otherwise, Pat's proof-reading expertise didn't extend to finding the petition spelling gaffe.

Nevertheless, the ladies of the Rugby Club mustered a good number of signatures on Saturday morning. Their spouses pleaded justifiable absence, as they had an away fixture against the Exebury Fliers in the afternoon. True enough, an away fixture did mean an early start to the day, but not early enough to excuse ducking out of a morning petition shift. For at least one of the team this proved a mistake. The ladies of the Roselake Rockets, the Town's hockey team, had also been dragged in to help with the signature collecting. They too had an away fixture, against the Broadcombe Broads, and claimed they needed an early start (in their case for pre-match fortification by spritzers rather than pints of modest-strength ale). A few of them sent their husbands onto the High Street as substitutes. The fraternisation of rugby widows and hockey widowers extended into a less than, or rather more than, fraternal relationship later in the day between Jane Ready and Shane Banks.

At the end of the day the teams had scored a creditable four hundred or thereabouts signatures.

Theirs was the only petition up for signing that day. The PRH, which as you may remember is the acronym for Preserve Roselake's Heritage group, had considered collecting more signatures for their own. They met on Friday night, in the London, to consider action. Numbers had dwindled. Graham and Lawrence were absent, for a start. Their campaign on Beggars Way was practically won, so Lawrence believed, and although Graham hadn't the same confidence he wasn't prepared to go to the meeting alone. After the violence at the council meeting he felt the PRH was a bit too militant for his comfort, and he had no interest in the wider issues, which he imagined would dominate the meeting.

In this Graham was right. When Len suggested getting more signatures on the petition he faced mutiny in the dwindled ranks. Ellen Parfitt said surely the pressing need now was to combat the threatened encroachment onto the Green. Garth Symes said he thought the reason the group had formed was simply to oppose the elimination of historic street names. Ellen disagreed. She said the group should never have adopted her suggestion for its name if it were to become a blinkered single-issue pressure group. The discussion between Ellen and Garth became quite agitated, ending in Ellen telling Garth that she hoped he were not about to start assaulting her like he had that man at the Town Council meeting or that man in the High Street. Which of course only served to inflame Garth, who considered himself the innocent party in the High Street altercation, even if he were not blameless in the Town Council mêlée.

Len did indeed, as Lawrence had remarked a week or two ago, have his head screwed on. He saw this was going nowhere. Neither was PRH.

'I suggest it may be better, given the events referred to, for us to adopt a low profile and forget any petitioning,' he said. 'In fact I suggest if Ms Parfitt wishes to convene another meeting to discuss the future of this group she does just that. Without my help. You can do what you like. I'm off home.'

Len finished his pint and did exactly what he said he was going to do.

If the Preserve Roselake's Heritage group was falling apart, so too were the campaigns to change the names Butts Close and Isis Close. Both parties received a push on Monday morning from Hilary, who intended to deter them from taking action. Hilary, naturally, avoided putting any of this in writing by passing on her prompts by telephone.

Hilary told Celia Pascoe that she fully expected the Council, at its next meeting, to pass the recommendation that only in exceptional circumstances would the Council approve changes to names with historical associations, and that the full costs of any approved changes, which might be considerable, would have to be borne by those seeking change.

'And, between you and me,' she told Celia, 'if I were you I would be concerned as to whether raising a big fuss about the name would be counterproductive.'

'What do you mean?' Celia asked.

'I mean that by raising the profile of the name and its connotations, you would only be making the situation – as you see it, I hasten to add - worse. Personally I see nothing wrong with the name. You might consider that the Close would attract precisely the sort of attention and ribald jokes that you are trying to avoid.'

'You really think so?' Celia asked warily.

'Most definitely,' Hilary replied. 'On more than one occasion already I have heard the Close being made the, er, object of rude jokes. This will only get worse if you persist.'

'I'll have to discuss this with my neighbours and get back to you, Ms Jessop. Thanks for the tip.'

'Don't mention it,' said Hilary, smiling to herself. She was sure that those few minutes on the phone would save her endless trouble and paperwork later. She looked up Ted Slater's number.

Celia was as good as her word. She convened a meeting at Gwen Thorwood's. Gwen told her it had better be a short meeting as her daughter Helen was staying with her. Celia agreed and called their neighbour Karen Coombes to join them. Karen was reluctant, but promised to be there for a short while.

Helen served the ladies tea and biscuits.

Celia outlined the conversation she had had with Hilary.

'Hmm,' Karen said, ambiguously.

'Yes, the ginger hobnobs are rather good, aren't they,' said Gwen.

'Yummy,' said Karen, ending any confusion of whether her hmm had been in appreciation of the hobnobs or signifying understanding of what Celia had told them. 'Where did you get them?'

'At Hunts Deli,' Gwen replied. 'But you won't find them there any more. These were at half price since Hunts were closing down half their shelf space to make room for tables and chairs for the mini café.'

'I really must ask whether Roselake needs yet another tea shop,' Karen said.

'Ladies,' Celia said, a note of irritation in her voice. 'Can we please keep to the subject of Butts Close.'

'Well I think Ms Jessop may have a point,' Gwen announced. 'The more we go on about it the worse it will get. That concerned me at the time, when we started, I mean.'

'Well you didn't say so then,' Celia complained, oblivious to the fact that Gwen had originally only followed Celia's lead out of friendship. 'What do you say, Karen?'

Karen had been wondering whether to dare ask for another hobnob, aware now they were a limited supply. 'Er, right, I'm not sure. I mean, if it would cost a lot of money anyway, that's a bit worrying. I don't think Bob would like the idea of paying. It would cost enough to have our personal stationery redesigned and printed, not to mention the cost of mailing the address change out to all my friends.'

'You could send the change out with Christmas cards,' Celia suggested.

'But that would mean all the cards we received would be wrongly addressed.'

'Surely it isn't beyond the wit of the Post Office to keep the old address going for a while,' Celia said.

'Better safe than sorry, though,' Karen said. 'I wouldn't want to lose contact with half my friends because their cards had disappeared down a black hole. Or wherever mail addressed to Santa Claus gets delivered. I'm sure my friends wouldn't like the idea of a fake Father Christmas reading all the details of the last year's events and the progress of their illnesses.'

'But what about the question I asked. Would we be doing more harm than good? Making ourselves a laughing stock?'

Helen poked her head round the door. 'Any more tea needed?'

Helen was an attractive young woman with a pert nose which men found cute, a good body which men found cuddlable, and a head of chestnut hair which men enjoyed running their fingers through. Although much sought-after for her looks and bubbly personality, Helen had one defect, her poor choice in men. Her second marriage was about to break up, which was why she had asked to stay a while with her mother.

'Why don't we ask Helen? An unbiased view?' Karen suggested.

'Ask what?' Helen queried.

'The name Butts Close. Do you think it's too risqué?' Celia asked.

Helen lived in London, or at least had until two days ago. She laughed.

'You mean it conjures up visions of contests between Billy goats for Nanny goats' affections?'

'No, not that type of butt,' Celia persisted.

'Ah you mean people expect to see discarded cigarette ends everywhere!' Helen declared innocently, a smile wrinkling her nose.

'No, dear,' Celia sighed. 'The other meaning.'

Helen shrugged. 'I can't think what you mean. Any more tea?'

Celia gave up trying. She helped herself to a ginger nut. It was clear her campaign had run up against the buffers.

Almost to the hour, since Sami Hussain's work started at lunchtime, and Ted Slater - being retired - could pick and choose his time, Ted and Sami were having a similar discussion. But not about hobnobs, and Sami turned down the offer of a ham sandwich with his tea without comment.

Hilary had also planted severe doubts in Ted's mind.

'The point this Jessop woman made is that the name Isis has had its day as what the press are calling the terrorists. The papers are fickle, a couple of weeks ago it was Isis, last week it was Daesh, this week it's ISIL or just Islamic State. Who knows what it will be next week? I think she has a good point.'

Sami's instinct told him Isis would stick, not that he followed Middle East politics, but he saw where the conversation was going. He personally had no wish to dig deep into his pocket on what had seemed a good idea a week or two ago but now looked less attractive.

'Right,' he confirmed.

'Ms Jessop says people will forget and just go back to thinking of posh nobs poling punts or rowing on the river at Cambridge. A nice image, she said, in her opinion.'

'Right,' Sami nodded. Sami was well aware that the Isis flowed through Oxford, but the point was not worth arguing. 'Or think of an Egyptian goddess,' he suggested.

Ted didn't know about that, and said so. The only other link that he could think of somehow involved Bob Dylan, but he couldn't put his finger on it.

'So what do we do, Sami? Do we ask to get the name changed or say we'll stick with it?'

'What would we change it to?' Sami asked. 'We never really thought about that.'

'Good point,' said Ted. He thought for a minute. 'Any ideas?'

'No.'

'Me neither. That's that then.'

Despite a "Reopening on Monday" sign which Hilary had stuck on the new office door, she was not besieged with visitors. In fact she had none at all for the first couple of hours that morning. Which suited Hilary fine, she was able to get on with the backlog of unfinished tasks. But at twelve the first pair of feet came through the door.

A lady whom we would have to describe (were we trying to be accurate rather than polite) as elderly and in a certain state of decrepitude walked over to Hilary's makeshift den and placed an object on her desk.

'It doesn't work any more. I want my money back,' the woman said.

Hilary was not entirely sure what the object was but had a pretty good idea.

'I can refer you to the trading standards office,' Hilary said with a little twitch of her face.

'I don't want no trading standards, I want my money back. I've only had it two months and it's dead. No use to man nor beast.'

Hilary's mind flickered over the idea that the article was not designed for man, nor, she thought with a shudder for beast.

'I'm afraid all I can suggest is trading standards,' Hilary repeated.

'And I'm saying I bought it here and I want my money back. I saw the sign reopening Monday. I've been waiting all weekend.'

'But this is the Town Council office, not the, er, His 'n' Hers.'

'But it says "His 'n' Hers" above the window. And you said "reopening". You can't get away with pulling the wool over my eyes like that.'

'If you had read the small print it would have been patently clear that the reopening referred to the Town Council offices after the fire just down the road.'

'Small print? I can't be reading small print with my eyes. You expect people to walk down the street with a magnifying glass in hand?'

Hilary tried a different tack. 'Have you tried changing the batteries?'

'Of course I have. I'm not daft. The first couple of times I changed the batteries everything was fine. Then it just went dead on me. New batteries didn't work. I paid a good price for them too. Duracell. Not those cheap packets for a pound down the market. Full price, from Boots. Now I want my money back.'

'So you said. And I have told you this is the Town Council offices.'

'You're just trying to hoodwink me and shirk your responsibilities. If my husband Don was still alive he'd soon sort you out.'

'For the last time, I am the Town Council clerk. See?' Hilary pulled out an identity card on a chain from her right hand drawer and held it up.

'I can't see without glasses, I told you,' the woman complained.

'Then I'll tell you what it says. It says Hilary Jessop, Roselake Town Council. Look – there's the Town Council logo. And that's my photo.'

The woman squinted at the card.

'So where's the sex shop gone?' she asked.

'Went broke. Packed in. The owner went to Australia,' Hilary added, a complete lie but one designed to reinforce the point that the sex shop was no more and the woman had as much chance of getting her money refunded as winning a million on the lottery. Less, in fact, if that is possible.

'Bloody hell. That's twenty quid down the drain then,' the woman moaned. She turned and went towards the door.

'Er, can you take that, thing, with you please,' Hilary said, but she was talking to the woman's back.

The woman half turned. 'You keep it. Maybe you can get it to work.' The doorbell rang as she exited.

For a minute or two Hilary pondered what to do with this odious deposit on her desk. She went to the toilet and got a big bunch of tissue. She was gingerly and with distaste attempting to pick the object up without touching it by hand when the doorbell rang and a second visitor walked in. It was Gloria Paynton.

'Oh,' Gloria said. 'I came to talk to you about next week's meeting, but I see it's an awkward time. I'll come back later.'

Gloria turned and left. Hilary seethed with her anger and embarrassment vying for number one emotion. Fortunately for her she had already concocted and distributed the agenda for tonight's Emergency Committee meeting, so she decided she was entitled to shut up shop for a while and cross the road to the Lamb and Flag to take a little refreshment until she had regained her composure.

The Emergency Committee met that evening as scheduled. Since Brian had effectively done all the work himself without consultation, there was little to do but approve the mayor's actions. Derek Hunt raised the expected grumbles about how much this was all going to cost, and how it was going to deplete the Council's finances and the emergency fund in particular. Brian told Derek it was his responsibility then as Finance Chairman to work up the insurance claim to make sure it adequately covered the Council's losses. Derek humphed. He preferred bluster to hard work. Judy Harker said she would oppose any depletion of the Emergency Fund provision, as Climate Change was already well in evidence and the present government's actions were likely to make the town's preparation for wartime or environmental emergencies very pertinent for review. A few comments were made round the table in response to this little speech, most of the "silly woman" variety that could not be raised as formal comment and recorded in the minutes.

The main purpose of the meeting from Brian's point of view was to check out the accommodation in the Scouts Hall, so that next week's full and important full council meeting would run smoothly.

The members found the venue satisfactory. There was a slight upset when Judy Harker screeched and said she had seen a rat running along the far wall towards the kitchen. Peter Galway, who as troop leader had an interest in preserving the reputation of the Scouts Hall, and the prospective income from hosting the Town Council for an indefinite time to come, was in two minds as to what to say. It was an awkward predicament. Sitting next to Judy, Peter had also seen the supposed rat. Judy's rodent and weasel recognition skills being on a par with her tree recognition skills,

Peter was more than doubtful about her identification. But to be fair to Judy, Peter did have some foreknowledge.

On Saturday the Hall had welcomed the annual show of the Roselake Ferret Appreciation Society. After the show it was discovered that one of the prize-winners, a ferret by the name of Alfie, had gone missing. His owner, Hal Masters, had assumed Alfie would not stray far, and had informed Peter about the loss. Hal would have been very upset to know that Alfie had been confused with a rodent.

Peter excused himself from the meeting, and took himself off to the kitchen to see if he could find Alfie. Hal had let Peter know that his ferret was partial to Freddy's Famous Ferret Fare, and had left a couple of cans at the hall for use in tempting Alfie out of hiding, along with a portable ferret cage. Peter emerged from the kitchen five minutes later having successfully tempted and caged Alfie, receiving only a friendly nip in the process. The bite which Jackie, the Scout Hall cleaning lady, had received on Monday morning had been neither friendly nor tolerantly received, and Peter, after liaising with Hal, had spent quite some time persuading Jackie that she did not need to attend casualty for a course of rabies injections, since Alfie had not broken skin. Jackie was only persuaded to a calmer view after Peter offered her a rise to forestall her resignation.

'My nephew's pet ferret,' Peter lied to the councillors. 'I forgot to put him back in his cage. I offered to take him to the vets this afternoon for a dental checkup and only picked him up shortly before the meeting. Sorry about the scare, Judy.'

Peter was desperately hoping his innocent explanation would pass without further comment, and as Brian was anxious to move on and close proceedings, it did.

'Now about next Monday's meeting,' Brian announced. 'It's vital things go well. It is an important agenda and I expect a good turnout from the public. I have the promise of a police community support officer's attendance. And as belt and braces I have asked the Vicar to remain throughout the proceedings. Hopefully the public will be too fearful of arrest, and too respectful of the clergy, to indulge in any of the behaviour we saw at the last meeting. And I have also asked a member of the Red Cross to be in attendance. But if any of you feel unwell on Monday, stay home, just in case.'

'At least there would be someone on hand for last rites,' Peter Galway muttered to Judy. Judy did not respond. She didn't approve of Peter's humour. Or Brian's, if humour was what he intended.

Brian raised his gavel. 'Well that's it. Thank you for coming.'

'Mr Mayor!' Frank Parton moved to speak by leaping to his feet. 'I am amazed you want to close the meeting without us discussing this news about the District Council wanting to build on Roselake Green.'

'That's because firstly it is not on the agenda, and secondly it is not news, it's just tittle-tattle,' Brian declared.

'But this is an emergency,' Frank insisted. 'We just can't allow the District Council to walk roughshod over us.'

Brian stood up. 'Please sit down, Councillor Parton. With respect, you are doing this Council no good by repeating in front of the press,' Brian glanced over at Anna, who was briefed by Brian to appear at the meeting, 'what appears only to be a rumour circulating around the town.'

'There's no smoke without fire, Mr Mayor.'

'Councillor Parton. Please. This committee can not usurp the role of the full Council. There is no mandate to treat wild rumours as emergencies, and to grace them with discussion would be irresponsible. I promise you the Council will discuss the matter next week. I have asked Ms Jessop to place the item on the agenda. By then we shall also have more information on the truth or otherwise of the matter. This meeting is closed.' Brian banged his gavel.

'Make sure you get that bit in about next week's agenda, please,' Brian asked Anna, as they said goodnight. She left him and rushed off to go buttonhole Peter Galway. The appearance of the ferret at the council meeting would make a good human interest story. Peter was caught on the hop. He had to improvise. But then not for nothing did the Scout motto imply a liveliness of mind. And Peter, an unmarried man, found Anna rather charming. She asked for a photograph, which meant Peter had to release Alfie from the cage temporarily. Unfortunately Alfie preferred freedom to encagement, and, with Peter not being an expert ferret handler, wriggled easily out of his grasp, giving him another nip in the process, fortunately not drawing blood. Anna got an interesting photograph.

Peter was left to try and tempt Alfie back, deciding that Alfie's free run had to end tonight. He wasn't sure how to entice a ferret. Did you say 'Here Alfie'? Did Alfie know his name? Peter called Hal for advice and to give him an update. Hal let Peter know in clear terms what he thought about Alfie being captured only to be released again. It was not complimentary, and Peter thought the chastisement went a little too far. Hal asked Peter if he was calling on a smartphone. Peter said yes.

'In that case,' Hal said, 'I'm not coming out tonight. You can stay there and get Alfie back yourself. Google "Top Games to Play With Your Ferret" for ideas. But Alfie particularly likes a tug of war. There must be a tea towel in the kitchen. Wave that about a bit. That'll probably do the trick.' Hal put the phone down.

CHAPTER 15

The Gazette's was another interesting edition that week. Although the Roselake Green rumour did not make the front page, which was occupied by an illustrated story about a pensioner who had been given a Community Protection Notice for feeding birds, Brian was pleased to find on page three a picture of himself in stern finger-wagging mode under the headline "WILL GREEN GO GREY?".

As Brian had hoped, the article hit the right note of formal denial of any plan to build on the Green against informal rumour impressive in its detail. And most importantly, dissociation of Brian from any scheme to deprive Roselake of one of its major assets, as the article called the Green. The net result was exactly what was required, leaving the majority of the article's readers to agree with Frank Parton that there was no smoke without fire.

Brian had to turn to page seven before he saw Anna's account of the ferret incident, which featured before and after photos. The first was of a cute Alfie nesting in Peter's grasp, the next a click of a visibly horrified Peter as Alfie leapt to the floor in a blur. "Scout Leader in Ferret Fun" was the headline, and the text made further play on whether Peter should have been "prepared".

Peter felt quite cross at this and rang Anna the next day to complain. Anna turned on the charm and offered to buy Peter lunch to make up for any offence. Peter said yes, and it is pleasing to report that things between them turned out fine at the end of the day. Alfie had enjoyed Peter's company and didn't mind being taken back to Peter's for the night, having made a new friend. By that evening almost the same sentence could be written and applied to Anna.

En route to page seven Brian had been surprised to find the Gazette devoting a page and a half to an outbreak of vandalism in the district. Carla could not ignore the spread from Roselake of defacement of street signs, particularly as a number of residents had called the paper asking why a police helicopter was buzzing towns at night strobing the roads with searchlights. Now all was revealed. Well not everything, as some of the pictures of defaced signs had to be blurred to hide the full nature of the disfigurement and leave some things to the readers' imagination.

It didn't take too much imagination to realise what offensive modification could be made to Tucker Drive and Cunningham Road in Rosebridge, or Argus Close, Back Lane, Lovelace Crescent and, still on a bodily note, Copse Avenue in Exebury. The modification to North Street there, deleting the final consonant and inserting one at the beginning, perhaps only made sense to the people of Exebury who knew the street was used for the illegal drugs trade. Similarly the conversion of Duke Way would only make sense to those who knew it was a shortcut home for the town youths who had been out carousing on a Saturday night. Bushes Lane was illustrated by the addition only of an exclamation mark. The conversion of Stanley Walk to Stanley Knife, being one of the least racy, was allowed to be shown in full in the paper.

'This is no more than petty vandalism,' a County Councillor for Exebury declared when asked for a quote. 'It is not funny. Exebury is not the set of a Carry On film. I hope the police will come down like a ton of bricks on those responsible for this deplorable outbreak. I am taking it up with the Police and Crime Commissioner this very day.'

Unfortunately for Councillor Painter he was photographed for the quote standing in front of an (undefaced) Exebury road sign, his head obscuring much of the writing of "Turner Road", half a dozen of the letters, to be precise. Whether the photo was snapped that way deliberately, whether the gaffe appeared in the paper by accident, and indeed whether the choice of the unpopular Councillor Painter to give the interview was with purpose, it caused much amusement, not to mention a tongue-in-cheek apology in the following week's edition.

Whilst the County Councillor may have been chosen because of the County's involvement with police services, the burden of the vandalism would fall on the District Council, and the leader found it appropriate to comment, in return for the promise of a photograph which showed him in a rather flattering light awarding prizes to Rosebridge's newly elected Carnival queen and princess (it being the start of the district's carnival season). His quote was in measured tones, regretting that the cost of the vandalism would fall on the hard-pressed council, which was under severe pressure from government to tailor its finances. Needless to say he did not add that this was the government of his own party, and this, which some might term hypocrisy, like the defacements of some of the signs shown in the article, had to be left to the reader's imagination.

More worrying were a paragraph or two at the end of the article. A "member of the public" was quoted as saying that if the police couldn't patrol Exebury streets and keep them safe from mindless vandalism then the public would. Asked for a comment on this, the area superintendent George Broughty said that his community officers welcomed support from the public. Schemes like Neighbourhood Watch had contributed greatly to a sense of security in the community. (Which was perhaps true, although it had done zilch to combat actual crime).

Had George taken a more considered view before responding, he might have realised he was encouraging the setting up by this particular member of the public, and others, of vigilante groups. This unfortunate suggestion was taken up, and when the statistics were eventually published, the vigilantes turned out to have committed more breaches of the law and occupied more of his officers' time than the vandals.

The worst incident involved a poor innocent decorator who was caught by one such group. Debagged and painted with the contents of one of the pots in the back of his unmarked van, he was left to dry for hours. It would be a long time until he was able to sit comfortably. The emergency unit treatment involved surgical spirit and a very stiff brush. Fortunately the unit did not stock paint stripper, which could have been a lot worse.

Whilst not paid-up members of the tar-and-feathering brigade, and no longer part of a militant posse distrustful of Dave Grant's intentions, Graham and Lawrence had formed their own version of a vigilante group. Actually this was more akin to neighbourhood watch, with lace curtains being drawn apart at regular intervals to make sure no further funny goings-on were occurring in Beggars Way, and the addition of a regular patrol, in the duo's case to and from the Carvery once an evening.

Laura had grown tired of remonstrating with Graham, either because of his continued worry about the name change business, or, not unlinked, his increased drinking in partnership with Lawrence. In vain she had tried to convince Graham that he himself had told her that the Town Council could not now support the change of name to Cypress Avenue. She reminded Graham that Hilary had told him she was hopeful the Town Council would endorse a policy supporting the town's heritage and opposed in principle to name changes.

Graham dismissed Laura's arguments, saying he trusted Dave Grant as much as he trusted a venomous snake. Laura asked how many venomous snakes Graham had come across and how many had bitten him. Graham was flummoxed as the correct answer was zero. But then Graham had never been much of an adventurer, and had only seen a venomous snake from the other side of glass in a zoo. His knowledge of snakes was based on not much more than reading The Speckled Band as a youngster.

Unfortunately Hilary had lost Graham's telephone number and had thought herself too busy to go to the trouble of writing to him to advise that she understood Dave to have dropped the whole idea of changing the Beggars Way name, which would have eased Graham's mind considerably.

Graham's worrying was heightening as the next council meeting approached. To get him out of her hair on Friday morning, after a breakfast ruined in her eyes by his chuntering on about the Grants and the whole affair, Laura sent Graham off to the council offices, to find out whether there was any news. As this was the first constructive comment Laura had made on the issue, Graham found it hard to refuse.

Hilary was busy and not in a good mood. Her rift with Brian was still in effect, and contrary to her expectation and half-wish Dave

Grant had not been in touch. Brian had not come through with any proposal to boost her salary in view of the extra work she was facing, and she no longer had any interest in the Beggars Way affair. She thought it was settled. So when Graham appeared at the office asking for an update on the Council's position, she told him rather bluntly there was none.

'You will have to wait until Monday. I can't possibly predict how the Council will vote on the new policy regarding name changes.'

'But I understood....'

'I told you from the start I don't make the decisions.'

'I didn't mean that. I was going to say, firstly, can you confirm that Cypress Avenue is now definitely a non-starter?'

'Certainly. I would have thought that was clear.'

'But that doesn't rule out changing the name to something else?'

'That would depend on any new application received. And whether it fitted the new policy. Whatever that might be.'

'So Grant and his supporters could still try and get the name changed?'

Hilary was a little surprised she should be asked the question. Surely David Grant had meant what he said about giving the idea up? If so, why hadn't he informed his neighbours?

'I think it highly unlikely. But I can only suggest you contact Mr Grant to confirm that. If I can't predict what the Council may say I certainly can't answer for the town's population. Now if you will excuse me I have some work to do.'

Hilary's expression hardened. She opened her drawer and for effect removed a sheaf of A4 papers and placed it on her desk. Graham could not understand this frosty reception. 'Time of the month maybe', crossed Graham's mind, charitably in his own mind, sexist maybe others would think. He turned and left.

Graham's account of his unproductive meeting with Hilary elicited little sympathy from Laura when he returned home. 'Well you'd better do as she says and talk to Dave Grant directly, hadn't you?' was all she had to say.

'I'm not going cap in hand to that man,' Graham told Laura, who tutted.

'Just don't expect me to collect your repeat prescription for your blood pressure pills next time, is all I can say,' Laura told him before switching on the vacuum cleaner and terminating the conversation.

The morning of Roselake's day of reckoning finally dawned. Hilary arrived to open up the council office to find a couple of thickset shaven-headed men waiting for her. She reached in her handbag and instead of pulling out the keys put her hand on a small canister.

'I should warn you, I have a personal defence spray in my bag and am not afraid to use it,' Hilary told the two.

'Good for you,' Mike Holmans, the Mastiffs' loose head prop forward said with a grin.

'He likes a spunky woman,' Luke Ashford, the scrum half, advised Hilary with an even wider grin.

'We've been waiting for you,' Mike told her.

Hilary realised maybe she had misunderstood the pair's intention, now she saw them smiling.

'That's rather what I was afraid of,' she said, attempting a smile herself.

'Like it,' Mike said. 'But you watch too much television crime drama. We've got something for you in the car.'

'Oh?'

'Yes, we'll get them.' Mike and Luke popped round the corner. Hilary fumbled for her keys, her nerves only now recovering from her moment of fear, and opened up the office door.

Mike and Luke followed her in, carrying a couple of large cardboard boxes.

'Petition,' Mike explained. 'We got cracking this last weekend and have got shedloads of support. Over thirteen hundred signatures. Not that I've counted them myself, mind.'

'Ah, the petition.' Light dawned. Hilary was surprised at the number, though. She opened the first box and read the top sheet. "Keep the Green Green".

'That's right,' Mike said. That's what we want and that's what we'll get.'

'Well I'll certainly pass this on to the Council before tonight's meeting. They are discussing the matter, you know.'

'We know,' Mike said. 'You don't think we'd have spent all those hours on a cold windy High Street wasting good boozing time if we didn't know, do you?'

'Indeed not, Mr...?'

'Holman. Front row.'

'Front row?'

'Ah I see you're not a fan. Never mind.'

'Didn't this used to be the sex shop?' Luke asked, his eyes roaming round in search of any relics from that era.

'Correct,' Hilary replied. 'But not any more, thank goodness.'

'Goodness had nothing to do with it,' Luke said, attempting a Mae West impression. 'Isn't that what they say? Not that I ever patronised the place. I can only imagine what was sold here.'

'Because your wife told you,' Mike said teasingly.

'Bollocks,' Luke replied. 'Wives of scrum halves don't need any help with their sex lives. Not like you pansy forwards.'

'Gentlemen, I appreciate your coming, and your amusing banter, but I have work to do.'

'Any time you want to meet the lads, just give me a call,' Luke said, after his eyes had given Hilary a quick up-and-down.

Brian had been correct, the evening's meeting had attracted a good crowd. So good, in fact, that it was standing room only. He was pleased to see little evidence of rival placards or banners. In fact before the start of the meeting there was no display of placards of any kind. Maybe his commissioning the presence of Julie Woodman, the Community Support Officer, and Gloria Paynton, had been overkill. Town Crier Barry had refused to come, making the excuse that he was still suffering from the after effects of his last attendance. Brian spotted a few players he knew from the Rugby Club, which was reassuring, the lads being of course virtuous and upright pillars of the community, except for the rare transgression, and no doubt their presence would impose anyway a certain reluctance to indulge in an affray.

At the allotted time Brian banged his gavel and drew the meeting to order. Gloria offered prayers. She had spent many hours wondering whether she would make any reference to recent events which had interrupted council proceedings, or to the burning down of the Senior Citizens' Centre, but her heartache and seeking of divine guidance had been ended by Brian who in response to her enquiry on the matter told her bluntly to keep it short and sweet.

Short and sweet too was Hilary's race through the usual opening business, apologies from missing councillors, of which she announced none (the late member was in no position to offer them), and declarations of interest, which attracted a quartet of non-pecuniary interests from members of the Community Complex Association, Rugby Club and Hockey Club.

The minutes of the last meeting were passed without comment, unsurprising in view of the business transacted, or lack thereof. The mayor's announcements were reduced to reference to the minutes of the Emergency Committee. 'This has not been a period of mayoral social engagements,' Brian said to explain the lack of any other detail of his activities.

The item of reports from County and District Councillors was always on the agenda, but as always Hilary said 'None received.'

Frank Parton stood to object to this, saying how scandalous it was, given the last item on tonight's agenda which critically involved the District Council, that none of the three representatives had shown their face. Frank was, of course, making the point because of his perpetually thwarted attempts to achieve district councillor status. He lived in hope that one day his ambition would be realised. 'Hell will freeze over first' was a comment that had been heard more than once when Frank's electoral chances were discussed by others. Brian dismissed Frank with 'Noted' and asked Hilary to move on to the first main item of the agenda, adopting the Council's policy on street naming.

'Councillors, you have had the recommendations before you for some time now so I won't waste time spelling out the detail. For the public's benefit,' Hilary looked at the gallery and smiled ingratiatingly, 'the policy is to give priority to maintaining traditional and historic names unless there are exceptional circumstances. If names are changed, those requesting the name change will pay the full administrative and other costs of both this council and the district council. I only have to add that I am now advised that the requests for name changes for Beggars Way, Butts Close and Isis Close have been retracted and there are therefore no current requests before you.'

Brian was distracted for a moment by a display of audience enthusiasm. Two gentlemen of the public, a little past their prime, stood, raised and waved their fists in the air in triumph. A high-five followed. The motions may not have been included in Graham and Lawrence's normal body language repertoire, but were adequately performed and wouldn't have disgraced football supporters appreciating a goal. The pair sat down again.

'I move from the chair that we agree the policy as drafted,' Brian said, with deadpan expression.

'Seconded, Mr Mayor,' Paul Hart said.

'All agreed?' Brian asked.

Judy Harker stood up. 'Just one moment, Mr Mayor. I would like councillors to consider the implications of the policy regarding paying for the change of any name. Implications for local democracy.'

'Go on,' Brian said, inwardly groaning.

'It seems to me entirely unreasonable that under this policy residents should be asked to vote for or against the change of name of their street, when they know if they vote a certain way they will suffer a financial penalty. This is not only unfair, it undermines the democratic process.' Judy sat.

Hilary spoke up. 'May I remind councillors that the alternative, in view of the costs, is what is imposed at the moment under the District Council rules. Namely that every single person in the street would contribute towards the name change costs, whether they opposed the change or whether they agreed with it. The only other course would be for this Council to bear the full cost itself.'

Derek Hunt stood. 'There you have it, Mr Mayor. Unfair? Sounds damn unfair to me for people who don't want something to have to pay for it. That is what unfair means to me, Councillor Harker,' he said, turning to Judy.

'And can I add that if Councillor Harker thinks this Council can afford to pay out hundreds if not thousands of pounds to change street names on a whim, she had better start putting some work into understanding this council's finances. And understanding that democracy doesn't mean all the Town's ratepayers should have to cough up for snooty people to give their streets fancy names. I support the motion.' Derek sat down.

Judy blushed at this.

'Do you wish to come back?' Brian said to Judy, to rub in her embarrassment. Judy shook her head, although she would have liked to remind the old campaigner that rates were replaced by council tax years ago.

'I'm sorry I didn't hear that,' Brian said, rather unkindly, to increase Judy's discomfiture.

'No, thank you, Mr Mayor.'

'Good. In that case it has been proposed and seconded that the policy as drafted be adopted. All in favour?'

A chorus of "Aye"s went round the table.

'Any against?' No reply.

'One down, the big one to come,' thought Brian.

'That's passed then, nem con," he announced.

The pair who had distracted him earlier did so again, but this time by standing and making for the door. Graham and Lawrence had something to celebrate, and it would be only fair to draw a veil over the state of inebriation they were in when their celebration was over, and their acrimonious homecomings, when they were received with the questioning but not the joy of the wife of a returning Odysseus.

Brian's big victory was, he hoped, at hand, but still to come. 'Now for the next agenda item. The recommendation before us is to commission the construction of the new community complex. Ms Jessop.'

'Nothing to add to the report, Mr Mayor. Except to remind councillors and members of the public that to proceed with the construction of the complex would be entirely in keeping with previously agreed council policy.'

Brian smiled. Hilary was not straying from her brief. He wondered whether he should try harder to heal the rift between them.

Brian called Paul Hart to speak.

'I have little to add to the report either, Mr Mayor. Except to say that a couple of minor planning issues that were raised the last time this was discussed have been sorted out with the district planning officers and county highways officers, and I can assure councillors that there are no outstanding planning issues whatsoever. You have the financial details, which are up-to-date. I also realise that any delay at this stage may undermine our attempts to block any attempt to move the complex site at this late stage. I am aware that this related issue has been raised and placed on the agenda for the next and final item, but I want to express my personal conviction that we should act now. If we say yes tonight we can have the diggers on-site within a month. I move we adopt the resolution as printed.'

Paul's speech was the prompt for unfurling of banners and the holding up of a large number of placards. With minor variations, the message was clear – "No Building on the Green".

Brian looked at Hilary. This was going entirely according to plan. She delivered the rehearsed speech.

'Mr Mayor. Since the issue of building on the green has come up now, I will also mention this. You may have seen press reports that there seem to be plans in embryonic stage to not only build houses on the Green but relocate the new complex to this area. This might be an appropriate time to confirm that the council received this morning a large petition from people who want to preserve Roselake Green. I have, of course, not been able to perform a complete audit, but I have checked as much as I could in the time available. I have to say it appears that over one thousand three hundred residents of Roselake have signed the petition. I can also say that according to my records this is the clearest and largest expression of public opinion ever expressed in Roselake, outside election time, of course.'

With a dramatic hand gesture Hilary signalled an assistant who slipped into the kitchen and re-emerged carrying a pile of petition forms. Hilary had commandeered the Carnival Princess for the task. For the next two minutes Andrea Carpenter walked backwards and forwards to and from the kitchen area, each time reappearing with a new large sheaf of papers. Finally she stood with folded arms and received a huge round of applause from the public gallery, partly because her arm folding had exaggerated her cleavage on show. The pile of papers on the table behind the mayor was indeed impressive, even if some of the piles were not petition forms but blank A4 paper to pad out the piles for appearance's sake. Brian and Hilary had spent a long time today opening reams of printer paper and dishevelling it.

The only ones who suspected the subterfuge were Mike Holman and Luke Ashford. They might have suffered a little ear damage over their rugby years, but their brains were intact. They looked at each other and raised eyebrows. 'Don't say it,' counselled Mike. 'Works in our favour, right?'

Brian was on a roll. 'You've heard from Councillor Hart that the planning route is clear. It's green light for go. The finance is in place. And if we do this today we will send a clear message about Roselake Green.' A cheer rose from the audience.

'Have we a seconder for the motion as proposed, that we proceed immediately to contract the building of the community complex?'

The public display had its effect. Three hands were raised, giving Brian a choice. He chose Peter. 'Councillor Galway has seconded the motion. Are we ready to move to a vote?'

There is of course always one. In fact on this occasion there were two. As Brian had expected, Derek Hunt rose to speak.

'Mr Mayor, may I say I think this is being pushed through with undue haste. I am still concerned about the potential future financial liability.'

'Councillor Hunt, I will remind you that this issue has been before the town for nearly twenty years. The current plans have emerged over the last three years of consultation. Much money and time has been spent on getting consultants' reports, getting designs drawn up, and negotiating funding. Tonight's documents have been in front of councillors, who have had the opportunity outside the council meetings to seek clarification or make suggestions, for the last six weeks. I can not accept that this is haste. The only pressure on this council is that we now have no town hall. The best way to resolve that is by getting the complex built and moving in as soon as possible. And I'll remind you that the public loan board interest rates we can fix if we do this today are the lowest ever. This is the best deal the town will ever get. If you want to stand in the way of the town's progress, and don't care about its future, I can only suggest you step aside and let those who do get on with it. Let's get started on building a facility which we and our children can be proud of. Future generations will be the ones to benefit most. They will thank us for our determination and vision. But only if we take our courage in our hands and vote for Roselake's future today.'

Carried away by this rare example of speechifying, the audience gave an appreciative roar. Even Gloria was inclined to join in the applause, only failing to clap because she thought it inappropriate to be seen to be taking a view. She looked up to the roof and wondered if God had finally responded to her prayers.

Derek Hunt realised he was defeated and sat down.

It was left to Frank Parton to utter the last gasp of the sceptics.

'May I request a recorded vote, Mr Mayor?'

'I see no problem with that. History will look back at this day and remember those who have been instrumental in making Roselake a better place. And voters at the next elections may remember those who have stood in the way of progress. Agreed?'

A further round of audience applause was followed by a chorus of ayes from the councillors.

'So let's move on to the vote. All those in favour of the motion, to proceed immediately with commissioning the complex?'

Hilary surveyed the raised hands. It was going to be easier to count and record any dissenting votes.

'Any against?' No hands were raised.

'Any abstentions?' Brian asked, his heart at ease.

Frank Parton, having recognised defeat, raised his hand. Boos came from the audience.

'They had him sussed,' Donald Ridgeway said to his habitual neighbour Ken Baker, who, surprisingly and unusually, had remained awake during the proceedings. 'Bloody LibDems. Never could make up their mind about anything.'

In his excitement about one of his major ambitions being realised, Brian was on the point of pounding his gavel to close the meeting when a nudge from Hilary reminded him that there was still another item on the agenda. The one which had brought him the public gallery who, innocent of the knowledge that they were part of Brian's plan, had dominated the night's events and quashed Brian's opposition. The public which had brought him the gift of the community complex and the prospect of an extremely fat bank account.

It was left to Hilary to introduce the item, which she did, according to the agreed script.

'The Mayor requested that I place this item on the agenda because of press speculation that there is a plan to build on Roselake Green, and that this scheme involves relocating the rugby and hockey clubs and displacing them from the grounds they have enjoyed leases on for decades.'

Hilary paused for effect. This announcement was met by a silence. Largely because the gallery could not decide whether to applaud or boo.

'I have to advise councillors,' Hilary continued. 'that my inquiries have revealed that no such proposal is part of District Council policy. Your Mayor has also been active on the issue. I have been advised by officers that there are no such recommendations made by them to the district councillors, and nothing related to this scenario has been discussed at portfolio holder level nor is scheduled for discussion. But since the question has been brought up in public the Mayor is in my view right in including it on tonight's agenda so that the Town Council can make its opinion known.'

Having achieved his ambition for the evening, and mindful naturally of the public interest, Brian was willing to let the discussion meander. His smile and nodding during Hilary's introduction had already conveyed the information that if there had been any plan for the Green, his own intervention had squashed it, or at least put it on hold.

'Yes, Councillor Hunt.'

'With the utmost respect to Ms Jessop, to the District Council and to the Roselake representatives on the District Council who are not with us tonight, I have to say I don't trust a word that a District Council officer has said on this matter. Everybody knows that the officers toe the Tory line. They just parrot Tory policy.'

Derek was a little surprised that his statement received loud boos from the audience. He had thought to have a clear run, but his speech-planning skills were faulty, despite his years of experience, and he had wrong-footed himself. He was aiming to back the preservation of the Green, but in his haste to first take a Don Quixote political tilt he had failed to take into account the natural party political home of the most significant sector of his audience - the Rugby Club. Brian made no effort to stifle the public outcry.

'If I may continue, Mr Mayor,' Derek said.

'Please do,' said Brian to Derek. 'And go hang yourself,' he thought.

Derek proceeded to form a noose. His rant continued to upset the public, and by the time he reached the statement of support for preserving the Green his audience was uncharitable enough to boo him again when he finally sat.

It would be tedious to relate in their entirety the speeches of the other councillors, most of whom wished to speak merely in order to ingratiate themselves with the largest public audience a town council meeting had ever witnessed. Judy Harker of course concentrated on Roselake Green being vital lungs for the town, and how important it was to the environment to have plants and trees combating global warming.

'She must need glasses,' Don Ridgeway said as a not very quiet aside to Ken Baker, 'if she can't tell the bloody difference between a goalpost and a tree.'

Brian, who might in normal situations have banged his gavel and chided Donald, sat back relaxed and content. He even let Frank

Parton ramble on. And on. And on. It was of course expected that Frank would have delivered a lecture on the history of Roselake Green, from the Middle Ages through to modern times, with a meander or two on the way. He announced he would now give a potted history of the Rugby Club and its occupation of the Green. It was, however, a member of the Rugby Club who shouted out to Frank to can it, not pot it, enough already, to a chorus of 'hear, hear's and applause. Brian banged his gavel happily and suggested to Frank that he had made his point.

Less expected was the fact that Ken Baker signalled his intention to speak. This was almost unheard of in over twenty years of council business.

'Mr Mayor. My father founded the Rugby Club before Councillor Parton was born. I played on those hallowed fields while Councillor Parton was still waving his rattle in his pram. Some of us know how important the Club and the Green have been to Roselake. From personal experience, not by reading history books.' Ken sat down.

'Precise and to the point, Councillor Baker. An object lesson to us all,' Brian said, with a stern look in Frank's direction.

'Now is anyone else wishing to speak? Yes, Councillor Threlfall.'

'Mr Mayor, what I wanted to say has already been said, but I want to reinforce the point that...'

'If it's already been said why say it again?' Don grumbled.

'To continue,' Charles Threlfall continued. 'Almost without exception – and Councillor Hunt rambled on so much I wasn't clear what point he was making, since he seemed to have one leg over the financial side of the fence and the other on the grass - it seems we councillors here tonight opposed any building on the Green. I would remind councillors of the lateness of the hour and suggest that the public, like ourselves, have homes to go to...'

'And pubs,' Don interrupted, to a discreet round of clapping from the audience.

'Right,' Brian said. 'I take the point.'

'But I haven't finished,' Charles complained.

'I think you have,' Brian said. 'From the chair I move that this council writes to the District Council informing them that we oppose any plan to relocate the Rugby Club, we…'

'What about us?' came an anguished cry from a lady in the audience, Grace Farrow, captain of the ladies hockey team. She introduced herself by waving a hockey stick.

'Apologies. Yes, we oppose any relocation of the Rugby Club or the Hockey Club, we suggest the District Council consider making the clubs' leases in perpetuity…'

Brian halted for effect and applause, and was granted his wish.

'And this council opposes any building on Roselake Green, except for the provision of a new replacement clubhouse for the Rugby club. And,' Brian said, raising his voice to prevent any further waving of hockey sticks, for separate – and I stress separate – changing rooms and other facilities for the ladies hockey club.' The latter drew more applause and not a little laughter.

'I so move,' Brian said, delivering his last line with satisfaction.

'Seconded,' Paul Hart barked.

'Right then. No request for a recorded vote, Mr Parton? For the historical record?'

Frank shook his head in irritation.

'All those in favour?' Hands were raised. 'That looks unanimous to me,' Brian announced, to a roar of whoops and clapping. 'Thank you councillors. And may I thank the public for being an attentive audience. I hope to see many of you here again.'

Brian turned to Gloria, who had been sitting quietly. She would be the first to admit that she had found the evening rather entertaining.

'Thank you vicar. You must have used a double-strength prayer on our behalf tonight.'

Julie Woodman pulled out her police radio and called base. She reported all well and was given confirmation by the officer in charge that she was now off-duty. She smiled. She would ditch her bowler, cravat, radio and tunic in the car and join the rugby club lads for a celebration. A couple of them had taken her fancy, and she wouldn't have said no to either of them. Or both.

Brian spent some time after the meeting receiving sundry congratulations and thanks, and giving a short interview to Anna. He made the effort to thank Hilary for an excellent job, and whispered to her that with all the extra work the fire and relocation would involve, he considered a generous raise of salary was in order. Hilary was still unsure how to tackle her personal relationship with Brian. She restricted herself to expressing her gratitude by saying 'Thank you. Yes that did go rather well.' She did not expand on how she had thought the evening a great success, after all when you know how the magician has performed his tricks, there is less reason to gush enthusiasm.

CHAPTER 16

The next morning Graham was late rising. Laura had brought him a tea in bed, but they didn't exchange words until Graham presented himself at the breakfast table. He nodded gently when Laura asked if he wanted a coffee.

'How's your head this morning?' Laura asked, no inflexion of genuine concern in her voice. She pushed a button on the espresso machine, filled a cup and took it to the kitchen table.

'Fine,' Graham lied.

'Well I expect it will be even finer if you take a couple of paracetomol. Would you like egg and bacon? I got some nice beef sausages.'

Graham's stomach lurched. 'Not at the moment, thanks, I'll just have a glass of orange juice.'

'Well you know where it is.'

'Who was that on the phone?'

'Pat. She asked if I wanted to go shopping with her in Exeter this morning. I said yes.'

'You mean Pat Stone?'

'Yes. Of course.'

'I didn't know you were, er, friends like that.'

'Well maybe we weren't but we are today. We're going to buy some new clothes.'

'But you don't…'

'Oh yes I do. I need a treat after these last weeks with you with your head stuck up your rear about this Beggars Way business. Now it's over I'm going to celebrate.'

'By buying clothes?'

'That's what women do, Graham,' Laura sighed. 'You should know by now, a man of the world like you.'

'What about my breakfast?'

'You said you didn't want any.'

'Well I might do.'

'Well if you do you know where things are. You've lived in this house long enough. Oh,' Laura added, 'There's a list of things we need from the shops here. Perhaps you could get them. A bit of fresh air might do you some good. Talking of fresh air the garden has been suffering from neglect in the last few weeks. Now you haven't your campaigning to worry about maybe you could give a little thought to that. The grass needs cutting and the shrubs need pruning for a start.'

There was a rap at the door. Laura looked at her watch. 'That'll be Pat. I must go.'

Graham drank his coffee and mused. Maybe victory was not always as sweet as the victor expected. Once Pat and Laura were gone maybe he would compare notes with Lawrence. Maybe they could amble down the road to the Carvery for the hair of the dog.

Graham heard the front door opening, a couple of words spoken, and a short peal of laughter. Laura returned to the kitchen, gave Graham a thin smile and kissed the top of his head. 'And do go over today to thank that Mr Grant for being gracious enough to withdraw his application. I do not want to spend the rest of the year avoiding looking in his direction, or his wife's, if we meet.'

Graham groaned. 'Yes dear.'

Two days after the Roselake Town Council meeting, Brian was again summoned to meet Stuart Parkinson. To his surprise, the invitation was not to meet at the District Council offices but at the Fox and Hounds. He also wondered why Donald Cresswell was again sitting in on their meeting.

'Nice one, Brian,' was Stuart's opening remark, after the three had settled themselves at a table out of earshot of at the bar and any other customers. 'A good result.'

'Not too embarrassing for you, I hope, Stuart,' Brian asked, rather fearing the answer was yes, and this was what had brought about the meeting.

'Not at all, Brian,' Stuart replied, smiling. 'If old campaigners like us can't cope with ticklish questions from a junior reporter who can?'

'Not Keith Eastham, obviously,' Brian said.

Keith had been caught on the hop when contacted by Anna Shales asking for a quote on the Roselake Green issue. He had been out of town and not been in a position to respond to calls from his co-councillor Tony Goodman and an irate Jack Gray. In his ignorance of context he had made the mistake of misunderstanding the whole situation and praised to the roof the plan to give the Rugby Club a new home and put some money into the Council coffers. Through ignorance Keith had made himself Roselake's Enemy Number One.

'No,' Stuart agreed. 'I have a feeling his days as a District Councillor are numbered. There could be a way back in for you Brian. Very very soon, if I exert a bit of pressure. Which of course I will.'

Things were looking up for Brian. Getting back on to the District Council was an idea that had been lurking in his brain for a couple of years now. If he had Stuart's support he could reactivate the ambition at the drop of a hat.

'I'll drink to that,' Donald chirped up. 'It'd be like old times.' He raised his glass. He, Stuart and Brian clinked their glasses together.

'That rash of vandalism's been more than a bit of a nuisance for us,' Stuart said, changing the subject. 'Pity it had to break out in Roselake.'

'Oh,' thought Brian. 'Here comes the catch.' But he was wrong.

'However,' Stuart continued, 'when I looked at the stats it seemed Roselake went quiet after the first couple of sign defacements. The majority of offences took place in Exebury, Bradmouth and, I'm sorry to say, Rosebridge.'

'Maybe it's just that there were fewer opportunities in Roselake for perverting the real names,' Brian offered, smiling, knowing this probably wasn't the case, as he himself had spent some time perusing the town map and exercising a juvenile invention.

'The imagination of the dirty mind is boundless,' Donald commented. He thought he had once read that somewhere but could not think of the quote's origin.

'Be that as it may,' Stuart resumed. 'it hasn't turned out too badly. Of course the police have come in for some stick. On the other hand it's increased the pressure on our local MP to try and get something done about the funding deficit, and decreased the pressure on the superintendents to cut feet-on-street budgets, so George Broughty for one is happy. The police helicopter crew got some real-life town night-time flying training, and the trials of the infra red camera to find the hotspots of cannabis growing resulted in two big drug busts which will improve the area's crime detection rates. So overall no-one has nose out of joint except for us, the District Council, who will have to foot the bill for replacement signs.'

Brian pulled a face of sympathy.

'On the other hand,' Stuart resumed his speech after another sip of Crowsfoot, 'it suits my, er, our plans, down to the ground. The councillors from the other towns can't now go holier-than-thou and point to decadent and unruly Roselake. And the rural reps will be easy to manage. The officers of the senior management team are on board, of course. There's a good officer package on offer for relocation.'

'In other words you think it's pretty-well buttoned up, now?' asked Donald.

'I think this evening we'll get a result,' Stuart nodded. 'We'll know at the pre-meeting, of course, if there's any opposition to be ironed out, but I can't see anyone objecting now.'

'Except for the Rosebridge residents who will lose parkland.'

'Plenty of that about,' Stuart said dismissively. 'Don't worry about the public. Maybe we can take a leaf out of Brian's book and get it falling beneath their radar by inventing a threat.'

'But isn't the loss of recreational area a threat?' Donald wasn't convinced.

'We have to produce a bigger threat. What's worse than losing a bit of green grass?' Stuart asked.

'Beats me.' Donald said.

'Losing money?' Brian offered.

'Exactly, Brian. We'll think of some expensive scheme, maybe a multimillion plan to rebuild the sea defences against the threat of global warming, something like that. That will concentrate minds very well.'

'Wouldn't that be a good plan anyway?' Donald asked.

'Maybe. Good idea. Lots of money for some to be made out of multimillion schemes paid for out of the public purse. Talking of which, I wanted to speak to you this morning about the prospects from the District Council offices relocation. I am assuming you two have already done some preparatory thinking?'

'About?' Brian asked.

'Come on, Brian, I know you too well, remember? I mean do you have a plan to, shall we say, maximise the benefits of the scheme?'

'You mean to Roselake?' Brian played dumb.

'I mean to you. Or shall I say us. Let's stop beating about the bush. You two organise the detail, get your people in place to put in bids for contracts and the rest. I, for my part,will make sure this gets pushed through the Council without hindrance. In return, of course, I get my cut. A good cut. Agreed?'

Brian and Donald looked at each other. They knew they had little option. They both nodded. The trio clinked glasses once more.

At their next formal meeting, the District Council's Cabinet approved the plan to relocate to Roselake, with no members of the majority party breaking ranks. The minority party members went along with the plan, once again demonstrating their inability to provide any genuine opposition. A couple of Independents voted against, mainly with a view to improving their personal profiles in advance of the next elections.

The news broke in the evening and morning dailies, and Brian featured prominently, as agreed with Stuart, in the reports, welcoming a significant new opportunity for Roselake.

Keith Eastham's resignation (on grounds of ill health, or fears of them if he remained in Roselake) went largely unnoticed, except by those who regularly scanned the Town Council noticeboard which served the electoral department by advertising a vacancy for a new district council representative for St Andrews Ward.

Hilary saw the new spring in Brian's step and without knowing that Brian would be welcomed back into the District fold, and being still estranged from his affections, as he from hers, guessed he'd made progress in his ambitions. He had emerged as the town hero in that week's Midweek Gazette, with a picture of a smiling mayor below a frontpage headline "Roselake's Rosy Future". No doubt this was instrumental in causing her to reassess her future. Regaining Brian's affection, which would only require a small sacrifice on her part, namely eating a slice of humble pie, and providing an evening of hot sex, which was no sacrifice at all, really, was perhaps a more sensible course of action, more appropriate to her circumstances than embarking on an adventure with Dave. Brian now stood to make significant gain in finance as well as kudos. Brian had also behaved very nicely to her in the last couple of weeks, even though she suspected this was cupboard love. But then Dave was, after all, rather common, even if he were to prove able between the sheets.

Brian received many congratulations in the street. But on Friday he was accosted by a face which wasn't smiling. Father Patrick looked worried.

'Ah Mr Mayor,' he said. 'I'm glad I've bumped into you. I have a matter to discuss.'

'Fire away, Father, I have a little time.'

Father Patrick looked around at the pavement passers-by. 'It's a little delicate. A little personal.'

'No problem,' said Brian. 'Why don't I buy you a cup of coffee or tea at the Tea Room.'

'The wine bar is a little closer,' Father Patrick suggested.

'The wine bar it shall be,' agreed Brian.

Father Patrick was clearly no stranger to the wine bar, or its owner, Marcella. This was apparent when Marcella saw him, did a small duck down behind the bar which Brian interpreted as a possible curtsy, and asked if he would have his usual. Father Patrick said yes.

'And Brian, it has been so long,' Marcella purred. You never came here any more after you...'

What she prevented herself from saying in Father Patrick's presence was that Brian stopped frequenting the wine bar after he started his relationship with Hilary. That liaison might have escaped the notice of the town, but not of a mature dark-haired Italian woman well-versed in affairs of the heart who had thrown her cap at Brian and failed.

Brian shrugged. 'You know how it is, busy busy busy.'

Marcella shrugged in reply, wondering in just what activity Brian was claiming to have been busy.

'What car do you drive now?' Marcella asked Brian.

'A Porsche,' Brian said.

'Ah, the same Porsche,' Marcella said. 'Such a beautiful colour. I never did get a ride in it.'

Marcella liked fast cars.

'Actually I have a new one,' Brian said.

'I expect it too is a beautiful colour. Maybe you should offer me a ride in your new car. If you let me know the colour in advance I will coordinate my outfit. I so think dresses and cars shouldn't clash, don't you?'

Brian knew that although the last was in jest, Marcella was no doubt serious about having a ride in his car. For a moment he pictured her in a low-cut short emerald green dress bending down to slip into the passenger seat as he held the door open, then moving her legs, which were undoubtedly two of the most shapely that Brian had seen, over into the car as he closed the door.

'Will you have a corretto also?' Marcella asked Brian, disturbing his fantasy.

'A corretto?' Brian queried, surprised, his mind still on the Porsche, and his ear having picked up Carrera.

'Coffee with a nice shot of cognac.'

'Oh, I see, no thanks, just a black coffee for me, please.'

'Ah, you have not picked up the Italian habits, like the Padre here,' Marcella bubbled. 'He has spent much time in Rome on his holy missions. An Americano it shall be for you Brian.'

Brian pulled his wallet out and looked at Marcella with a questioning glance.

'Niente, caro,' Marcella said. 'We don't charge the clergy. Our clergy,' the emphasis on the our probably indicating that Gloria Paynton or the Methodist pastor would have had to reach for their wallets, receiving no dispensation. 'And yours is free too. In exchange for a ride in your Porsche, of course.'

'Sounds a deal,' Brian said, not having yet recovered from his mind wanderings.

'Good,' Marcella said, smiling and waving her finger. 'I'll keep you to your promise. I'll bring the coffees over to your table. Why don't you take the window seat?'

Brian and Father Patrick did just that. And after a minute or two Marcella brought over their drinks. Depositing them on the table required Marcella to bend down, causing both men to gulp. Marcella was an attractive woman, who was making the most of her years as a ripe beauty before any serious decline started. She had been watching Brian astutely out of the corner of her eye, and wondered what had happened to Hilary, if his interest in Marcella could be visibly rekindled so easily. She would make another play for Brian. And this time she would not fail.

Father Patrick lost no time downing his corretto. 'A good woman, Marcella,' he said, licking his lips. 'A great heart. A generous heart.'

'Er yes,' Brian said, not knowing how to interpret this. Surely Father Patrick was not referring to other parts of her body in close proximity to her heart? His embarrassment showed in his face.

Father Patrick saw the reddening and wondered if he had inadvertently put his foot in it. 'You haven't, er, aren't....' he asked.

'No no, of course not,' Brian blustered.

'Well if you do, no doubt I'll hear of it in confession,' Father Patrick said, smiling in confirmation that this was his little joke.

Brian wondered if he ought to offer the priest another corretto. He decided no. It was true Brian was not entirely familiar with Italian ways. A week on the pistes of the Dolomites hardly qualified him as an expert in Italian social graces. But he had had time to notice that drinking an espresso was never a prolonged affair and certainly didn't signify thirst.

'So, Father, you have a delicate matter to discuss?' he asked instead.

'Yes. Talking of confessions, it's rather along those lines.'

Brian, not being a Catholic, assumed Father Patrick did not mean him.

'Whose confession, surely not yours?'

'Sadly, yes.'

'And what is the sin?' Brian was almost tempted to add 'my son', as although having no personal knowledge of Catholic goings-on inside the confessional this seemed to be a normal add-on conversational line from the films he'd seen.

'I think out of the choices available I have to choose first procrastination. The fact is I have known about something for a couple of days now and have been summoning up courage to discuss it with you.'

'With me?' Brian asked in puzzlement. 'And you have choices of sins?'

'Whether mea culpa extends to more than procrastination rather depends on the answer to this question. Do you still have that statuette, that figurine of Christ that I gave you, or rather gave the Town Council?'

'No, I'm afraid not,' Brian replied. 'Unfortunately it was destroyed in the fire.'

'Ah,' was Father Patrick's rather uninformative reply.

'You are disappointed?'

'No, it is rather as I feared. Let me come to the point. That statuette was one of a number I purchased during my last trip to the Vatican. Two days ago I received a notification from the Vatican gift department - I am on their website mailing list - that they were withdrawing the particular item in question from sale, and advised purchasers to return any items they had purchased for a full refund. Unfortunately a few samples of the articles had proved to be defective. Some problem at the Korean factory.'

Brian groaned. He knew what was to come. And his mind strayed back to the night after the Council meeting two weeks ago when he had rather lost control of his senses for a while because of the union with Anna. The events flashed through his mind. He had turned Jesus on. Jesus had turned Anna on. Brian had switched the room light off, and at conclusion of the proceedings had turned the room light back on in order to rescue the bottles which had gone flying off the mayor's desk, fortunately landing safely, if empty, on the carpet. After the required dress adjustment and social niceties, Brian had escorted Anna out of the office, turning off the room lights at the switch by the door. He remembered admiring Anna's rear as she walked away and he closed the office door absentmindedly behind him. Brian now knew for certain he had not turned off the Jesus statuette.

He had hardly heard Father Patrick explaining the reported electrical defect in the holy souvenirs. But now he heard the priest's conclusion.

'So there it is. You leave it on for an extended period, it overheats, and…' Father Patrick, his hands having earlier adopted a praying position, now flew apart.

'Pooff!' Brian suggested.

'Exactly. So now I have to ask the difficult question. Have I played my part, albeit unwittingly, in the burning down of the Senior Citizens' Centre?'

Brian was not used to facing moral dilemmas, as his own ideas on morality were extremely flexible. But Father Patrick was clearly so distraught at the prospect of having burnt the centre down that Brian could not admit the link, especially since Brian's culpability was immeasurably greater. And there was a truth to ease a troubled mind.

'No, Father,' Brian said. 'I am sure you needn't reproach yourself at all. This has nothing to do with the fire. Burnt-out old wiring was blamed for starting the blaze. Possibly kitchen equipment blowing a fuse.'

'Oh, that's a relief,' Father Patrick said, drawing himself up in his chair as his self-respect returned. 'You *are* sure?'

'Absolutely. I can show you the fire investigation report if you doubt me. If anyone is to blame it's me for storing gifts of spirits from our friends across the Channel, our twin towns. Fed the blaze, unfortunately.'

261

'Ah,' Father Patrick said, his mind easing. 'We had a similar incident at St Walfrid's soon after I was ordained. We lost the church hall in almost identical circumstances.'

Brian did not ask why St Walfrid's found it necessary to store quantities of spirits. Whether he would have received an honest answer from Father Patrick we shall never know. The new incumbent at the church had inherited a legacy of kind and custom from his predecessor, who was driven to improvisation during the war years, bending a little the rules of a directive of the Congregation of the Inquisition on the addition of wine spirit to fermenting grape must.

'In any event,' Brian continued. 'Look at things this way. No-one was hurt in the fire. Only the insurance company will suffer.'

'And insurance companies have no souls,' Father Patrick said, reminded again of his experience at St Walfrid's.

'Exactly. But look at all the good that has come out of it. The senior citizens will have a cracking new centre built with modern facilities, proper wheelchair access at last and disabled toilets. Plus they will have medical services on-hand so they don't always have to get a taxi to get up the hill to the medical centre.'

Brian paused for effect, to let the benefits sink in. He was already persuading himself, too.

'On top of that, Roselake will have a new theatre, entertainment and social complex that the town will be proud of, to take us through the next decades. That project would likely have failed if not for the fire. And equally good for the town, if the District Council relocates its offices the town will have more jobs, plus more business for the town centre. I'll spare you the detail, but that, too, might not have happened if not for the events of a fortnight ago.'

After this speech Father Patrick was now convinced that the statuette did have some involvement in the fire, but equally he was convinced that Brian would not reveal all. Father Patrick would therefore not press him, but remain grateful for Brian's attempt to absolve him of responsibility and guilt. Father Patrick smiled.

'I hear what you say, Mr Mayor - Brian. There is a lot of truth in the old adage about clouds and silver linings. If, and I mean just if, hypothetically, that statuette had been involved in the fire, one would inevitably be drawn to the conclusion of the truth of another saw. That God moves in mysterious ways.'

'Even if he is Korean?' Brian asked, teasingly.

'God's bounty is everywhere,' Father Patrick said, his gaze having been drawn to Marcella's approaching cleavage as she came over to ask if the pair wanted anything else this morning.

Alan Tootill

MORE BOOKS BY ALAN TOOTILL

The Martin Cole Novels
Cole In The Country
Cole And The Cat Woman
Cole And The Corgi Killer
Cole And The Cactus Thief
Cole And The Clairvoyant

The Blackpool Novels
Marton Mere
Payback Call
Fracking The Fylde
Frackworld
Five Blackpool Tales

Non-Fiction
Fracking The UK
Fracking The UK 2 – The storm rages on

For more information visit
www.alantootill.com

Cole And The Clairvoyant

The latest in the Martin Cole novels series, set in Roselake

In the fifth of the Martin Cole novels Martin is called in by a local businessman to look into a series of thefts from his warehouse. But the investigation is interrupted by the killing of one of the suspects. Are the thefts and the murder related? Are the police right in thinking there is a drug connection? Or should Martin follow clairvoyant Delia's advice to look for a mysterious triangle?

Once again Martin's search for the truth poses many questions for him. Should he become careers advisor to the drugs industry? How much should he pay for his visit to Roselake's brothel? Should he paint the vicar's ceiling? The truth about the murder might be hard to discover and unpleasant, but as usual Martin makes some new friends along the way.

For more information visit
www.alantootill.com

Printed in Great Britain
by Amazon